FROM THE KITCHEN OF:

_____

_____

pulp

pulp

A PRACTICAL GUIDE TO COOKING WITH FRUIT
215+ SWEET AND SAVORY RECIPES AND VARIATIONS,
INCLUDING A BAKER'S TOOLKIT

by abra berens

PHOTOGRAPHS BY EE BERGER
ILLUSTRATIONS BY LUCY ENGELMAN
FOREWORD BY TIM MAZUREK

CHRONICLE BOOKS
SAN FRANCISCO

Text copyright © 2023 by Abra Berens.

Photographs copyright © 2023 by EE Berger.

Illustrations copyright © 2023 by Lucy Engelman.

All rights reserved. No part of this book may be reproduced in any form without written permission from the publisher.

Library of Congress Cataloging-in-Publication Data

Names: Berens, Abra, author. | Berger, EE, photographer. | Engelman, Lucy, illustrator.
Title: Pulp : a practical guide to cooking with fruit : 215+ sweet and savory recipes and variations, including a baker's toolkit / by Abra Berens ; photographs by EE Berger ; illusturations by Lucy Engelman ; foreword by Tim Mazurek.
Description: First. | San Francisco : Chronicle Books, 2023. | Includes index.
Identifiers: LCCN 2022045922 | ISBN 9781797207148
Subjects: LCSH: Cooking (Fruit) | Desserts. | CYAC: Cooking (Vegetables) | LCGFT: Cookbooks.
Classification: LCC TX811 .B5 2023 | DDC 641.6/4--dc23/eng/20220922
LC record available at https://lccn.loc.gov/2022045922

Manufactured in China.

Prop contributions from Meilen Ceramics, Debbie Carlos, Monsoon Pottery, Felt + Fat.

Food and prop styling by Mollie Hayward.

Design by Sara Schneider.

Typesetting by Frank Brayton.

Benzomatic is a registered trademark of Worthington Torch, LLC. Diamond Crystal is a registered trademark licensed from Cargill, Inc. Doritos is a registered trademark of Frito Lay. Hudsonville Creamery is a registered trademark of Hudsonville Creamery and Ice Cream Company, LLC. Jell-O is a registered trademark of Kraft Heinz. King Arthur Flour is a registered trademark of King Arthur Baking Company, Inc. Morton is a registered trademark of Morton Salt, Inc. Maldon is a registered trademark of Maldon Crystal Salt Company Limited. Oxo Good Grips is a registered trademark of Helen of Troy Limited.

10 9 8 7 6 5 4 3 2

Chronicle books and gifts are available at special quantity discounts to corporations, professional associations, literacy programs, and other organizations. For details and discount information, please contact our premiums department at corporatesales@chroniclebooks.com or at 1-800-759-0190.

Chronicle Books LLC
680 Second Street
San Francisco, California 94107
www.chroniclebooks.com

MIX
Paper | Supporting responsible forestry
FSC™ C008047
FSC
www.fsc.org

Her hand moved behind his head and supported it.
Her fingers moved gently in his hair. She looked up
and across the barn, and her lips came together
and smiled mysteriously.
　　　　　　　　　—John Steinbeck

This book is dedicated to every person who does the
often invisible work of bringing food to our tables.
Specifically to those whom I've had the privilege of
working alongside over the years; thank you for making
space for me and for teaching me along the way.

foreword

BY TIM MAZUREK

The first time I met Abra, she sold me a pastry. At the time she was working at Chicago's Green City Market selling sweets for our mutual friend Sandra's beautiful bakery, Floriole. The pastry in question was a canelé, back when they were almost unheard of in the States. We bonded over our love for the custardy little umber-colored cakes, and she explained how they are made at the bakery using lovely copper molds from France. I am struck, in retrospect, by how much was revealed to me in that first brief conversation, which, for the record, Abra does not remember. Abra managed to establish camaraderie, gently educate me, and share excitement and wonder over food in the space of a few minutes. She probably also made a groan-worthy pun that I couldn't help but respect. It was energizing. It made me want to be her friend, which of course is what happened. More than a decade later, we are the best of friends, and I am here writing the foreword to her third cookbook, *Pulp*.

Pulp follows on the heels of Abra's first two books, *Ruffage* and *Grist,* completing a kind of trilogy. Like their older siblings, *Pulp* serves as, among other things, an homage to the agriculture of the Midwest, this time focused on its fruit. (You won't find a citrus chapter here.) The land looms large, and the stories and recipes are rooted in Abra's life, which has been spent primarily in Michigan and Chicago. The focus on the Midwest is noteworthy because it is a part of the country that Abra (and I!) love dearly and that remains underrepresented in food media. Few cookbooks originate here, and national media has tended to cover the Midwest condescendingly as a monoculture of hotdish, Jell-O salads, and pathological friendliness. Or with stories of perceived exceptionalism—can you believe this cool ceramicist lives in Michigan?! Yes. Yes, we can. Those of us who live here know that while there may be church potlucks and quilting circles, there are also experimental filmmakers, vegan pastry chefs, and people working to abolish the police. The Midwest, like anywhere, is a complicated convergence of people, cultures, and problems, and it is worth getting to know. But truly understanding anything requires patience, empathy, and effort. It is hard work and takes time, which is why people so often resort to clichés and stereotypes—to oversimplification.

Not Abra. The ability to sit with diverse, sometimes-conflicting ideas and seemingly unresolvable problems is one of the things I admire most about her. Instead of resolutions, she strives for understanding and connection. While many of us seek refuge in the black and white, Abra comfortably navigates the gray. She recognizes that solutions to problems, especially in complicated systems like food production, often create their own problems. She supports the work of farmers absolutely, and worked for years as a farmer, but where others might glamorize it, she admits to disliking the work. On a photoshoot for this very book, a Technicolor bag of commercially produced Gushers she picked up at the supermarket sat next to a homemade pie filled with local fruit. Does she contradict herself? Don't we all contain multitudes?

One of the challenges of introducing your friend's work, especially as someone prone to hyperbole, is that you might not believe me when I tell you that Abra is my favorite cook, but she is, truly. And I am fortunate to have enjoyed her cooking countless times in settings as diverse as fancy restaurants, lunch counters, and farmers' fields. But my favorite meals are the ones she serves at home, in her own kitchen. A meal at Abra's is always an exceptionally nice experience that she makes feel totally effortless. When you arrive she is relaxed and focused on you (where I am an anxious and distracted host). There are probably little plates of things to snack on and glasses of wine, and her husband, Erik, has some good music playing. At the right moment she asks if you are ready to eat and then suddenly salads are being plated, a roasting tin pulled from the oven, and you're sitting down to dinner. And of course the food is always memorable and inspiring and prompts you to ask questions, which Abra responds to enthusiastically with details of where the fruit came from or how she makes her pickle brine—reminding me always of the first time we met and making me feel pretty smug about my ability to pick friends.

And you should feel pretty good about your choice of cookbook. *Pulp* is a beautiful ride through the fields, orchards, and kitchens of the Midwest. Here you will find Abra doing what she does best: educating, examining big issues, sharing stories, making dumb jokes, and inspiring you in the kitchen. She's going to change the way you cook, and maybe even the way you think, not through dictates and demands, but through insight, encouragement, understanding, and connection. Enjoy it.

CONTENTS

PART 1
baker's toolkit

PART 2
fruits and how i prepare them

apples 119

introduction

I'm a talker. For better or worse, if something is on my mind, I'll probably bring it up. In talking with friends about this book, I heard one of two things in almost every conversation: "Fruit? Why would you need a book about it? Just eat it," or "Ugh, I never buy fruit because I don't know what to do with it besides just eating it and it goes bad so quickly." This is exactly why I wanted to write this book.

Fruit is simultaneously simple and frustrating. It can be so perfect that it needs nothing but a splash of cream and sprinkle of sugar to make the most ethereal dessert. It can also be disappointing and inconsistent, in which case there are very few techniques in most kitchens to help the ingredient along.

I also wanted to write this book because fruit is inextricable from my cooking. It shows up in dessert, yes, but, maybe more interestingly, throughout the meal. Think: A dark, leafy green salad studded with pops of juicy berries. A fatty cut of pork balanced by tart yet achingly tender roasted plums. Earthy lentils pepped with the sweetness of thin apple slices. The coddling softness of creamy cheeses kept in check by a pile of bracing currants to be eaten alongside.

It's possible there is so much fruit in my cooking because I'm from Michigan. The mitten state is the second-most agriculturally diverse state in the union, due in large part to the tremendous amount of fruit we grow. The climate of the west side of the state, a.k.a. the Fruit Belt, is moderated by Lake Michigan and so not prone to the temperature swings elsewhere in the state, let alone the Midwest. The glacially carved hills are the perfect landscape to protect delicate trees and vines providing good airflow and drainage.

Just as necessity is the mother of invention, so too can be abundance. When life gives you lemons, make lemonade, sure, but also lemon squares, preserved lemons, grilled lemon relish, and lemon curd. Fruit lends acidity, sweetness, color, and a range of different textures to dishes both sweet and savory. There are only so many blueberries I can eat out of hand, and so they find their way into my meals in other ways, leveraging their tang the way I might use vinegar or wine.

Pulp, like *Ruffage* and *Grist* before it, is a practical guide to particular ingredients, in this case fruit. This cookbook is practical because it gives everyday information on selecting and storing and because you'll never have to jump through tricky culinary hoops to achieve a Wednesday night dinner. My best cooking comes when I'm excited by an ingredient that is on hand, and I have a sense of different ways to prepare it and other flavors that partner well with it. I hope that this book helps guide your hand throughout the year, encouraging you to find new and interesting ways to showcase a cornucopia of fruits at your table.

farming, labor, climate, and the fruit industry

I find vapid discussions glorifying food while ignoring the people who grow or process our food very, ahem, frustrating. It is trite but true: no farms=no food. We have to go beyond a superficial rah-rah-rah for growers.

It's helpful to understand a bit about what goes into food production to understand why and how a particular product comes to market, and how everything from climate collapse, changes in immigration policy, infrastructure, market availability, and a globalized economy affect the already complex challenges facing growers.

Driving around Leelanau County, the center of Michigan's cherry heartland, it occurred to me that most of the visitors seeing these trees might not know that the fruit they produce doesn't go to a farmers' market or grocery store. There are vast differences in how farms and orchards are organized depending on whether a grower sells fruit on the fresh or commodity market.

Trees need to be planted and pruned differently if they are to be harvested by hand or by machine. The market dictates volume and diversity. A farmer can grow a lot of one thing that sells for a relatively low price to be converted into a value-added product, or grow a lot of different things at a higher retail price. Almost no one does both. That leads to decisions about infrastructure and equipment and the type of labor the grower hires and the loans needed.

Additionally, specific to the fruit industry, there are a lot of auxiliary businesses that are integral to how fruit is grown and handled in this country. We don't always think of items like wine, canned pie filling, or baby food as being agricultural products, but when the main ingredient is 100 percent fruit, you bet your blueberries that the end product is an agricultural product affected by the same whims as the grower.

local-seasonal

Like Samneric in *Lord of the Flies*, the adjectives *local* and *seasonal* have been lumped together so frequently they've blended into one concept. They are, in fact, different. Local food is grown within the boundaries of a particular region. Seasonal food refers to food that is harvested in the season when it is grown—think about strawberries that ripen on the vine for part of the year as opposed to strawberries that

are grown out of season in artificial conditions to provide a year-round product. You can have seasonal, non-local fruit. You can have unseasonal, local fruit. You can have unseasonal, non-local fruit. You can have local, seasonal fruit. There are a lot of value judgments placed on these two terms, which should be examined if not outright challenged.

FLAVOR:

Anyone who tells you that a local, seasonal piece of fruit is always better has either been duped or is selling you something. I think you are most likely to get a flavorful, fresh fruit if it is grown seasonally and within your region, but it is not a guarantee. Again, these are agricultural products that are subject to the whims of an increasingly volatile environment. I will say that I have found the most flavorful fruit by shopping at farmers' markets not because the food is intrinsically better, but because I can have a conversation with the grower about what is tasting best and be introduced to new-to-me varieties that are what I'm looking for. Again, it's about the grower, not the system. Frozen or canned produce is often harvested at peak ripeness and processed to withstand time and travel, so it is a great option for full flavor and year-round availability.

COST:

Somehow the terms *local* and *seasonal* have become indicators of price simultaneously both low and high. Low because when fresh fruit floods the market it is often sold at lower rates than the fruit distributed evenly across the food system. High because most produce at a farmers' market is more expensive than what you see in a national grocery store.

Before you scoff, consider what goes into fruit production. Unlike vegetables, all the fruits covered in this book are perennials. Many of those trees and vines take years to bear maximum yields, yet the costs associated with production do not go down. If a farmer is going to make that sort of investment, they most likely want to own the land so as to not get kicked off a lease right as their trees are hitting peak production. That takes a lot of capital. Capital and lending are not universally accessible, especially to minority growers. Add in that fruit seems to grow best in some of the most beautiful places on Earth, which means both that fruit land is more expensive than traditional agricultural land and that land is sought after by homeowners in addition to growers. Low mortgage rates and the rise of Airbnb have spurred on second home buying in a lot of these regions, making it more expensive to live in fruit-producing areas on traditionally lower wage farm jobs.

Speaking of farm jobs, all produce requires many touches by farmworkers to get to market: winter pruning, spring spraying, or bud thinning; mid-season maintenance; harvest, which can take several weeks to capture fruit that ripens at different rates; packing, getting it to market, and standing there selling it. It should come as no surprise that the United States is struggling with farm labor shortages. Farmers are retiring without clear plans for succession as their children are more hesitant to take over a family business that seems riskier and riskier. Immigration policy changes have made foreign and guest workers harder and more expensive to secure. Yikes.

So yes, growing fruit is expensive. Local food is often more expensive because the true cost of the production of that food is passed directly on to the consumer. You'll have to decide whether you want to allocate your resources to it.

HEALTH:

I believe the science that we are healthier when we eat unprocessed ingredients. The local-seasonal market traffics in just such ingredients. Note that the word *organic* is not a part of the local-seasonal mash-up. Some local-seasonal produce is organic; some is not. There are reasons for both. Buying on the local-seasonal market gives you the opportunity to ask growers why they practice what they do. It should be stated clearly that organic food is not proven to be more nutritious than non-organic. It does have a lower environmental impact than non-organic and that, combined with the decreased rate of chronic disease among organic growers, is why I buy organic when I don't know the grower. When I know the grower, I have the opportunity to ask and decide. For me, a certification is not a replacement for a relationship. You'll have to decide for yourself.

ENVIRONMENTAL IMPACT:

Fruit growing affects our environment in similar ways to other crops, be it vegetables, grains, or legumes. Organic and low-spray practices minimize pollution of waterways and promote soil health. Tree fruits are slightly different, as they are perennial crops and sequester carbon in their roots whether the fruit they produce is eaten within their growing region or not. To my mind the biggest environmental issue surrounding fruit in a regional way is that it is energy intensive to ship highly perishable fruits around the planet. It is also energy intensive to have a bunch of folks driving their cars to a million different farmers' markets. It seems to me that we should fix the energy crisis and then evaluate from there. Until we do that, there are, as far as I can tell, environmental benefits from minimizing the fossil fuel consumption to transport fragile fruits around the world by focusing on what is grown in your region.

ECONOMIC IMPACT:

This is the only local-seasonal argument that resonates with me. Food purchased within the local economy does more to sustain fiscal viability than not. I'm not just talking about farmers' markets, though being able to charge a retail price directly to consumers does ensure that more money for those products goes into the farmer's bank account, which then goes into their employees' bank accounts, and so on. I'm also talking about regional grocery chains. It is much more likely that a regional grocery chain will purchase from regional producers because they are not as reliant on the economies of scale that large corporations require to ensure profitability. I can go to my local grocery and get Michigan produce more frequently and in more abundance than at a national chain. Plus, a regional grocer is more likely to adapt to your desires as a consumer than a national one. If you don't see what you're looking for, speak up and these folks just might listen.

All that said, this is only true for growers selling on the fresh fruit market versus the commodity market—where fruit is consumed as a primary ingredient or used as a part of a value-added product. Think eating a quart of fresh cherries versus buying a can of cherry pie filling. The only thing you can do to help growers who grow at a scale where the commodity market makes sense is to be sure you are buying domestically grown and produced canned goods, and to be sure that your elected official supports domestic food production over cheaply produced imports, especially those of dubious certification.

In short, I think there are a lot of good reasons to participate in your local-seasonal food economy, but it does not make you more worthy. For me, the goal is to encourage cooking at home, ideally with loved ones, and anything that makes that possible is aces. If the convenience of buying out-of-season, non-local berries means that you and your family will cook a pie together, buy those berries! I will never pooh-pooh anyone's decision on how to feed their family until I have spent time in their kitchen, and quite frankly, neither should you.

midwestern fruit

One time at Vie Restaurant, where I cooked for a handful of years, we hosted a chef from New Orleans. I don't remember all the dishes he made, but I have a sparkling memory of there being something with foie gras, pineapple, and Espelette pepper. After the course went out, my friend (and the woman who taught me how to be a line cook) Amber Blatt and I gobbled up the leftover pineapple. The chef asked if we wanted to try the foie gras. In unison we passed. The pineapple, so sweet and tart and tropical in the middle of a Midwestern winter, was all we were after.

It is often said that writers should stick to what they know. Well, as a born-and-bred Michigander, I know the fruit grown here. I have a sense of when those fruits turn up at the market and how best to store them. I have an unending slew of ideas on how I would want to eat them, and a deep appreciation that comes from the abundance and austerity of Midwestern seasons. I don't know jackfruit about cooking with pineapple.

I also don't know the people who grow pineapples. I don't know their struggles and successes. I'd love to know how growing pineapples is different from growing apples. This book is focused on the fruit of my region; thankfully, it is a region robust and diverse enough in its bounty to fill a book. I hope that the interest in fruit as more than just something to snack on grows so that writers from other regions will tell the story of the fruit on their tables. Those are books I'd like to read.

food waste

A friend told me once that the number one reason she doesn't buy fresh fruit regularly is because it always goes to waste. Admittedly, I struggle with the same thing and so do most other households. In 2019, 35 percent (229 million tons) of the food produced in America was unsold or uneaten. Thirty-seven percent of that food is wasted in homes, with fruit and vegetables constituting 34 percent of the total of wasted food. The average household spends $1,800 per year on food that gets thrown away. Yuck. Food waste strains our agricultural system, our environment, and our budgets. We will never be rid of waste entirely, but we can always do better, and that starts with being conscious of the issue and open to solutions.

Throughout this book, I've taken care to include places where less-than-perfect fruit can shine. Each chapter also has a section on preserving fruit. I hope that these ideas help give you the tools to catch fruit before it is too far gone and turn it into something for later. This is not a deep dive on home canning, but instead, quick recipes that can be made in small batches. When in doubt, freeze it. It will buy you time.

As I write this, I'm looking out my window at my neighbor's apple tree in full, pink-bloomed, springtime glory while eating a non-local apple slathered with peanut butter. Food issues are weighty and complex and will only become more so as we adapt to a climate growing ever more tired of us. Thank goodness food is also lovely and a privilege to eat. Food won't magically heal the wounds in our world and bring us together in some sort of kumbaya nirvana. That said, I do believe that if we think and talk deliberately about the food we eat and pay for with our dollars, the effects radiate outward into every societal issue we confront. That is a worthy cause and will be spurred on over a delicious fruity meal.

how to use this book—and some things to know

This book is organized alphabetically by fruit. Within each chapter there is a Notes Box that gives guidance on signs of ripeness, how to select from the market, and storage notes. Next there is a series of preparation techniques. Each technique has a savory and a sweet variation. The savory variation is a pretty straightforward cookbook-style recipe. The sweet variation most regularly relies on a recipe from the Baker's Toolkit (see page 33) (more on that in a bit). The sweet recipes are more of a suggested pairing rather than a strict (or as strict as I get) collection of necessary components. If you want to swap custard for ice cream, feel not only free but encouraged to do so. Please note: The recipes in this book generally serve four people of average hunger (unless otherwise noted).

Along with this practical information, there are also several interviews with growers, food producers, and those deeply entrenched in the food movement. I hope that these conversations help you engage with the ingredients and make all of us appreciate the sheer scope of work, challenges, successes, and ingenuity that goes into food production, especially as growers around the world navigate a changing climate that is upending farming practices and migration patterns and forcing very tough conversations about sustainability and longevity.

glossary of terms

equipment

Everyone has a favorite pot or pan, and my favorite need not be yours. That said, there are a couple of things to know especially when cooking fruit.

NONREACTIVE METALS:
Fruit tends to be acidic and so interacts with many metals, especially aluminum and iron. When cooking fruit, it is best to use stainless steel or other nonreactive materials, such as glass or glazed ceramic, to prevent the metallic flavor from leaching into the food and pitting the surface of the cookware itself.

HEAVY BOTTOMS:
Who doesn't love a heavy bottom? A thick surface between the heat element and the food ensures that heat distributes evenly and is less likely to burn the sweet fruit. There is debate about using the long-favored copper jam pot. Copper is the best conductor of heat, and so jams cook evenly and quickly, helping to prevent burning and resulting in a brighter flavor. Copper also interacts with acidity and many worry about toxicity levels. It turns out the sugar in the jam mixture prevents the fruit acid from interacting with the metal. While it isn't necessary to shell out a month's rent for a beautiful copper pot, it may encourage you to make preserves, which is a good thing, and always including sugar in your jam will keep toxicity levels low and safe.

BLOWTORCHES:
I don't know how anyone singes a meringue, caramelizes the top of crème brûlée, or loosens a very stuck-to-the-bottom-of-a-cake-pan cake without a blowtorch. They are used in restaurants all the time. Skip the fancy "kitchen torches"—they break and are a beast to fill with fuel. Go to the hardware store and get a Bernzomatic 16 oz [480 ml] propane torch. They last forever, they cost in the ballpark of $30 (at last check), the tanks simply screw into the nozzle, and they can be used for a variety of other around-the-house projects. If you aren't up for a blowtorch, you can use a broiler, but the results will be hard to control. It will work, but you won't achieve the burnished result showcased in glossy magazines.

KITCHEN SCALES:
I believe in kitchen scales and weighing ingredients. We use scales in restaurant kitchens because they provide more precise measurements and make it much easier to scale a recipe to make one pie or ten. If you don't own a kitchen scale, please consider buying one. My favorite is the OXO Good Grips Five-Pound Food Scale with Pull-Out Display. I've had mine for years. It is accurate, doesn't burn through batteries, costs around $30, and hasn't broken yet.

HOW TO MEASURE:
My friend Tim Mazurek (passionate about many things, including baking) insists that the best way to volume-measure flour is to scoop (with a spoon) into a measuring cup and then level the cup. He's usually right, so when I can't weigh, I do it his way.

salt

There is a lot of hubbub about different types of salt, and mostly for good reason. Different salts taste and behave differently because they too are an agricultural product harvested either from the sea or from underground mineral deposits.

IODIZED TABLE SALT:
I don't use this in my cooking unless I'm desperate. Table salt is most often harvested from mineral deposits in places where naturally occurring iodine is minimal. Salt began being fortified with iodine in the United States in 1924 to eliminate the effects of iodine deficiency (goiters, along with intellectual and developmental deficiencies) in the population. I find the taste metallic and the salt less nuanced in flavor. It also contains the most sodium of all table salts.

KOSHER SALT:

This is table salt but without the additives. There is a range of textures available, from fine to coarse, as well as differing salinity levels between brands. Many people are in the Con Agra Diamond Crystal camp because it is the finest in texture and dissolves the most quickly and evenly in baking projects. Diamond Crystal is also less salty than other salts, so I often almost double the amount called for in recipes. I tend to buy Morton Kosher Salt because it is coarser and so does well as a finishing salt when I'm out of flake salt. It is the saltiest of the koshers, so I end up using about half as much as other salts. You'll have to taste around and decide to which tribe you belong.

SEA SALT:

Like kosher salt, sea salt comes in a variety of textures and flavor profiles. I tend to use the very fine sea salt where I would kosher, and the chunky crunchier sea salts, like Maldon, to finish a dish where you want a big pop of salinity to cut through rich or sweet flavors.

general cooking terms

ACIDULATED WATER:
Water that has some sort of an acid in it, used to keep things like fennel or artichokes from oxidizing. To make, add 2 Tbsp of vinegar (usually apple cider or white wine; avoid dark vinegars such as balsamic or sherry) to 2 cups [480 ml] of cool water. You can also use lemon juice or white wine, but I always have vinegar on hand, and it is the cheapest of the options.

ALBUMIN:
The protein that is found in egg whites or in the liquid of cooked chickpeas that is often used as an egg white replacement.

BAIN-MARIE:
A container filled with hot water into which another vessel is placed to cook the contents gently. To translate, *bain* means *bath* in French. This technique is most often used to bake delicate custards and cheesecakes. The hot water bath provides an even temperature that keeps the protein from cooking quickly, which can shorten the protein strands and result in a grainy or curdled texture where a silky, luscious mouthfeel is desired.

BAKED:
Specific to this book, cooking fruit by placing into a moderately hot oven, often with other ingredients, until soft but juicy.

BATTER BRUISING:
When a dough or batter gets dark splotches across it from berry juice. There's nothing wrong with the end result beyond aesthetics.

CARTOUCHE:
A circular paper lid placed over a stewing pot of fruit to allow some slow evaporation. To make, fold a piece of parchment in half and then in half again to make a square. Then fold in halves to make a triangle. Place the folded tip end of the triangle at the center of the pot and then trim the loose edges of the parchment to the width of the pot. Unfold and press into the pot in direct contact with the cooking fruit. You can also just use a stray butter wrapper and not worry about the exact shape.

CHALAZA:
One of the two twisted, white protein strands that tethers the yolk to the shell in a chicken or duck egg.

CHEF'S TREAT:
Treats that only chefs (or kitchen cooks) get to eat because they are not fancy enough to serve or there's not enough to share. My favorite in this book is the meringue that clings to the whisk, which is then toasted with a blowtorch to make a marshmallowy tidbit that never leaves the kitchen.

CLINGSTONE VERSUS FREESTONE:
Refers to whether the flesh of a stone fruit is bonded to (clinging) or loose (free) from the pit. Often dictated by variety or time of season; usually the later the fruit ripens in the season, the more likely it is to be freestone. The benefit of freestones is that after cutting around the circumference of the fruit, you can twist the sides apart easily. Clingstones need to be cut almost as apples because the flesh will never separate cleanly from the pit.

CREAMING METHOD:
Batter made by creaming together butter and sugar until light and fluffy either by hand or with a stand mixer. Start with soft butter. Don't rush it, and keep beating until the mixture is truly a shade or two lighter in color and the sugar no longer feels grainy.

DEGLAZE:
The act of releasing the browned fond from a pan after searing an ingredient (traditionally meat); usually done with wine or water and then used as the base for a sauce.

DOUBLE BOILER:
Placing a heatproof bowl over a pot with 1 to 2 in [2.5 to 5 cm] of boiling water in the bottom to gently heat items with steam. This method is used for ingredients like chocolate or eggs to keep them from burning (or melting or cooking too quickly). Be sure that the bottom of the bowl does not touch the water.

EGG WASH:
Whip 1 egg with a splash of water, milk, or cream to paint on baked goods to give a good shine. The more fat (cream versus water) in the wash, the darker the finished glaze will be.

FOND:
The browned bits clinging to a pan after searing an ingredient (traditionally meat), usually loosened with wine or water in the deglazing process.

FRUIT GOO:
Thickened juices made from macerating fruit, draining the juice away from the fruit itself, and then cooking the juice separately to thicken. A term used almost exclusively for pies.

GEL POINT:
The temperature at which jams "set," which means that they've foamed and continued thickening from a loose liquid into a more-viscous, jammier consistency; see Wrinkle Test (page 31). Almost universally, jams cook until they reach 220°F [105°C]. If the fruit is low in pectin, it can still not firm up at that temperature, and may need to be taken as high as 240°F [115°C] but 220°F [105°C] is a good place to start.

GELATIN:
Gelatin comes in either powdered or sheet form and needs to be softened to blend evenly. For powdered or granulated gelatin, sprinkle over cold water to rehydrate. For sheet gelatin, place in ice water until it is soft, then wring out any excess moisture and add to the recipe.

GLUG:
The amount of liquid it takes for the liquid to hit the top of the jug and make a glugging sound—anywhere from 2 Tbsp to ¼ cup [60 ml]. Really just means throw a bit of whatever into the pan and move along.

GRILL:
To cook unilaterally via direct heat, often over fire or the flame of a broiler.

INDIVIDUALLY FREEZE:
The act of laying out pieces of fruit (in this case) on a tray to freeze as individual units, after which they can be bagged, ensuring that the fruit freezes as separate pieces instead of a giant block.

JUICE MANAGEMENT:
The act of regulating the amount of juice in a fruity baked good, often through thickening, draining, or evaporation.

KNIFE TEST:
The act of piercing the center of a cake with a thin (usually paring) knife to see if the cake is done. If the knife comes out clean, it's done. Hooray! If it comes out with batter clinging to it, it isn't done. Be patient and put it back in the oven. This can also be done with a toothpick or skewer, but I rarely have those on hand, so knives it is.

NEUTRAL OIL:
A flavorless oil that has a high smoke point and so is good for searing and frying. Examples are (my favored) grapeseed, rice bran, safflower, canola, peanut, and vegetable oils.

NONREACTIVE:
A material that will not chemically react with the acidity in fruit. Usually stainless steel, ceramic, or glass. Avoid aluminum or copper when cooking fruits (though see the note about using copper for jams on page 27).

POACH:
To cook gently by simmering in flavorful liquid at a moderate temperature until the fruit is tender. It is then removed from the liquid and served on its own.

PRESERVE:
To process fruit so that it doesn't spoil, either by pickling (submerging in an acidic solution), jamming (stewing with enough sugar to stabilize), drying (evaporating enough moisture to prevent rot), or freezing (making cold enough that the cells can't break down).

PROOF:
In baking, the act of allowing the yeast in a recipe to leaven the dough. The warmer the environment, the faster this will happen. Always loosely cover a proofing dough with plastic wrap or a damp kitchen towel to prevent the top of the dough from drying out during the proof.

RAW:
Applying no technique to heat; leaving fruit uncooked.

RIG:
A catchall phrase for a chunky, acidic relish that enhances everything it is spooned over. It is one part relish, one part vinaigrette, three parts awesome.

ROAST:
To cook fruit in a dry, hot environment (either an oven or a pan) with enough space around it to quickly evaporate the juice, collapse the interior, and caramelize the exterior.

SCALD:
The act of heating dairy to just below a boil. This is often done to either infuse a flavor (like vanilla) or to properly temper into eggs (like for custard).

SET:
The point at which a jam or preserve is no longer runny, usually after it has reached the gel point of temperature or passed the wrinkle test.

SHRUB:
Both a bushy plant and (for our purposes) a sweet-tart, fruit-infused liquid. To make, dissolve 1 cup [200 g] of sugar in 1 cup [240 ml] of vinegar (usually apple cider, white, or red wine) and then add any number of fruits or fruit juices to infuse for a few days, until it is to your taste. Then use immediately or store in the fridge for several weeks or until it doesn't taste good to you anymore.

SIDECAR:
A small, low vehicle attached to a motorcycle for carrying passengers, or a stack of cookies served alongside a delicious fruit dessert.

SLURRY:
A loose, liquidy mixture or a mixture made by whisking together a liquid and cornstarch to dissolve the cornstarch and thicken something like pastry cream. Make a slurry, instead of dumping the powdered cornstarch directly into the pastry cream, to avoid lumps in the finished product (this is also true for Thanksgiving gravy).

SNACKY DINNER:
A complete dinner made up of a variety of items that are traditionally eaten as snacks, such as cured meats, cheeses, pickles, nuts, dried fruit, bread, crackers, green salad, and a couple of other random vegetable dishes.

STEW:
To cook fruit gently by simmering with other ingredients that will all be served together.

SUCCULENTÉ:
A term coined by Chef Michel Nischan to describe food that is simultaneously succulent, excellent, and prized. It is best said while making the "chef's kiss!" gesture with the fingertips.

TEMPER:
The act of adding a hot liquid to whisked eggs in a slow and steady stream while whisking constantly to gently bring the temperature of the eggs up without constricting the proteins and scrambling the eggs. Most often referenced in custard and pudding making. Tempering is also used in chocolate making to ensure good shine and crack, but details on that are for another book.

TIP AND TAIL:
Cutting off the top and bottom of a vegetable or fruit as the first step in preparation.

WRINKLE TEST:
Another way to tell if jam has set (see "Set," left). Place a plate in the freezer. When it is cold (and you think your jam has cooked to the right point), place a tablespoon or so of the jam on the cold plate and let it sit for a couple of minutes to cool. Then nudge the pool of jam with your finger and see if it wrinkles. If it does, the jam will be thick when it cools. If it doesn't, keep cooking the jam, return the plate to the freezer, and test again in 10 minutes.

PART 1
baker's toolkit

I am not a natural baker. I don't tend to delight in the process or the product of a long arduous pastry session. I like simple desserts, especially those in which fruit is the star component. Over the years, several recipes have come in and out of my life, and I've collected a body of foundational recipes that showcase fruit well. I've retested and organized them in this book to share with you.

This is my quiver of arrows at the ready to support a meal's fruity finale. I have organized the recipes into groups—cakes, cookies, creamy things, etc.—to highlight their roles on the plate. Feel encouraged to swap them around and find your own preferred combinations. These recipes are a mishmash of ones I've tasted at restaurants or seen online, but most often come straight from the many talented bakers with whom I've had the privilege of working in close proximity. I have benefited from them sharing their knowledge and craft and have noted them by name in the headnotes, not only as an appreciation, but also because it is their work, not mine, that has given these recipes life. I hope that you utilize them as much as I have over the years.

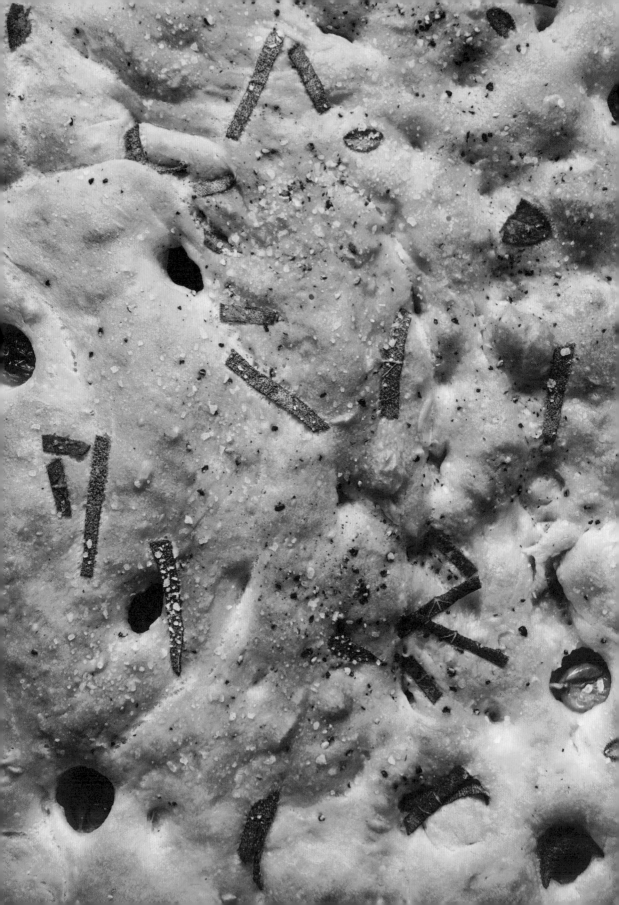

BREADS

focaccia

I prefer a focaccia made with a pre-ferment or poolish, which adds depth of flavor. If you don't have the time or interest to prepare this, simply add all of the ingredients together at the start of mixing and carry on. I'm most used to focaccias with ingredients draped over the top just before baking. If adding ingredients to the center of the focaccia, add in before pressing into the pan. This recipe is adapted from Frank Carollo and Amy Emberling from Zingerman's Bakehouse and their incredible cookbook.

MAKES 1 FOCACCIA

POOLISH

¾ cup [115 g] all-purpose flour

⅛ tsp instant yeast

DOUGH

¼ cup [60 ml] olive oil, plus more for drizzling

½ tsp instant yeast

3 cups [425 g] all-purpose flour

2 tsp salt

Crunchy salt, for sprinkling

To make the poolish: In a medium bowl, mix the flour, ½ cup [120 ml] of water, and the yeast together and ferment, covered with plastic wrap, at room temperature for 8 hours.

To make the dough: In a large bowl, combine 1 cup [240 ml] of water, the poolish, olive oil, and yeast. Stir to form a slurry (see page 31). Add the flour and salt. Knead until smooth, about 8 minutes. Transfer to a bowl, cover with plastic wrap, and let proof at room temperature until doubled in size, about 75 minutes. Punch down the dough, add any ingredient mix-ins and press into an oiled baking sheet. Let rest for 10 minutes and then press into

continued

the prepared baking sheet a second time, gently stretching the dough to reach into the corners. Cover loosely with plastic wrap and proof (see page 30) until just about doubled in size, about 1 hour.

Preheat the oven to 450°F [230°C]. Dimple the surface of the focaccia with your fingers to make little valleys, drizzle with olive oil, and sprinkle with crunchy salt. Bake until golden brown and cooked through, about 20 minutes. Cool to room temperature before slicing and serving. Focaccia is best the day it is baked.

milk bread

I first started making milk bread after seeing it on my Instagram feed. I found a handful of recipes online and ended up using the one from Julia Moskin of the *New York Times* the most. This recipe is twice the volume of hers because I have two loaf pans; it freezes well, so I don't see the point of not making two loaves when the oven is already on. While this recipe includes making a starter dough, don't be put off. It isn't a sourdough and doesn't take much time, but you can't skip it, or the bread won't have the same pillowy texture. It uses a Japanese cooking technique, tangzhong, that is being utilized more and more commonly throughout the world of baking to attain this specific texture in doughs.

MAKES 2 LOAVES

STARTER

⅓ cup [45 g] bread flour

½ cup [120 ml] whole milk

DOUGH

1 cup [240 ml] whole milk, plus more for brushing

5 cups [700 g] bread flour

½ cup [100 g] sugar

4 tsp dry active yeast (2 packets)

2 tsp salt

2 eggs

8 Tbsp (4 oz [120 g]) butter, at room temperature

To make the starter: In a small saucepan, whisk together the flour and milk until smooth. Bring to a simmer over medium heat, stirring until thickened but still pourable, about 12 minutes. It will continue to thicken as it cools. Transfer the starter to a bowl and press a piece of plastic wrap or wax paper onto the surface (as for pudding). Let cool to room temperature.

To make the dough: In a small saucepan, warm the milk until the side of the pot is warm to the touch (or the milk is about 100°F [35°C]). In the bowl of a stand mixer, combine the flour, sugar, yeast, and salt. Add the eggs, warm milk, and cooled starter. With a dough hook, knead the mixture on medium-low speed for 5 minutes. With the mixer on low, add the butter a few knobs at a time

continued

until incorporated. Increase the speed to medium and knead for 10 minutes more, until the dough is silky and springy. Cover the bowl with plastic wrap or a damp kitchen towel and let proof in a warm place—such as your oven with the heat turned off—until doubled in size, 45 to 60 minutes. With wet hands (to keep the dough from sticking), lift the dough and divide into four equal balls. Cover with a damp kitchen towel and let rest for 15 minutes.

Preheat the oven to 350°F [180°C]. Grease two 9 by 5 in [23 by 12 cm] loaf pans.

Using a rolling pin on a lightly floured surface, roll each ball of dough into a 12 by 6 in [30.5 by 15 cm] oval with the long side running north-south on your table. Fold the top 3 in [7.5 cm] of the oval down and the bottom 3 in [7.5 cm] up, making a rough square. Starting on the left, roll the square to the right to make a fat log. Place the log in the loaf pan, seam-side down and perpendicular to the long side of the pan. Repeat with the other balls, nestling two logs into each pan. Cover the pans with damp kitchen towels and let proof until the dough rises almost to the top edge of the loaf pan, 30 to 60 minutes, depending on the temperature of your kitchen.

Brush the top of the dough with a splash of milk for a glossy crust. Transfer to the oven and bake until golden brown and the internal temperature is 200°F [95°C], 35 to 45 minutes, rotating the pans after 20 minutes. Remove from the oven, let rest for 10 minutes, then unmold from the pans and let cool completely on a wire rack before slicing. After completely cool, store covered for up to 5 days or wrap well and freeze for up to 2 months.

pumpernickel

I grew up in a household that loved pumpernickel bread, especially when the round loaf was hollowed out and filled with spinach artichoke dip and the just-removed center was toasted for dipping into said dip. It has become harder and harder to find in my town and, apart from ordering online from Zingerman's Mail Order, I haven't liked the online versions I've tried. Classic pumpernickel bread is made with whole-grain rye flour—the bran and endosperm are left in the flour, making the dark color.

This recipe is a mishmash of different recipes from over the years and uses cocoa powder to approximate the dark color of classic pumpernickel in case you can't find whole-grain, dark-rye flour. Note: At last check, King Arthur Flour has true pumpernickel flour available in a 3 lb [1.4 kg] bag—but I still add the cocoa powder.

MAKES 1 LOAF

3 cups [420 g] bread flour	1 Tbsp salt	1 Tbsp dry active yeast
2 cups [280 g] dark-rye flour	2 cups [480 ml] whole milk	¼ cup [80 g] molasses
2 Tbsp unsweetened cocoa powder	1½ Tbsp brown sugar	3 Tbsp butter, at room temperature

In the bowl of a stand mixer, combine the bread flour, rye flour, cocoa powder, and salt.

In a small saucepan, warm the milk over medium heat until the side of the pan is warm to the touch (or the milk is about 100°F [35°C]). Add the brown sugar, yeast, and molasses to the milk and whisk to combine. Let sit for 5 minutes to bloom the yeast (it will start to foam).

Add the milk-yeast mixture to the dry ingredients and knead on medium-low speed for about 6 minutes (the dough will start to pull cleanly from the sides of the bowl). On medium speed, add

continued

the butter, a knob at a time, until incorporated. Continue mixing at low speed until the dough is smooth and springs back to the touch, 10 to 12 minutes more. Cover the bowl with plastic wrap or a damp kitchen towel and let proof until doubled in size, about 45 minutes in a warm kitchen.

Grease a 9 by 5 in [23 by 12 cm] loaf pan. Lift the dough from the bowl and, on a lightly floured surface, pat the dough into a rough 9 in [23 cm] square. Roll the dough into a fat log, pinching the seam together. Place the log into the prepared loaf pan, seam-side down. Cover again with plastic wrap or a damp kitchen towel and let proof until doubled in size, about 45 minutes.

Preheat the oven to 375°F [190°C]. When the loaf has doubled in size, remove the covering and bake until the crust is dark brown and the internal temperature is 200°F [95°C], 35 to 45 minutes. Cool for 10 minutes before removing from the pan and turn out onto a wire rack to cool completely before slicing. Store, well wrapped, for up to 5 days or freeze for forever.

BATTERS

brown butter custard batter

My friend and mentor Sandra Holl of Floriole Cafe & Bakery in Chicago uses this filling to bind tart plum galettes. It is simple enough that even I can make it and it pairs well with any number of tart fruits, making it the perfect addition to the Baker's Toolkit.

MAKES 1 CUP

8 Tbsp (4 oz [120 g]) butter

½ cup [100 g] sugar

2 eggs

¼ cup [35 g] all-purpose flour

¼ tsp salt

In a small frying pan, warm the butter over medium-high heat until it foams and then starts to brown, about 7 minutes. Remove from the heat and let cool to room temperature.

In a medium bowl, whisk together the sugar and eggs until pale, thick, and fluffy, 3 minutes. Add the flour and salt. Whisk to remove any lumps. Add the brown butter and whisk to combine. Use immediately, or store, covered, in the fridge for up to a week.

clafoutis batter

My neighbor and cherry farmer Kathy Garthe introduced me to clafoutis because she would make dozens every summer through-out the height of cherry season. Traditionally, the cherries would be baked with their pits intact because it perfumes the custard with the bitter almond scent found in the pits. Plus, spitting cherry pits into the grass after a long lunch eaten outside in the summer sun is as genteel as I'll ever want to be. This is her recipe that has become my standard-bearer. Don't be surprised if the clafoutis deflates a bit as it cools—that's just the way of things.

MAKES ONE 9 BY 9 IN [23 BY 23 CM] CLAFOUTIS

1 lb [455 g] fruit of your choosing

½ cup [70 g] all-purpose flour

¼ tsp salt

2 eggs

½ cup [100 g] sugar

¾ cup [180 ml] milk

1 Tbsp butter, melted

½ tsp vanilla extract

1 Tbsp booze (brandy, cognac, rum, calvados, whiskey, etc.)

Preheat the oven to 400°F [200°C]. Evenly fill a 9 in [23 cm] square baking dish with the fruit and set aside.

In a large bowl, whisk together all the ingredients. Pour over the fruit. Place in the oven and immediately reduce the oven temperature to 350°F [180°C]. Bake until the custard is set and lightly browned, about 25 minutes. Cool to warm or room temperature, then slice and serve. Leftovers can be stored refrigerated for up to 2 days; reheat before serving.

cobbler batter

This is the first dessert recipe I ever memorized. It comes straight from the kitchen of Chef Rodger Bowser at Zingerman's Deli in Ann Arbor, Michigan. I know we made a bunch of different versions, but the one I love best is peach and blueberry. Since those days, it has reigned supreme as a summer fruit dessert crowd-pleaser. Don't skimp on the butter dots before baking or else Bowser will know and won't hesitate to check that the kitchen isn't out of butter because that's the ONLY reason there could be for not using a full stick.

MAKES ONE 9 BY 9 IN [23 BY 23 CM] COBBLER

2 lb [910 g] summer fruit (any variety or mixture of multiple)

1 cup [140 g] all-purpose flour

1 cup [200 g] sugar, plus extra for sprinkling

1 cup [240 ml] milk

1 Tbsp baking powder

Pinch of salt

8 Tbsp (4oz [120 g]) butter, cut into small pieces

Cream or sour cream, for serving (optional)

Preheat the oven to 350°F [180°C]. Place the fruit into a 9 by 9 in [23 by 23 cm] baking dish.

In a large bowl, whisk together the flour, sugar, milk, baking powder, and salt. Pour this batter over the fruit. Dot the butter all over, especially in the corners of the pan. Sprinkle a handful of sugar over the top and bake until the cobbler is set, about 45 minutes. Cool for 15 minutes to set the fruit before serving.

To serve, I like to finish it with a heavy pour of ice-cold cream or a spoonful of sour cream on top. Leftovers can be stored refrigerated or at room temperature for up to 2 days.

crepe batter

My favorite task in the Zingerman's Deli kitchen was making crepes. It always happened toward the end of the shift and we made what seemed like a hundred at a time. Muscle memory is the key to a lot of skills in kitchens, and the best way to develop muscle memory is certainly to make things a hundred at a time. It takes a little while to get the temperature of the pan right—not too hot but hot enough to get a nice sizzle—but the "mistake" crepes can be eaten gleefully, slathered in butter and sprinkled with sugar. Not that I ever did that while on the clock. Nope. Never.

MAKES 14 CREPES

1¾ cups [420 ml] whole milk

2 Tbsp butter, melted

3 eggs

1 cup [140 g] all-purpose flour

Pinch of salt

In a blender, combine the milk, butter, eggs, flour, and salt. Blend until well combined. Rest the batter for a minimum of 1 hour.

Before starting to cook the crepes, line a baking sheet with parchment paper for a landing pad as the crepes come out of the pan. Have a few more pieces of parchment nearby so you can stack the crepes up with parchment between the layers to prevent sticking. Heat a small frying pan (or two if you are up for it) over medium heat until warm. Ladle about 1 oz [30 ml] of batter into the pan. Swirl it around to evenly coat the pan, return the pan to the heat, and decrease the heat to medium-low. Cook until the crepe is dry in the center, about 1 minute. Using a small butter knife or spatula, lift the crepe and flip it to lightly cook the other side, about 10 seconds. Slide the crepe to the lined tray. Repeat with the remainder of the batter.

Crepes can be layered between sheets of parchment or wax paper, then wrapped and frozen for storage for up to 2 months.

dutch baby batter

I always forget about Dutch babies. They are super easy, super fast, and their puffy, eggy, bubbly edges are endlessly delightful to eat.

SERVES 4 TO 6

| 3 eggs | ½ cup [120 ml] milk | Pinch of salt |
| ½ cup [70 g] all-purpose flour | 1 Tbsp sugar | 3 Tbsp butter |

Preheat the oven to 425°F [220°C].

In a large bowl, whisk or blend the eggs, flour, milk, sugar, and salt into a smooth batter.

Place a large frying pan in the oven to preheat, 7 to 10 minutes. Leaving the pan in the oven, add the butter and let it melt, being careful to not let it burn. When the butter is melted and foamy, pour in the batter. Bake until the pancake is puffed and the center is cooked through, about 20 minutes. Remove from the oven and cut into wedges to serve.

muffin batter

I'm pretty sure that this recipe is based off of the blueberry muffin batter from *Joy of Cooking*, though it seems to have gone through a few twists and turns over the years. I like to substitute whole-grain flours for the all-purpose flour, especially spelt or barley, which are naturally lower in gluten and so make a tender muffin that still has structure. If you don't have milk, I have substituted buttermilk or thinned-out yogurt with good results. Finally, I add the fruit to each individual muffin instead of adding to the batter to prevent batter bruising (see page 29).

MAKES 12 MUFFINS

2 cups [280 g] all-purpose or lower gluten flour

⅓ cup [65 g] sugar

1 Tbsp baking powder

1 tsp salt

1 cup [240 ml] milk or buttermilk

2 eggs

3 Tbsp butter, melted

2 Tbsp [30 g] fruit per muffin unless specified in the specific recipe

SSS (page 78), optional

Preheat the oven to 375°F [190°C]. Grease a 12-cup muffin tin or line with baking papers.

In a large bowl, whisk together the flour, sugar, baking powder, and salt.

In a small bowl, whisk together the milk, eggs, and melted butter.

Pour the wet ingredients into the dry and stir until just combined. Scoop the batter into the prepared muffin tin. Add the fruit to each muffin cup. Top with a sprinkle of SSS (if using). Bake until the knife test (see page 30) comes out clean, 15 to 20 minutes.

Cool completely before serving. Muffins keep in an airtight container at room temperature for up to 2 days.

CRACKERS

pat's crackers

I got this recipe from Pat Mullins of Three Oaks, Michigan. He is one of the best cooks I know, mastering everything from high-end dining to running a one-of-a-kind butcher shop to making the most perfect slice of pizza at Patellies. I'm lucky to be his friend, and you are lucky he shared his cracker recipe with me. I like baking the crackers in large sheets and then breaking them into irregular shards. If you want a more uniform cracker, cut into the desired shape after rolling but before baking.

MAKES A LOT OF CRACKERS

SPONGE

1 tsp dry active yeast

¼ tsp sugar

2¼ cups [320 g] all-purpose flour

DOUGH

3¾ cups [520 g] all-purpose flour

⅔ cup [160 ml] olive oil

2 tsp salt

Flake salt and freshly ground black pepper

To make the sponge: In a large bowl, dissolve the yeast and sugar in 2¼ cups [530 ml] of warm water. Add the 2¼ cups [320 g] flour and mix to combine. Let proof in a warm place for 1 hour.

To make the dough: Add the 3¾ cups [525 g] flour, olive oil, and salt to the sponge. Mix to bring together into a smooth dough. Proof until doubled in size, about 1 hour.

Preheat the oven to 375°F [190°C]. Line a baking sheet with a silicone mat or parchment paper.

continued

Flip the dough out onto a lightly floured work surface and cut in half. Roll one half of the dough until it is ¼ in [6 mm] thick. Transfer to the prepared baking sheet and sprinkle with flake salt and pepper. Bake until golden brown and cooked through, about 7 minutes.

Repeat with the other half of the dough. Cool until you can handle the dough, then break into irregular pieces. Serve at room temperature or store in an airtight container until they get soft, up to 2 weeks.

variations

To make herby crackers: Add 4 tsp chopped herbs to the dough during the second mixing and continue on.

To make seedy crackers: Add 4 tsp seeds to the dough during the second mixing and continue on. I like to use an even mixture of poppy, fennel, chia, and flax seeds.

To make everything crackers: Add 1 Tbsp sesame seed, 1 Tbsp poppy seed, 1 tsp dried onion flakes, ½ tsp dried garlic flakes, and ½ tsp coarse salt to the dough during the second mixing and carry on.

graham crackers

I love the entire genre of digestive biscuit, some weird version of health food that is really just a less sweet cookie. I credit Amy Emberling and Frank Carollo for reinforcing that something that you thought you knew tastes a world apart when made with high-quality ingredients. It turns out you really can taste the difference. This recipe is based on Amy and Frank's, but tweaked to suit what I have in my kitchen.

MAKES 40 CRACKERS

1 cup (8 oz [230 g]) butter

½ cup [100 g] granulated sugar

½ cup [100 g] brown sugar

1 egg

1 Tbsp honey

2 cups [280 g] spelt or all-purpose flour

¾ cup [105 g] whole-wheat flour

1 tsp baking soda

1 tsp five-spice powder (or substitute ground cinnamon)

1 tsp ground ginger

¼ tsp salt

In the bowl of a stand mixer, beat the butter and sugars until light and fluffy. Add the egg and honey and continue beating until incorporated and creamy.

In a medium bowl, whisk together the flours, baking soda, five-spice powder, ginger, and salt. Add this mixture to the butter-sugar mixture and beat to combine. Tip the mixture onto a lightly floured work surface and gently knead it until it forms a smooth dough. Divide the dough in half, wrap, and chill for 30 minutes.

Preheat the oven to 350°F [180°C]. Line a baking sheet with a silicone mat or parchment paper.

Unwrap the chilled dough (one block at a time), dust the work surface with flour, and roll until ¼ in [6 mm] thick. Cut into squares and transfer to the prepared baking sheet. Bake until the crackers are golden brown and fragrant, about 10 minutes.

Cool completely before serving, or store in an airtight container until they get soft, up to 2 weeks.

oatcakes

Oatcakes are another version of the digestive biscuit hailing from the oat-loving (and growing) Scots. Is it a cracker? Is it a cookie? Both, I guess, which is why I try to keep some on hand for a daily late-afternoon snack or as an accompaniment to a cheese plate for guests. I'm pretty sure I was reacquainted with oatcakes via Jessica Battilana's wonderfully useful book *Repertoire* and I'm sure her recipe has influenced the one I use.

MAKES LOTS OF OATCAKES

1½ cups [210 g] whole-wheat or spelt flour

1 cup [100 g] rolled oats, old fashioned, not instant

½ tsp baking soda

½ tsp salt, plus more for sprinkling

8 Tbsp (4 oz [120 g]) butter, cut into cubes

¼ cup [85 g] maple syrup or honey

Preheat the oven to 350°F [180°C]. Line a baking sheet with a silicone mat or parchment paper.

In a large bowl, combine the flour, oats, baking soda, and salt. Rub in the butter with your fingertips until the mixture looks like coarse cornmeal. Add the maple syrup and ¼ cup [60 ml] of water and use your hands to bring the mass together into a shaggy dough.

Tip the dough out onto a lightly floured workspace and work into a ball. Roll it out to a thickness of ¼ in [6 mm]. Cut into rounds or squares, placing them on the prepared baking sheet at least 1 in [2.5 cm] apart. Gather up the pieces one time and roll again to make more. Sprinkle lightly with salt. Bake until browned and fragrant, 12 to 15 minutes. Cool on a wire rack.

Store in an airtight container for a few days (or until they go soft). The unbaked dough freezes well for up to 2 months, just be sure it comes back to room temperature before you try to roll it.

CRUSTS

hazelnut crust

This crust comes from the long line of graham cracker and cookie crusts, but uses hazelnut meal as the base. Should you want to make it with graham crackers, do so by all means. If you can't find hazelnut meal, use almond flour.

MAKES ONE 9 IN [23 CM] CRUST

2 cups [240 g] hazelnut flour or meal

1 Tbsp sugar

1 tsp salt

1 egg

Preheat the oven to 350°F [180°C]. Grease a 9 in [23 cm] pie pan.

In a medium bowl, combine the hazelnut flour, sugar, and salt. Mix in the egg to bring the dough together. Press into the prepared pie pan in an even layer. Bake for 15 minutes for par-baked or 25 minutes for fully baked. Cool completely before filling.

pretzel crust

Claudia Fleming, through her iconic cookbook *The Last Course*, first introduced me to leveraging salt to play against sweet in desserts. Then my friend and fellow cook Danielle Jamnik introduced me to her family's pretzel pie: a pretzel crumb crust topped with a very Midwestern cheesecake-style dessert. The pretzel crust quickly became my desert island dessert of choice.

MAKES ONE 9 IN [23 CM] CRUST

3 cups [120 g] pretzels, finely ground or smashed

¾ cup (6 oz [70 g]) butter, melted

3 Tbsp sugar

Preheat the oven to 350°F [180°C]. Lightly grease a 9 in [23 cm] pie pan.

In a medium bowl, mix the pretzels, butter, and sugar until it comes together. Press into the prepared pie pan. Bake for 10 minutes for par-baked or 20 minutes for fully baked. Cool completely before filling.

DOUGHS

I have wondered (often aloud) at the baker's magic of taking the same ingredients and combining them in different ways to yield such different end results. This may be no truer than in making dough. Every dough consists of flour, fat, and water. How the butter interacts with the flour and melts during baking changes the texture.

If you want a super-tender short crust, the butter needs to be creamed to bind the flour together, so it will enrich and set the flour. If you want an ultra-flaky pie, the fat needs to stay in little pieces within the dough, so when it melts during baking, emitting steam, it leaves little air holes that translate to flakes of pastry.

A puffy puff dough is layer built upon layer, meaning you need to laminate (or fold) the butter over itself within the dough so it forms organized layers rather than air-pocket flakes. Any flaky or puff dough needs to be chilled after mixing to set the butter flecks but then come back to a cool room temp to roll without just crumbling or tearing or being so hard that you want to throw it at a wall.

To get shatteringly crisp layered phyllo crust, you must brush a layer of fat between each layer of the fat-free phyllo dough. If two sheets of phyllo are stacked on top of each other without a buffer layer of fat, they will bake together as one thick sheet with no crisp or crackle.

These are my go-to dough recipes with notes on how the fat is incorporated and other bits and bobs along the way.

choux/cream puff dough

Choux dough is a technique worth mastering because of its versatility. This dough is the basis for cream puffs, French profiteroles, gougères, eclairs, churros, Paris-Brest torte, and a form of gnocchi.

MAKES 4 TO 12 CREAM PUFFS, DEPENDING ON THE SIZE

8 Tbsp (4 oz [120 g]) butter

½ tsp salt

1 cup [140 g] all-purpose flour

4 eggs

Preheat the oven to 375°F [190°C]. Line a baking sheet with a silicone mat or parchment paper.

In a medium saucepan, bring the butter, salt, and 1 cup [240 ml] of water to a boil over high heat. Lower the heat to medium and simmer until the butter is melted.

Add the flour and vigorously stir the mixture until the flour is completely absorbed and starting to cook in the pan. The pan will begin to "fir"—this is when the flour starts to gently stick to the bottom of the pot. Cook until the dough starts to smell cooked and takes on a slightly golden color, about 3 minutes more. Transfer the dough to a stand mixer bowl (or a large bowl) and let cool slightly, about 4 minutes.

Add the eggs one by one, beating to fully incorporate after each addition. The dough will be sticky and stiff enough to hold a peak when you lift the beater out of it.

Spoon the dough in ½ cup [30 g] mounds onto the prepared baking sheet. Gently press each into a circle, smoothing any pointy tips with a wet finger. Bake until the puffs are fully golden brown and set, 35 to 45 minutes (without opening the oven, which encourages collapse).

Cool completely on a wire rack before filling. Store in an airtight container for up 3 days, re-crisping in a moderate oven for 10 minutes as needed.

cream scone dough

This recipe is one of my favorites from *Joy of Cooking*. It is fool-proof because scones are hard to overwork—the fat in the heavy cream insulates the protein in the flour from developing too much gluten. Plus, you can mix in just about anything to flavor these. I've used this dough over the years to make everything from fruit scones to savory Cheddar biscuits. And unbaked scones freeze perfectly, so I mix them in big batches, freeze on a parchment- or silicone mat–lined baking sheet, and bake off one or two as needed.

MAKES 12 MEDIUM SCONES OR A LOT MORE IF YOU MAKE THEM SMALLER

4 cups [575 g] all-purpose flour

⅔ cup [165 g] sugar

2 Tbsp baking powder

1 tsp salt

2½ cups [600 ml] heavy cream

Preheat the oven to 350°F [180°C]. Line a baking sheet with a silicone mat or parchment paper.

In a large bowl, combine the flour, sugar, baking powder, and salt. Add the cream and mix until it forms a shaggy but cohesive dough. Scoop into ½ cup [115 g] balls, leaving 2 to 3 in [5 to 7.5 cm] apart on the prepared baking sheet. Lightly press to flatten them. Transfer to the freezer and freeze for a minimum of 30 minutes to set the dough.

Bake from frozen until lightly browned and set through, 17 to 20 minutes, rotating the tray halfway through baking. Serve warm, or cool completely and store in an airtight container for 2 days.

cream cheese dough

This dough is my go-to all-purpose dough. It makes a nice pie and isn't too sweet for a savory pot pie. It can be used to make kolache by folding a bit of jam into the center of cookie-size pieces. It is also foolproof because there is no tricky addition of water, only two fats that insulate the wheat proteins, making overworking (and thereby toughening) the dough less likely. This also means the scraps can be rerolled a couple of times without getting too tough to enjoy. I learned this dough from Paula Haney, who learned it from the famous pastry chef Della Gossett. We used it at Hoosier Mama Pie Company to make hand pies. I use it all the time in my day-to-day baking, often substituting in alternative flours such as rye or spelt for added flavor.

MAKES TWO 9 IN [23 CM] CRUSTS

10 oz [185 g] flour, all-purpose or alternative

¼ tsp salt

¼ tsp sugar

6 oz [170 g] cold butter, cut into cubes

6 oz [170 g] cream cheese, at room temperature

In a large bowl, combine the flour, salt, and sugar. Rub or cut in the butter until the mixture is in pea-size pieces. Add the cream cheese and bring together into a slightly shaggy dough. Divide the dough in half and pat into rounds, wrap in plastic, and chillax for at least 30 minutes.

Remove from the fridge and bring to room temperature (for ease of rolling). On a lightly floured surface, roll out the dough to a ¼ in [6 mm] thickness and proceed with your recipe. This dough freezes very well as a disc for future use.

phyllo dough

There are recipes on the internet to make your own phyllo dough, but I have never tried. I don't really see the point except for the novelty of it, so I buy it from the freezer section. The most important things to know about phyllo dough are:

- It dries out if left uncovered, so always cover with a slightly damp kitchen towel while working with it.

- It needs a layer of fat between each sheet. Most recipes call for melted butter but for some reason that always annoys me, so I usually just drizzle with olive oil and spread with a pastry brush.

- Most phyllo doughs are made without salt, so I always sprinkle a bit of salt and pepper between each layer.

- Phyllo dough can be thawed and refrozen. Because it doesn't have fat or leavening agents it is A-OK to thaw, use a few sheets, and then refreeze what you haven't used. Just be sure to keep it covered the whole time.

- If you get a bunch of dried-out, cracking phyllo, look up a recipe for knafeh on the internet and use it for that. It is delicious, but I don't need to reinvent the wheel for you.

- I've never used whole-wheat phyllo but presumably it will work interchangably because the flaky layers come from the layer of fat between the dough and therefore will not be hurt by some extra bran.

- When comparing brands at the store, I always just look for the one that has the fewest ingredients.

biscuit dough

This recipe is adapted from America's Test Kitchen and like so many things is just genius because it rethinks how to achieve what you need (little pockets of butter) in an easier way (creating butter flecks by cooling melted butter in cold buttermilk instead of cutting the butter in like pie dough). Because a tender biscuit is the goal, I like swapping in lower gluten flours such as spelt or barley flour, which also adds depth of flavor.

MAKES ABOUT 16 BISCUITS

6½ cups [925 g] all-purpose flour (or 50/50 all-purpose and alternative flour such as spelt or barley)

1 Tbsp baking powder

1 tsp baking soda

1 Tbsp sugar

2 tsp salt, plus more for sprinkling

8 oz [230 g] butter, melted and cooled to warm

2 cups [480 ml] buttermilk

Line a baking sheet with a silicone mat or parchment paper.

In a large bowl, combine the flour, baking powder, baking soda, sugar, and salt.

In a medium bowl, pour the warm melted butter into the cold buttermilk so that it makes little clumps as it cools.

Pour the buttermilk mixture into the dry ingredients and mix together (I use my hands or a wooden spoon) to make a shaggy dough. Turn it out onto a lightly floured surface and gently bring it together by hand. Pat and roll the dough into a 1½ in [4 cm] thick mass. Using a 2 in [5 cm] wide biscuit cutter or glass, punch out the biscuits and transfer to the prepared baking sheet, leaving 1 in [2.5 cm] between the biscuits. Press the scraps together and punch out as many more biscuits as you can. Wrap and chill the biscuits for a minimum of 30 minutes and up to overnight.

Preheat the oven to 475°F [240°C]. Sprinkle the tops of the biscuits with a pinch of salt and bake until golden brown, about 20 minutes. Serve warm or cool completely before storing in an airtight container for up to 3 days.

pie dough

Like all things pie in my life, my training came from Paula Haney of Hoosier Mama Pie Company in Chicago, Illinois. I am confident that this is her dough recipe, though maybe I've changed it. I can't really remember. The key is to keep the butter very cold while bringing the dough together. The flecks of butter melt during baking, leaving little air pockets that yield the flaky texture.

If you work the butter into the dough, it will be much more like a short crust—the butter enriching the dough, making it tender, not flaky. To be sure to get the butter pockets, I often add the butter in two additions, three-quarters of it in the first go-around, working it into the dough with my fingers or a pastry cutter. When that mixture is almost pea-size, I add the last little bit and work it in. Alternatively, when it is crazy hot in the summer, I super-chill everything: grate and freeze the butter before adding, ice the water, and chill the flour mixture for 20 minutes before mixing.

MAKES TWO 9 IN [23 CM] CRUSTS

2½ cups [350 g] all-purpose flour

1½ tsp sugar

1½ tsp salt

13 Tbsp (6.5 oz [195 g]) fat (butter or lard or a 50/50 mix)

1 Tbsp vinegar (any variety except balsamic)

In a medium bowl, combine the flour, sugar, and salt.

Cut the fat into cubes (the smaller you cut them, the faster they work into the dough). With a pastry cutter or your hands, rub the butter into the flour mixture, making shaggy flecks about the size of a pea.

Add ½ cup [120 ml] of water and the vinegar and bring together into a craggy dough. Turn out onto a lightly floured surface and gently yet quickly knead until the dough just comes together—I like there to still be streaks of butter in the dough. Divide into two even pieces, pat into rounds, wrap, and chill for at least 30 minutes and up to 1 week to set the butter. Roll out to the size specified in the recipe and proceed.

puff pastry dough

Lamination—the process of folding butter into dough to achieve multiple layers—is the key to a proper puff pastry dough. Traditional puff pastry requires taking a big block of butter and wrapping it in dough and then doing a hundred million folds and rolls. This recipe is for "Ruff Puff" and what I've always seen used in restaurant kitchens. It is faster and no less puffy. The only way to make it "puff" is to do all of the folds and rests in between. This process arranges the layers of butter on top of each other so that when they melt in the hot oven, organized, stacked pockets of air result. Without the lamination, you'll just get the chaotic air pockets of flaky pie dough. To be totally honest, you could probably use pie dough and just laminate it to make the layers and it would work as well. I've always used this ratio, and so I am including it here, but I'm confident that it is less about the butter ratio and more about making the layers.

MAKES 14 OZ [400 G] DOUGH	1¼ cups [175 g] all-purpose flour	½ tsp salt	13 Tbsp (6.5 oz [195 g]) butter, frozen

In a medium bowl, combine the flour and salt. Grate the frozen butter on the largest tooth of a box grater and add to the flour mixture. Toss the butter in the flour to coat. Add 6 Tbsp [90 ml] of water and bring together into a cohesive dough (at this point it will feel a lot like pie dough). Pat into a 5 in [12 cm] square, cover, and chill for 30 minutes.

Roll out on a lightly floured surface into an 8 by 15 in [20 by 38 cm] rectangle and then fold into thirds like you're folding a letter. Cover and chill for 30 minutes. Repeat folding and chilling two more times. Chill for 1 hour to fully set the butter, then roll and use as the recipe calls for.

CAKES

almond orange cake

This cake is an old James Beard classic that I found via his founda-tion's cookbook, *Waste Not*. The only thing that can be a bit of a hassle is boiling the oranges and puréeing them. I've started doing that whenever I have a couple of oranges or clementines that are getting a little sad, then freeze the purée, which gives me the ability to whip up this cake on a whim.

MAKES ONE 9 IN [23 CM] CAKE

2 whole oranges or 1 cup [240 ml] orange purée

6 eggs

1½ cups [180 g] ground almonds

1 cup [100 g] sugar

1 tsp baking powder

Pinch of salt

Preheat the oven to 400°F [200°C]. Line a 9 in [23 cm] cake pan with parchment or grease with butter or cooking spray.

Fully submerge the oranges (peels and all) in a pot of salted water. Bring to a boil, decrease to a simmer, and cook until the oranges are soft, about 30 minutes. Transfer the oranges from the water to a food processor and process into a fairly fine paste.

In a medium bowl, whisk the eggs until foamy. Add the almonds, sugar, baking powder, orange purée, and salt and stir to combine. Tip the batter into the prepared cake pan. Bake in the middle of the oven until the cake is starting to brown, feels firm to the touch, and a knife test (see page 30) comes out clean, about 1 hour. Cool for 10 minutes, then loosen the cake from the sides of the pan and flip it out onto a wire rack to cool completely. Serve at room temperature. Store in an airtight container at room temperature for up to 7 days.

angel food cake

I inevitably have a container of stray egg whites in the back of my fridge. This cake is the perfect way to hoover up those whites, and the stark-white, spongy cake pairs well with just about any fruit you have on hand.

MAKES ONE 9 IN [23 CM] CAKE

1 cup [140 g] all-purpose flour

1 cup [120 g] powdered sugar

12 egg whites

1½ tsp cream of tartar

¼ tsp salt

1 cup [200 g] granulated sugar

½ tsp vanilla extract

Preheat the oven to 375°F [190°C].

Into a medium bowl, sift together the flour and powdered sugar.

In the bowl of a stand mixer fitted with the whisk attachment or using a handheld electric beater, whip the egg whites until foamy. Add the cream of tartar and salt and continue whipping on high speed until soft peaks start to form. Decrease the mixer speed to medium and start adding the granulated sugar a spoonful at a time. The whites will turn firm and glossy. With the mixer on low speed, whisk in the vanilla.

Sift the flour mixture over the whites and gently fold together (I usually use the whisk from the mixer but you can also do it by hand) until no streaks of egg whites or pockets of flour remain in the batter.

Pour the batter into an ungreased angel food cake tube pan (it is critical that the pan be ungreased because otherwise the cake can't creep up the side and set, and the fat will also deflate the whipped egg whites). Bake until the cake is golden brown and has pulled back from the sides of the pan, and a knife test (see page 30) comes out clean. Flip the pan upside down onto a wire rack and let the cake cool completely before removing it from the pan.

Store in an airtight container for up to 7 days.

basque cheesecake

This burnished and tangy cheesecake is fluffier than a traditional New York cheesecake and pairs just as well with any fruit, so this is a recipe to keep in your back pocket when nothing else is jumping out at you. I don't own a springform cake pan, so I bake this in a regular cake pan and it works fine. Maybe it is harder to get the first slice out, but that's really about it. If you have a springform pan, now's a good time to use it. This recipe is adapted from Genevieve Ko of the *Los Angeles Times*.

**MAKES ONE 9 IN
[23 CM] CAKE**

Olive oil

1½ lb [685 g] cream
   cheese

1½ cups [360 g] sour
   cream

7 egg yolks

¾ cup [150 g] sugar

½ tsp salt

Preheat the oven to 425°F [220°C]. Grease a 9 in [23 cm] springform or traditional cake pan with olive oil.

In the bowl of a stand mixer fitted with the paddle attachment, beat the cream cheese until light and fluffy. Add the sour cream, egg yolks, sugar, and salt. Beat again until perfectly combined.

Tip the batter into the prepared pan and bake until the top is deeply browned and the sides are set, but the center is still soft, about 20 minutes. Cool to room temperature. Cover and chill overnight.

Remove from the pan and serve cold. Store refrigerated and tightly covered for up to 7 days.

cornbread cake

This mixture can be used as slightly sweet cornbread or as the base for a not-very-sweet cake. Like all cornbread, it dries out quickly, so store in an airtight container and eat it up.

MAKES ONE 9 BY 5 IN [23 BY 12 CM] LOAF CAKE OR 9 IN [23 CM] ROUND CAKE

2 cups [280 g] cornmeal

2 cups [280 g] all-purpose flour

2 tsp baking powder

1 tsp baking soda

1 tsp salt

2 cups [480 ml] buttermilk

10 oz [300 g] butter, melted

2 eggs

¼ cup [50 g] brown sugar

¼ cup [85 g] honey

Preheat the oven to 375°F [190°C]. Grease (with any fat you have on hand—butter, bacon fat, pan spray) a 9 by 5 in [23 by 12 cm] loaf pan or a 9 in [23 cm] cake pan.

In a large bowl, combine the cornmeal, flour, baking powder, baking soda, and salt.

In a separate large bowl, whisk together the buttermilk, butter, eggs, brown sugar, and honey.

Add the wet ingredients to the dry ingredients and stir until well combined.

Pour the batter into the prepared pan. Bake until golden brown and a knife test (see page 30) comes out clean, 25 to 30 minutes for the cake pan, 30 to 45 minutes for the loaf pan.

Cool on a wire rack. Serve warm or store in an airtight container for up to 2 days.

ginger honey cake

I'm not generally one for "warming spices." I find them cloying and too much like pumpkin pie–scented candles. Ginger, on the other hand, is a horse of a different color: warming, yes, but spicy. My friend and talented baker Sierra Smith was the first one to introduce me to adding ginger and cayenne to a molasses dough, and I'm better for it and her friendship. This cake is moist, snappy, and pairs well with a variety of fruits. And it's not too shabby on its own. Note: This makes for a very tall cake, so place the cake pan on a baking sheet to catch any inadvertent overflow.

MAKES ONE 9 IN [23 CM] CAKE

2½ cups [350 g] all-purpose flour

1 tsp ground ginger

¾ tsp finely ground black pepper

⅛ tsp ground cayenne

¾ cup [240 g] molasses or sorghum syrup

¼ cup [85 g] honey

1 cup [200 g] sugar

1 cup [240 ml] neutral oil

2 oz [55 g] fresh ginger, peeled and grated

2 tsp baking soda

2 eggs

Preheat the oven to 350°F [180°C]. Line a 9 in [23 cm] cake pan with a circle of parchment paper.

In a medium bowl, combine the flour, ginger, black pepper, and cayenne.

In a large bowl, combine the molasses, honey, sugar, and oil.

In a small saucepan, bring 1 cup [240 ml] of water to a boil. Add the fresh ginger and the baking soda, stirring to dissolve. Add to the molasses mixture, then whisk in the dry ingredients. Add the eggs and whisk until well combined.

Tip the batter into the prepared cake pan. Bake until it is cooked through and a knife test (see page 30) comes out clean, 60 to 90 minutes. Cool the cake on a wire rack for 10 minutes. Loosen the edges and flip onto a platter. Cool to room temperature before serving, and store in an airtight container for up to 7 days.

maple pudding cake

I found this cake as I was researching cake traditions of the northern Midwest. I think of it as something akin to a tres leches cake. The butter in the cake batter will be fully submerged in the maple syrup mixture when it goes into the oven and then invert while baking so the cake is floating on top of a thickened maple glaze. I like to make this as individual cakes baked in ramekins, but it works just as well with less hassle baked in a regular baking dish.

MAKES ONE 9 IN [23 CM] SQUARE CAKE OR 6 MINI CAKES

¾ cup [180 ml] maple syrup (I like grade B for extra dark, rich flavor)

⅓ cup [80 ml] heavy cream

2 Tbsp apple cider vinegar

6 Tbsp (3 oz [85 g]) butter, at room temperature

2 Tbsp sugar

1 egg

½ tsp vanilla extract

1¼ cups [175 g] all-purpose flour

1 tsp baking powder

½ tsp salt

Preheat the oven to 350°F [180°C].

In a small saucepan, bring the maple syrup, heavy cream, and vinegar to a simmer over medium heat. Cook until slightly thickened, about 5 minutes.

Either in a stand mixer or by hand, cream the butter and sugar until fluffy. Scrape down the sides of the bowl and add the egg and vanilla. Beat until combined. Add the flour, baking powder, and salt. Combine gently until it just comes together into a stiff dough.

Pour two-thirds of the maple-cream mixture into a 9 by 9 [23 by 23 cm] unprepared (as in plain, not startled) baking dish. Top with the cake batter, pushing it to the edges and into the corners of the baking dish. Pour the remaining maple-cream mixture on top of the cake batter. Bake until a knife test (see page 30) comes out clean, about 35 minutes. If baking as mini cakes, do the same thing in those dishes but the cake will take less time to bake; start checking with the knife test after 12 minutes. Cool for 10 minutes. This cake does not store well, so make and eat on the same day.

upside-down cake

Like most of the best things in my life, I'm pretty sure I got this off of my friend Tim Mazurek's blog, *Lottie + Doof*, from his pineapple upside-down cake recipe. It has now become my go-to buttery, tender cake batter that does well baked over the top of just about any fruit topping, including jam when fresh fruit isn't available. Of course, if you happen to have a lot of pineapple on your hands, go find the original recipe and go that route instead.

**MAKES ONE 9 IN
[23 CM] CAKE**

2 cups [240 g] fruit, unless directed differently in the specific fruit recipe

9 Tbsp (4.5 oz [135 g]) butter, at room temperature

¼ cup [60 ml] buttermilk

¼ cup [60 g] sour cream

3 egg yolks

1 tsp vanilla extract

1½ cups [210 g] all-purpose flour

⅔ cup [130 g] sugar

¾ tsp baking powder

½ tsp salt

Preheat the oven to 350°F [180°C] (unless otherwise directed in the main recipe). Line a greased 9 in [23 cm] cake pan with a parchment circle. Spread your fruit mixture across the bottom.

In a medium bowl, combine the butter, buttermilk, sour cream, egg yolks, and vanilla.

In a large bowl, combine the flour, sugar, baking powder, and salt.

Combine the wet ingredients with the dry. Beat for 2 minutes to develop the cake's structure.

Spread the batter over the fruit mixture in the prepared cake pan. Bake until golden brown and springy, and a knife test (see page 30) comes out clean when inserted in the center of the cake, about 25 minutes. The cake will store, covered, at room temperature for up to 3 days or wrapped and refrigerated for up to 5 days.

COOKIES

almond brutti ma buoni

Brutti ma buoni translates from Italian as "ugly but good" and really should read "ugly but good and easy and universally applicable" (I'm sure that would still sound quaint à la Italiana). These cookies are super straightforward, and I can't think of a single fruit that wouldn't taste good with some crushed almond cookies over the top. Note: They are equally as good made with hazelnut flour or shredded unsweetened coconut. Thank you to Chef John Asbaty for introducing me to these little gems.

MAKES ABOUT 18 COOKIES

3 egg whites (3 oz [85 g])

2 cups [240 g] fine almond flour

1½ cups [180 g] powdered sugar

1 tsp vanilla extract

Pinch of salt

Preheat the oven to 400°F [200°C]. Line two baking sheets with silicone mats or parchment paper.

In a large bowl, beat the egg whites until foamy but not peaking. Add the flour, sugar, vanilla, and salt. Stir to combine.

Scoop tablespoon-size balls onto the prepared baking sheets, spacing them 1 in [2.5 cm] apart. Bake until golden brown and fragrant, about 14 minutes (longer for dry cookies, shorter for chewy cookies).

Cool completely and serve with fruit. Store in an airtight container at room temperature for up to 7 days.

ginger thins

This recipe is based on the Belgium almond cookie, pain d'amande, but uses ginger instead of almonds. If you want to make the almond version, substitute vanilla for the ground ginger and sliced almonds for the candied ginger. I like them both ways, but an almond-ginger combo version is too much.

MAKES ABOUT 20 COOKIES

8 Tbsp (4 oz [120 g]) salted butter

⅔ cup [130 g] granulated sugar

⅔ cup [130 g] light brown sugar

½ tsp ground ginger

2⅓ cups [325 g] all-purpose flour

¾ cup [90 g] candied ginger, coarsely chopped

¼ tsp baking soda

Line a 9 in [23 cm] loaf pan with plastic wrap.

In a medium saucepan over medium-low heat, melt the butter with the sugars, ground ginger, and ⅓ cup [80 ml] of water. Heat only until the butter melts—the sugar won't dissolve—about 3 minutes. Remove from the heat.

In a large bowl, combine the flour, candied ginger, and baking soda. Add the melted butter mixture and stir until completely combined.

Press the dough into the prepared pan, smoothing the top. Chill until firm, at least 1 hour and up to 2 days, after which the dough oxidizes so I usually transfer to the freezer if I'm not going to bake for a long time.

Preheat the oven to 325°F [160°C]. Line two baking sheets with silicone mats or parchment paper.

Using a sharp chef's knife, slice the dough into thin rectangles, ideally ⅛ in [3 mm] thick.

Lay the cookies on the prepared baking sheets. Bake until the cookies feel firm and are starting to brown, about 10 minutes. Using an offset spatula, flip the cookies and bake for 10 to 15 minutes more, until golden brown all over and crisp.

Cool on a wire rack. Store in an airtight container at room temperature for up to 7 days.

pecan sandies

Pecans might be my favorite nuts. Buttery cookies might be my favorite cookies. Logic would go that a buttery cookie studded with pecans would be my favorite cookie, and these are! I like to roll the dough into a log, freeze it, and then slice it into coins to bake. This ensures perfectly round cookies as well as having a bit of cookie dough in the freezer whenever you find yourself with unexpected guests or some extra fruit that needs a crunchy counterpart.

**MAKES ABOUT
20 COOKIES**

8 Tbsp (4 oz [120 g]) butter, softened

½ cup [100 g] brown sugar

1½ tsp vanilla extract

1 cup [140 g] all-purpose flour

½ tsp salt

1 cup [120 g] pecans, roughly chopped

In a medium bowl or the bowl of a stand mixer, cream the butter and sugar until light and fluffy. Add the vanilla and beat to combine. Add the flour and salt and beat until just combined. Fold in the pecans.

Transfer the dough to a large sheet of parchment paper. Use the paper to help you form a log 1 to 2 in [2.5 to 5 cm] across. Or scoop into 1 in [2.5 cm] balls, transfer to a baking sheet lined with a silicone mat or parchment paper, and flatten the balls with the bottom of a glass. Chill the dough (either as a log or as flattened portions) for at least 30 minutes and up to 2 days.

Preheat the oven to 350°F [180°C].

If you chilled a log of dough, slice into 20 cookies about ¼ in [6 mm] thick. Place cookies on a baking sheet lined with a silicone mat or parchment paper, leaving at least ½ in [12 mm] of space between cookies. Bake until golden brown, 15 to 18 minutes, rotating the sheet halfway through.

Let cool on a wire rack. Store in an airtight container for up to 7 days.

pie dough cookies

This is my favorite way to use up the trim from making a pie. Take the leftover scraps and gently knead them back into a cohesive disc. On a lightly floured surface, roll it out to ¼ in [6 mm] thick. Cut into shapes with traditional cookie cutters or simply cut into rectangles or squares of whatever size you like. Transfer to a baking sheet lined with a silicone mat or parchment paper. Brush with heavy cream and sprinkle with SSS (page 78) or any other sugar/spice mixture. Bake in a 350°F [180°C] oven until golden brown, about 12 minutes. Let cool on a wire rack and then snack away or store in an airtight container for up to 7 days.

---

puff pastry tortas de aceite

Favorite cook's treats right here. This is something that I just throw together because it is so good, but it's a bit unrefined so it rarely sees the light of a formal table.

Preheat the oven to 400°F [200°C].

Roll pieces of Puff Pastry Dough (page 61) to ¼ in [6 mm] thick and cut into wide strips or squares. Transfer to a baking sheet lined with a silicone mat or parchment paper. Brush the dough with olive oil and sprinkle with SSS (page 78). Bake until puffed and golden brown, about 12 minutes. Allow to cool and then eat by yourself standing over the sink or share with your friends.

CRUNCHY STUFF + TOPPINGS

candied fennel seeds

The idea for these came when I couldn't find the candied anise seed commonly served at Indian restaurants for dessert. While they lack the brightly colored candy coating, the flavor is there. Note: This ratio can be used for more simply candied nuts (without spices); just replace the volume of fennel seeds with the nut of your choosing.

MAKES ⅓ CUP [75 G]

2 Tbsp sugar	¼ cup [60 g] fennel seeds	¼ tsp salt

In a small frying pan over medium heat, combine the sugar and 2 Tbsp of water. Simmer until the mixture reduces and becomes syrupy. Add the fennel seeds. Stir continuously until the mixture crystalizes. Add the salt. Remove the pan from the heat to let cool. Store indefinitely tightly covered at room temperature.

candied nuts

This is a slightly more elaborate version of classic candied nuts. If you don't want to do the extra steps, use the Candied Fennel Seeds recipe (facing page) multiplied up for the volume of nuts you want to candy. I'm not a huge fan of warming spices and so I rarely add them, but I have included them in this recipe in case you want to make a big bowl of spiced nuts for the holidays.

MAKES 2 CUPS [250 G]

4 Tbsp (2 oz [60 g]) butter

8 oz [230 g] nuts (any variety or a mix)

½ cup [100 g] sugar

¼ tsp ground black pepper

1 tsp ground cinnamon (optional)

½ tsp ground ginger (optional)

¼ tsp ground clove (optional)

¼ tsp ground black cardamom (optional)

½ tsp salt

In a large frying pan, melt the butter over medium heat. Add the nuts and stir to coat. Add the sugar and black pepper (and other spices, if using) and stir to coat. Continue stirring until the sugar caramelizes and starts to crystalize. Remove from the heat, add the salt, and stir to distribute. Transfer the mixture to a parchment- or silicone mat–lined baking sheet to cool. Store tightly covered at room temperature for upwards of 2 weeks or really until the nuts go rancid.

crumble topping

Crumble topping is one of my favorite things because it is end-lessly adaptable to what's in the kitchen—I've made it with just flour, flour and oats, oats and nuts, and on and on. This is my base recipe, and I'll add in other ingredients on a whim. As long as the end texture stays the same, you shouldn't have any trouble.

MAKES 3 CUPS [300 G]

1 cup [140 g] all-purpose flour

1 cup [100 g] old-fashioned rolled oats, not instant

1 cup [200 g] brown sugar

¼ tsp salt

8 Tbsp (4 oz [120 g]) butter, cubed

In a medium bowl, combine the flour, oats, brown sugar, and salt. Rub in the butter like you would for pie dough until the crumble holds together like a loose snowball when gripped. Chill for 30 minutes.

Use to top pies, or bake on its own by spreading onto a parchment- or silicone mat–lined baking sheet, and baking in a 375°F [190°C] oven until golden brown, about 20 minutes. Scatter on a big bowl of fruit. Store tightly covered at room temperature for 7 days, rewarming in the oven if the crumble loses its crisp.

honeycomb brittle

My Grandma Hazel used to dip this in chocolate and call it sea foam candy. Undipped, it is usually called honeycomb. It is effectively peanut brittle without the peanuts and flavored with honey. I rarely eat big pieces of it anymore, but instead use it to add texture to simple desserts.

MAKES 4 CUPS [400 G]	1½ cups [300 g] sugar	¼ cup [85 g] honey	1 Tbsp baking soda

Spray a baking sheet with cooking spray or line with parchment paper or a silicone mat.

In a large saucepan, combine the sugar, honey, and ¼ cup [60 ml] of water and bring to a boil over high heat, stirring regularly, until the sugar is dissolved. Stop stirring (to keep the sugar from crystalizing on the side of the pot) and cook until the mixture reaches 300°F [150°C] on a candy thermometer, about 4 minutes. Add the baking soda and stir once with a whisk to distribute as it foams up (more stirring will pop all of the bubbles).

Pour the mixture onto the prepared baking sheet without spreading (which will also pop the bubbles) and let cool completely. Break into pieces and eat or store at room temperature in an airtight container for up to a week or until it gets sticky, which happens more when it's humid out.

salty sugar sprinkle (sss)

This is less of a recipe and more of an idea. For every 1 cup [200 g] of sugar, add a ½ tsp of salt and then use that mixture to top any number of sweet things, including cookies, pies, dough-nuts, etc., for a nice mix of salty-spiked sweetness. Store for the rest of your life covered at room temperature anywhere cool enough to not melt the sugar.

---

salty nuts

I like to add these salty nuts to the top of something creamy or a butter cake to add texture, nuttiness, and a hit of olive oil and salt.

MAKES 1 CUP [140 G]

1 cup [140 g] nuts (I usually use pecans but use what's on hand, or what you like), toasted	2 Tbsp olive oil	Salt

Toss the toasted nuts with the olive oil and a big pinch of salt and then top away. Store covered at room temperature for upwards of 2 weeks or really until the nuts go rancid.

CREAMY STUFF
(though not always made w/dairy)

crème brûlée

Like many of my favorite foods, crème brûlée is elegant in its simplicity, which leaves little to hide behind if poorly executed. Tips: Take care with the custard. Always bake in a bain-marie (see page 29). It is a bit fiddly but provides the even, gentle heat needed to best support a silken filling. Cook the custards less than you might think. The filling should have a jiggle in the center when gently shaken to test for doneness; cooking for longer results in a grainy, curdled mouthfeel. Chill completely because you can't properly swirl the ramekin for the caramel crust if it is a hot soup. For the crust, most kitchens use a standard hardware store blowtorch, but an oven broiler will also work. Sprinkle a teaspoon or so of sugar on the custard and then shake to evenly distribute. Torch and fully caramelize the sugar, swirling the ramekin to spread the caramel. Then repeat. The two-step caramelizing is the best way to get a nice thickness of caramel and an even coating.

MAKES FOUR 10 OZ [300 ML] RAMEKINS

2 cups [480 ml] heavy cream

1 cup [240 ml] milk

5 Tbsp [75 g] sugar, plus more for sprinkling

½ tsp vanilla paste or ½ vanilla bean, split and seeds scraped

6 egg yolks

Preheat the oven to 300°F [150°C].

In a large saucepan over medium heat, combine the cream, milk, sugar, and vanilla. Bring to a scald (see page 31), allowing the sugar to dissolve.

continued

In the bowl of a stand mixer fitted with the whisk attachment (or using a hand mixer), whip the sugar and egg yolks until pale in color, fluffy in texture, and the whisk leaves a trail when lifted, about 5 minutes.

Temper (see page 31) the cream mixture into the egg yolks and then strain into a pitcher. Place the ramekins in an ovenproof baking dish. Divide the filling among the ramekins.

Bring a teapot of water to a boil and pour the hot water into the baking dish to surround the ramekins. Bake until just set, about 30 minutes. Carefully remove the ramekins from the baking dish and let cool to room temperature (or for about an hour), then chill for 4 hours or up to 4 days.

Just before serving, sprinkle the top of each custard with a couple spoonfuls of sugar. Using a blowtorch or the oven broiler, caramelize the sugar, swirling the ramekins to move the caramel evenly across the surface. If using the broiler, carefully remove from the oven one ramekin at a time and swirl while holding with a pot holder. Repeat a second time (top with sugar, caramelize, and swirl) to fully coat, creating a true glass crust. Serve immediately.

custard

This custard is the ice cream base that my mentor Skye Gyngell taught me when I worked for her at Petersham Nurseries in London. I use it for all my ice creams and for unfrozen custard sauces. I've never used a different one, and I probably never will. Be sure not to whisk the egg yolks and sugar together until just before you're ready to add the hot cream as the sugar can "cook" the yolk, making lumps.

2 cups [480 ml] heavy cream	1 tsp vanilla paste, preferably with the seeds in it	6 egg yolks
¾ cup [180 ml] whole milk		1¼ cups [250 g] sugar
		Pinch of salt

In a medium saucepan, combine the cream, milk, and vanilla over medium heat. Bring to a scald (see page 31). Just as the cream mixture starts to bubble, remove from the heat and set aside.

In a large mixing bowl, whisk together the egg yolks, sugar, and salt. Beat until pale and fluffy, about 2 minutes.

Temper (see page 31) the cream into the egg yolks.

Return the mixture to the saucepan and cook over low heat while stirring in a figure-8 motion the entire time. The mixture will start to thicken after 6 to 8 minutes. Continue cooking until the custard is thick enough to coat the back of a wooden spoon and leave a clean line when you drag a finger through it. Remove from the heat, then strain the mixture through a fine-mesh sieve into a clean bowl. Cover with plastic wrap, pressing the wrap to the surface of the custard, like you would for a pudding. Cool to room temperature and then refrigerate until completely cool before using. Store refrigerated for 7 days or until it sours.

continued

ginger custard

Add ¼ cup [55 g] chopped candied ginger and 1 tsp ground ginger to the cream mixture when scalding.

sherry custard

Add ¼ cup [60 ml] of sweet sherry (like Pedro Ximénez or cream sherry) to the custard at the end before chilling.

fool

Fool (originally spelled foole) is a decidedly English dessert. It is made from any fruit (though usually tart and always cooked or macerated) folded in equal parts with whipped cream or whipped custard. Most references for fool couch it as a summertime dessert; I tend to make it more in the winter, utilizing frozen fruit and serving with a plate of crunchy cookies. I particularly like using frozen fruit because the fruit is naturally soft and juicy after it thaws, so no cooking is required. Below is my template recipe for most fruits. Taste the fruit filling before layering with the cream to be sure it is both tart and sweet, remembering that the bland creaminess of whipped cream will dampen the intensity of the fruit.

1 cup [140 g] frozen fruit

¼ cup [50 g] sugar

Pinch of salt

2 Tbsp some sort of acid (lemon juice, sherry vinegar, balsamic vinegar, etc.)

1 cup [240 ml] heavy cream

In a medium bowl, combine the fruit, sugar, salt, and acid. Mash with the back of a fork, then let sit for 5 minutes or so to combine.

In a separate mediuim bowl, whip the cream to medium stiff peaks (slightly more than if you were whipping for dolloping) so that it holds up when layered with the fruit.

Either gently fold the fruit and the whipped cream and swirl to make a lovely color OR layer in a tall glass: first fruit, then cream, and repeat in layers. Let your guests mix as they eat. Serve immediately and don't let it hang around like a fool.

panna cotta

There's an old industry joke: "How can you tell a restaurant doesn't have a pastry chef on staff?" Answer: "Panna cotta." It's usually true because panna cottas are easy and don't require a ton of technique to achieve beyond using gelatin successfully. It also always feels like a decadent treat despite its simplicity, which makes it perfect for home entertaining. Note: If using sheet gelatin instead of powdered, replace the gelatin packet with three sheets, soften the gelatin in ice water, and omit the 3 Tbsp of cold water.

1 oz [30 g] unflavored powdered gelatin	2 cups [480 ml] heavy cream 1 cup [240 ml] whole milk	⅓ cup [75 g] sugar 1 tsp vanilla paste or extract

In a small saucepan, sprinkle the gelatin over 3 Tbsp of cold water to bloom. Heat gently over low heat to dissolve. Add the cream, milk, sugar, and vanilla. Bring to a scald (see page 31). Divide evenly among four containers (jars, glasses, bowls, whatever you want and think looks good) and refrigerate until set, at least 4 hours and ideally overnight. Serve cold within a couple of days, storing cold until serving.

pastry cream

I have no idea where this recipe came from. It is a random spread sheet in the "random recipes" folder on my computer. Judging by the quality of the spreadsheet formulas (for costing purposes), I think this came from Danielle Jamnik, a wonderful baker from whom I've learned so much over the years. Danielle, is this yours? If so, thanks! If not, do you know where it came from?

2 cups [480 ml] whole milk

4 Tbsp (2 oz [55 g]) butter

1¼ cups [250 g] sugar

1 tsp salt

¼ cup [35 g] cornstarch

7 egg yolks (4 oz [120 g])

1 tsp vanilla extract

In a medium saucepan over medium heat, combine the milk, butter, half of the sugar, and the salt. Bring to a scald (see page 31).

In a large bowl, whisk together the cornstarch and remaining sugar. Add the egg yolks and vanilla to the cornstarch mixture and whisk to combine. Temper (see page 31) in the scalded milk mixture.

Strain the tempered egg mixture back into the pan and return to medium-high heat.

Bring the mixture to a boil for 30 seconds to cook out the cornstarch, stirring constantly. Remove from the heat.

Strain (one more time) into a metal bowl or baking dish. Press plastic wrap or wax paper onto the surface of the pastry cream, allow to cool to room temperature, and place in the fridge to cool completely. Store refrigerated for up to 5 days or until it smells/tastes sour.

ricotta

I love ricotta and often buy it, but when I have a lot of whole milk, I'll make it and feel very proud of myself. Admittedly, the milk is usually on its way out of date, so ricotta is the last chance to keep it from spoiling—the heat and acidity often killing off any bacteria that has built up in the milk. The process is simple but also leaves you with a lot of whey, which can be used to brine chicken or marinate vegetables. I credit Dana Cree with that last idea. I had a dish of hers once with whey-marinated carrots that was delightful. She also makes incredible ice cream. If you find yourself in Chicago, head to Pretty Cool Ice Cream for a treat.

4 cups [1 L] whole milk	½ cup [120 ml] heavy cream	Lemon zest, chili flakes, herbes de Provence, or Aleppo pepper (optional)
¼ cup [60 ml] apple cider vinegar	Salt	
	Ground black pepper	

In a large saucepan over medium heat, bring the milk to a scald (see page 31).

Remove from the heat, add the vinegar, and give it a whisk. The curds should separate easily and float in the whey. If after 10 minutes the liquid is still milky, add another 1 Tbsp of vinegar.

Pour through a fine-mesh strainer set inside a metal or glass bowl to strain the curds from the whey. Place the curds in a bowl, add the cream, and season with salt and pepper to taste. Add additional flavors such as lemon zest, chili flakes, herbs de Provence, or Aleppo pepper (if using). Ricotta will store for upwards of 2 weeks (if the milk was fresh), refrigerated in an airtight container.

sabayon (french), zabaione (italian), sabajón (spanish)

This globe-trotting dish is an eggnog-like custard made by whipping egg yolks, sugar, and wine or spirits into a frothy, creamy treat. Every time I read a sabayon recipe, I don't think it will work but it does. You have to use a double boiler to ensure that the heat doesn't scramble the eggs. You have to whisk continuously and with gusto to both aerate and not curdle the eggs. You can add whipped cream to the finished product to make it richer, but I don't.

sweet sherry sabayon

3 egg yolks	¼ cup [50 g] sugar	2 Tbsp lemon juice (about ½ a lemon)
½ cup [120 ml] cream sherry or marsala	Pinch of salt	

In the bowl of a double boiler (see page 29), combine the egg yolks, sherry, and sugar. Whisk continuously and vigorously until completely frothy, emulsified, and doubled in volume, 8 to 12 minutes. Be sure to get the sides when whisking to prevent the egg yolks from cooking and curdling. Add the salt and lemon juice and whisk to combine. Serve warm, at room temperature, or chilled. Store refrigerated for 2 days, but the mixture will deflate some.

goat cheese sabayon

3 egg yolks	½ cup [120 ml] hard cider or white wine	Pinch of salt
		3 oz [85 g] fresh goat cheese

Follow the instructions for sweet sherry sabayon, substituting hard cider for sherry and adding the goat cheese with the salt. Serve warm or chilled. Store refrigerated for a couple of days, but it will deflate some.

salted caramel sauce

Sandra Holl of Floriole Cafe and Bakery taught me the secret to a complex caramel sauce is to hold your nerve and really let it smoke from the center. I've taken it further than I care to admit and have never had a caramel sauce that tastes burnt, so when in doubt, try to channel your inner daredevil and let it go. The only thing to note is to use a deeper pot than you might imagine because it really does bubble up violently when the cream is added (because the moisture in the cream will immediately convert to steam when hitting the extremely hot caramel). This is also a way to preserve cream that might be close to going off, so feel free to scale up the batch.

1¼ cups [250 g] sugar	1 cup [240 ml] heavy cream	1 tsp salt

In a deep pot over medium-high heat, combine the sugar and ½ cup [120 ml] of water. Heat without stirring until the sugar dissolves, swirling the whole pan to encourage the sugar to dissolve. Use a pastry brush wetted with water to brush down the sides of the pot if crystals begin to form on the sides.

When the sugar has dissolved, increase the heat to high and continue not stirring (which encourages crystal formation). The sugar will start to caramelize (probably in the center). Occasionally lift the pot and give a light swirl to caramelize evenly. When the caramel is dark brown and starting to smoke from the center (which will be later than from the edges), remove from the heat and add the cream (remember it will bubble violently, so don't be startled or burned by the steam). The mixture will be chunky and look broken and awful; don't worry, just return it to the heat over medium-low and stir until smoothed out. Continue cooking until the caramel reaches 225°F [110°C], about 3 minutes after the sugar dissolves. Add the salt, stir, and pour into a heatproof container to cool and serve. Store covered in the fridge for upwards of a month or until it tastes sour.

Note: If you want to make caramel candies, bring the mixture to 245°F [115°C] and add a knob of butter (about 2 Tbsp) at the end. Then pour into a lined baking sheet to form a block, sprinkle the top with sea salt, and allow to cool completely. Cut into bite-size pieces and wrap in plastic wrap or wax paper to serve. Store at room temperature (out of high humidity) for weeks or until they taste sour.

sour cream

Truth be told, I usually buy sour cream and just give it a good whip before using. I use it more often than whipped cream because the tang helps balance sweet desserts. However, if you want to make it (or crème fraîche for that matter), take 1 part cultured buttermilk or yogurt and whisk it into 4 parts fresh heavy cream (so that's ½ cup [120 ml] buttermilk and 2 cups [480 ml] heavy cream), cover with cheesecloth, and leave, unrefrigerated, until it is firm like sour cream (usually 2 to 4 days).

Some things to know:

· Be sure to use cultured buttermilk and live yogurt because it is the bacteria in the buttermilk that will multiply, acidulate, and stiffen the cream.

· Leave it unrefrigerated while fermenting because bacteria grow best at warm temperatures—too cold and they won't multiply.

· Wait until it is as stiff (or tangy) as you want because if you refrigerate it too quickly, it suspends the bacteria growth and won't ever stiffen up.

· Don't worry if it separates and is thicker at the top and liquidy at the bottom; that is just the more buoyant fat rising to the top. Just whisk it together and chill.

· Store covered in the fridge until it molds or tastes bad (usually upwards of a month).

syllabub

Syllabubs are in the same light and creamy dairy desserts category where sabayon and fools like to hang out. A syllabub is different than a sabayon in that there is no egg, only wine and citrus flavoring the sweetened cream. It is different from a fool, which is plain whipped cream with an equal part of fruit added in. All of these sound kind of bad on paper, but are really delightful to eat and dead simple to prepare.

½ cup [120 ml] sweet sherry or masala (I often use late-harvest Riesling)

½ cup [100 g] sugar

2 Tbsp dark rum or brandy

2 lemons (about 3 oz [90 ml]), zest and juice

1 cup [240 ml] heavy cream

Pinch of salt

In a large mixing bowl, combine the sherry, sugar, rum, and lemon zest and juice and stir until the sugar is dissolved. Add the cream while continuously stirring to keep from curdling. Whisk the mixture until it holds soft peaks, about 5 minutes. Add the salt and stir to distribute.

Divide the mixture among four glasses and either chill or serve immediately.

whipped cream

Darina Allen's fingerprints are all over my food. Almost every dessert at Ballymaloe Cookery School is served with a "dollop of softly whipped cream," and to this day desserts often feel a bit underdressed without it. Whipped cream always makes me think of cooking school because it was the one time that Darina was genuinely let down by my performance. I whipped the cream too stiffly, and, upon tasting, she made an expression as if the cream had cut her mouth. She then literally said, "Abra, that cream is a disappointment." I was shattered but have never overwhipped cream since. TL/DR: Stop right as the whisk starts to leave billows in the cream. Note: If you want to whip cream in advance, store in the fridge and then simply rewhip if it is liquidy on the bottom.

plain

I grew up in a household that liked very sweet whipped cream— you could feel the grains of sugar crunching in your teeth. It took me some time to come around to plain whipped cream (no sugar, no flavor add-ins), but I'm here now and I really love it. Take 1 cup [240 ml] or so of cream and whisk into soft billows.

Below are add-ins you can use to gussy up this plain-Jane whipped cream.

boozy

Whip the the cream until it begins to thicken, then add 3 Tbsp of sugar and 1 Tbsp of booze (cognac, rum, whiskey, brandy, etc.) and continue whipping to very soft peaks. Note: If you use more cream, it will be less boozy; less cream, more boozy.

continued

maple

Add ¼ cup [60 ml] of maple syrup to the cream before whipping.

vanilla

Add 1 Tbsp of sugar and 1 tsp of vanilla paste or extract to the cream before whipping.

overwhipped cream a.k.a. butter

If you whip cream too much, the proteins will seize, expel the water bound in the protein (technically buttermilk), and make butter. I've made "small batch" butter too many times to count (blame the divided attention known as multitasking).

Some things to know:

- Drain/press the water from the butter—it firms the butter and makes it more stable.

- I like to salt after pressing the water away and then give a final squeeze when the salt has pulled even more moisture from the protein.

- The buttermilk released is not good for making sour cream or crème fraîche because it isn't cultured and so does not have the all-important bacteria.

- If you want to make butter from crème fraîche, it will work the same but be tangier, and that buttermilk should work to make your next batch of crème fraîche.

- It is worth making "small batch" butter at least once because it is really special even if it is sort of a pain.

CURDS

I love making curds in part because they are perfectly tart and sweet, in part because they have an unbelievably silky texture, and in part because it is funny when something that is so good has such an unpleasant-sounding name. Also, one of the best snacks ever is taking a thick slice of baguette, toasting or grilling it until it is lightly charred, letting it cool for a sec, and then slathering it with curd. It is the perfect treat.

MAKES ¾ CUP [180 ML]

lemon curd

½ cup [100 g] sugar	¼ cup [18 g] lemon zest	Pinch of salt
½ cup [120 ml] lemon juice (about 2 lemons)	2 egg yolks	4 Tbsp (2 oz [55 g] butter

In a small saucepan over medium heat, combine the sugar, lemon juice, lemon zest, egg yolks, and salt. Cook, whisking continuously, until the mixture thickens and bubbles, about 7 minutes. Whisk in the butter. Strain through a fine-mesh sieve into a storage container, press plastic wrap to the surface of the curd, and chill until firm. You can serve it warm, but it tends to feel thin in the mouth.

Store in the fridge for a week or until the lemon starts to taste metallic.

tart fruit curd

1 cup [240 ml] fruit juice (cranberry, currant, rhubarb, etc.), strained of any solids

⅔ cup [130 g] sugar

4 egg yolks

8 Tbsp (4 oz [120 g]) butter

In a small saucepan over medium heat, combine the fruit juice, sugar, and egg yolks. Cook, whisking continuously, until the mixture thickens and small bubbles start to form, about 7 minutes. Whisk in the butter. Strain through a fine-mesh sieve into a storage container, press plastic wrap to the surface of the curd, and chill until firm.

Store in the fridge for a week or so.

FROZEN STUFF

There's maybe nothing better than something frozen against sun-warmed fruit. There's also nothing easier than pulling an already made frozen dessert to the table as an easy finish to a party (or hard day).

ice cream base

Use the Custard (page 81) from the Creamy Stuff section. Churn and freeze per your ice cream maker's instructions.

sorbet

Below is my "should work" ratio to make sorbet from any fruit. That said, every fruit is different, so you'll have to taste the liquid before freezing and adjust it, which can take a few times to get right. Remember that freezing dampens flavor, so you want the sorbet to be sweeter and more tart than you think it should be before freezing it.

3 cups [720 ml] fruit juice   1 cup [240 ml] Simple Syrup (page 109)   ¼ cup [60 ml] lemon juice

Pinch of salt

In a large bowl, whisk together the fruit juice, simple syrup, lemon juice, and salt. Taste and adjust, adding more syrup or lemon juice to suit. Churn and freeze per your ice cream maker's instructions.

lime sorbet

Citrus-only sorbets don't conform to the "should work" ratio, so I use this recipe for lime or lemon sorbet. I like ginger with lime, but not so much with lemon. For lemon sorbet, I make it the same way and just skip the ginger ale.

¾ cup [150 g] sugar

Zest of 1 lime

¾ cup [180 ml] lime juice, freshly squeezed, not bottled

¼ cup [60 ml] ginger ale, the spicier the better (preferably Blenheim or Vernors)

Dissolve the sugar in 1½ cups [375 ml] of water, stirring or shaking to encourage it to dissolve. Add the lime zest, lime juice, and ginger ale and stir to combine. Churn and freeze per your ice cream maker's instructions.

---

sherbet

The beautiful compromise between ice cream and sorbet, sherbet is effectively sorbet with a bit of milk added in for creaminess. I look for creaminess from the dairy and tang from something else, be it buttermilk, citrus, or sour fruit.

buttermilk sherbet

Although buttermilk is often paired with lemon, I prefer a subtler tang of just straight buttermilk.

½ cup [100 g] sugar

2½ cups [600 ml] buttermilk

Pinch of salt

continued

In a medium saucepan over medium-high heat, bring ⅓ cup [80 ml] of water to a boil. Add the sugar, lower the heat to low, and dissolve the sugar. Whisk into the cold buttermilk. Add the salt, stir to combine, and freeze and churn per your ice cream maker's instructions.

fruit sherbet

This basic recipe is a good jumping-off point for just about any fruit sherbet. I make Concord grape the most often, but orange and grapefruit are also in regular rotation.

2 cups [480 ml] fruit juice   ½ cup [100 g] sugar   2 cups [480 ml] whole
3 Tbsp lemon juice   milk or buttermilk

Combine the fruit juice, lemon juice, and sugar and stir until dissolved. Add the milk, stir to combine, and freeze and churn per your ice cream maker's instructions.

MERINGUE

Meringue can be a bit of a tricky devil because it's only made of three ingredients: egg whites, cream of tartar, and sugar (and maybe some flavors). This means technique plays a critical role. That said, once the technique is mastered, meringue serves many purposes in a kitchen. It can be the marshmallowy topping for a curd tart (often lemon) or pie. It can be dried out and used for texture on a strawberry sundae. It can even be filled with chopped nuts and baked for a cookie-like option.

Some things to know about meringue:

- For foolproof meringue, use cream of tartar or a squeeze of lemon to help acidulate and stabilize the eggs. It makes a world of difference.

- The mixer bowl and whisk need to be free of any sort of fat or dish detergent or the whites won't whip.

- The whites need to be free of any stray egg yolk.

- Don't be tempted to turn up the heat in the oven—the meringue won't dry out faster, it will simply brown and be gummy underneath.

- Even the most perfectly dried meringue will get gummy when exposed to high humidity. Always store in an airtight container at room temperature and use silica packets if you really need to keep it dry—though that is often reserved for restaurant scenarios.

- If using for a soft meringue topping, make the same way but instead of baking, spoon the meringue onto your tart (or whatever) and go forth.

- My favorite way to minimize food waste: Burn the meringue left on the whisk with a blowtorch for a toasted marshmallow cook's treat.

- There is a recipe for Swiss meringue out there in which you heat the egg and sugar over a water bath to cook the egg whites before whisking. I don't bother doing that anymore, but if you are worried about the egg whites, either cook them or buy better eggs.

continued

3 egg whites (3 oz [85 g])   ¼ tsp cream of tartar   ¾ cup [150 g] sugar

Preheat the oven to 250°F [110°C]. Line a baking sheet with a silicone mat or parchment paper.

In a large bowl or the bowl of a stand mixer, whisk the egg whites and cream of tartar on medium speed until soft peaks start to form. Decrease the mixer speed to medium-low and add the sugar one spoonful at a time, continually whisking until the meringue is stiff and glossy.

Pipe or spread on the prepared baking sheet and bake until puffed and fully dry, 2 hours. In restaurants, we would also bake meringues last thing and then turn off the oven, prop the door open with a wooden spoon, and let slowly cool and dry out overnight.

PIE FILLING

Grand pie master Paula Haney has a truly revolutionary way of handling juice management in apple pies. She taught me to cut up the apples, toss them in the required sugar, spices, and starch, and let macerate for 25 minutes. Let the resulting liquid drain for 25 minutes before cooking that starch-rich juice into a thick fruit goo. Then (and only then) do you build the pie. This process helps pull out the bulk of the liquid, in advance of baking, that would normally leech from the fruit and make the pie crust soggy. Because of the nature of thickeners (especially cornstarch), the goo will thin as it heats during baking, mix with the rest of the fruit (and the juice that will continue to leach as the fruit cooks), and result in a cohesive filling by the time the crust is golden brown.

I've taken Paula's instruction and adapted it to account for just about any fruit, depending on juiciness—apples require less thickening than cherries. Admittedly, this system is a way to always be able to jigger some sort of pie. If you want more specific ratios for specific fruits, consider getting Paula's *The Hoosier Mama Book of Pie* or Lisa Ludwinski's *Sister Pie* cookbook. Both are incredible resources from incredible women.

super juicy fruit pie filling (for peaches, apricots, berries, cherries, rhubarb, etc.)

2 lb [910 g] fruit, pitted and cut up	1 tsp flavor or spices of choice (vanilla extract, ground ginger, citrus zest, etc.) (optional)	¼ cup [35 g] cornstarch
1 cup [200 g] sugar		½ tsp salt

less juicy fruit pie filling (for apples, pears, etc.)

2 lb [910 g] fruit (I usually keep the peels on but cut the seeds away and then cut into large chunks)	1 cup [200 g] sugar	2 Tbsp cornstarch
	1 tsp flavor or spices of choice (cinnamon, five-spice powder, pie spice, etc.) (optional)	½ tsp salt

In a large bowl, toss the fruit with the sugar, flavor of choice (if using), cornstarch, and salt. Let sit at room temperature for 25 minutes.

Place a colander over a large bowl and tip the fruit mixture into the colander. Let sit for another 25 minutes. Collect the drained liquid from under the colander and transfer to a small saucepan. Place over medium heat and bring to a simmer. Cook until thick, about 8 minutes. Remove from the heat and cool to room temperature.

While the goo is cooling, roll out the pie dough and place the dough round in a 9 in [23 cm] pie pan. Place the fruit in the pie pan, top with the cooled goo, add a double crust or a lattice top, and crimp the edges with a fork. Freeze the assembled pie for a minimum of 30 minutes (but better if overnight).

Preheat the oven to 350°F [180°C].

Brush the crust with egg wash (see page 30) or heavy cream and sprinkle a little extra sugar on top. Bake until the crust is golden brown and the filling is bubbling from the center, usually about an hour. Fruit pies can be stored at room temperature for a couple of days or until the crust gets soggy or the fruit moldy. You can keep in the fridge too, but allow to come to room temperature or warm before eating for best flavor.

PUDDINGS

Some things to know about puddings:

- Puddings (in my opinion) are one of the most underlauded desserts around. You can make them in big batches to feed a crowd. They pair easily with fresh or preserved fruit. They are, in short, a treat.

- Puddings will usually continue to thicken as they cool and the starches set, so I generally like to pull them from the heat when they are starting to show signs of thickening, but before they are fully there.

- If the pudding is too thin after the fact, you can always re-cook it to thicken further (it's just a bit of a hassle).

- If a pudding is too thick, you can always thin it with a bit of cream. I whip the cream if I want to add lightness or body to the pudding or you can just use liquid cream if you want it to be looser. Any pudding should have a piece of plastic wrap, wax paper, or parchment paper pressed to the top of the pudding as it cools to prevent a skin from forming. Some people are really into pudding skin. I am not. Find your own joy.

- Store puddings covered in the fridge for upwards of a week or until they taste sour.

butterscotch pudding

While we're talking about underappreciated, enter butterscotch pudding. I love it. Others say it reminds them of grandparents (implying some sort of ageist insult). Most have never had real butterscotch pudding. So here goes. Read the instructions twice because it will look bad, but if you follow along, it will come together. Like all things caramel, hold your nerve and let the caramel really smoke. This is the only chance you have to control the darkness and flavor of the finished pudding. Even a bit scorched is really good, so don't be a pale pudding wimp.

Note: I've kept the vanilla optional because, with climate change and labor issues, vanilla has gotten very expensive and the pudding works without it, though the flavor is more complex with it. You'll have to decide for yourself; I just didn't want you to feel obligated to use it.

2½ cups [600 ml] whole milk

¼ cup [35 g] cornstarch

½ tsp salt

3 eggs

4 Tbsp (2 oz [60 g]) butter

¾ cup [150 g] brown sugar

1 cup [240 ml] heavy cream

1 tsp vanilla extract (optional)

In a large bowl, combine the milk, cornstarch, and salt to make a smooth slurry. Whisk the eggs into the milk mixture and set aside.

In a deep stockpot, melt the butter over medium-high heat. Add the brown sugar and whisk; the mixture will be grainy at first and split. Keep cooking; it will eventually be a cohesive, liquid, bubbling mass. Continue cooking until it starts to smoke, then remove from the heat. Add the cream. It will bubble violently, so watch out; this is why you use a deep stockpot. Return the pot to low heat. Whisk until the sugar has dissolved.

Temper (see page 31) the hot cream to the milk-cornstarch mixture and strain back into the pot. Increase the heat to medium-high. Bring the mixture to a boil, whisking constantly. Boil until thickened, about 1 minute. Remove from the heat and add the vanilla (if using).

Strain one more time through a fine-mesh sieve into a clean bowl. Press plastic wrap, wax paper, or parchment against the surface of the pudding. Let cool completely to room temperature or chill in the fridge before transferring to serving dishes. Store refrigerated for up to 7 days.

chocolate pudding

This is a very rich chocolate pudding, probably more like a mousse. It isn't technically a mousse (I'm not really sure why, but a pastry chef once assured me it wasn't). If it is too chocolaty for you (as it often is for me), whip additional cream and fold it in to thin the chocolate flavor.

2 cups [480 ml] whole milk

1 cup [240 ml] heavy cream

3 Tbsp cornstarch

2 eggs

½ cup [100 g] sugar

10 oz [280 g] 60 percent dark chocolate

4 Tbsp (2 oz [60 g]) butter

1 Tbsp rum

1 tsp vanilla extract

Pinch of salt

In a medium saucepan, scald (see page 31) 1 cup [240 ml] of the milk and the cream over medium heat, being sure not to scorch the bottom.

In a large bowl, whisk the remaining 1 cup [240 ml] of milk with the cornstarch to make a slurry. Whisk in the eggs and sugar until smooth. Temper (see page 31) in the scalded milk mixture, then return to the saucepan and cook over medium heat, whisking constantly until it begins to thicken and boil, about 5 minutes. Whisk at a boil for an additional 2 minutes to cook out the cornstarch.

Remove from the heat and add the chocolate, butter, rum, vanilla, and salt. Whisk until everything is melted and combined, with no streaks.

Pour the chocolate mixture through a fine-mesh strainer into a bowl or pan. Press plastic wrap or wax paper to the surface of the pudding and chill in the fridge until firm, usually at least an hour but best if overnight.

To serve, whip the pudding to make it easier to scoop and transfer to serving dishes. Store refrigerated for up to 7 days.

rice pudding

Zingerman's Deli in Ann Arbor was such a formative place for me—I was taught all sorts about the power of small businesses, servant leadership, and rice pudding. Having only ever had cafeteria cups of stodgy, lumpy sweet stuff, I always thought that rice pudding was nasty. It turns out good ingredients and a bit of know-how really make a great product, or as Zingerman's would say, "You really can taste the difference."

4 cups [960 ml] whole milk

2 cups [480 ml] heavy cream

½ cup [100 g] Arborio rice

¼ cup [50 g] brown sugar

1 tsp ground cinnamon or five-spice powder

1 tsp ground ginger

1 tsp vanilla paste or extract

Pinch of salt

1 cup [140 g] dried cherries or raisins

Zest of 1 orange

In a large pot over medium heat, combine the milk, cream, rice, brown sugar, cinnamon, ginger, vanilla, and salt. Cook at a simmer until the rice is fall-apart tender and the porridge is thickened, about 30 minutes. The pudding will continue to thicken as it cools, so once the rice is cooked, it's usually good to go.

Remove from the heat, add the cherries and orange zest, and give a good stir. Press a bit of plastic wrap or parchment paper to the surface, let cool at room temperature, and then refrigerate.

Rice pudding can be made up to 7 days in advance, though the rice will continue to absorb the liquid. If it is too thick when you go to serve it, simply add more milk or cream (or half-and-half) to thin it out. Serve cold or warm.

tapioca pudding

Tapioca pudding is one of the most divisive desserts I've encountered. Many people are not fond of the texture, but many more just think they don't like it because there is a lot of bad tapioca puddings out there. Me? I love it. When made with good ingredients, it has all the pleasantries of a good custard with an extra bit of bubbly delight. Small pearl tapioca is my preferred size. Instant tapioca is too grainy and large pearls are distracting. This recipe was perfected by Becky Carson when we cooked together at Local Foods in Chicago, Illinois.

3 cups [720 ml] milk (half-and-half, coconut milk, oat milk)	¼ cup [35 g] small pearl tapioca	½ cup [100 g] sugar
	¼ tsp vanilla paste or extract	1 egg yolk
		¼ tsp salt

In a medium pot over medium-high heat, bring the milk, tapioca, and vanilla to a scald (see page 31).

In a medium bowl, whisk the sugar, egg yolk, and salt. Temper (see page 31) in the hot dairy mixture. Return the tempered mixture to the pot and cook over low heat, stirring constantly, until the custard is thickened and coats the back of a spoon, about 10 minutes.

Transfer to a bowl or storage container and press plastic wrap or wax paper to the surface of the pudding, cool to room temperature, and chill. When cool, whisk to check the texture; if it is unpleasantly thick, add a bit more dairy to loosen it up. Store refrigerated for up to 7 days.

SYRUPS

Like compound butters (which are just butter with stuff in it), syrups sound fancy but are really just a mix of sugar and water of varying sweetness and often infused with another flavor. They are easy to make and keep forever. I often store mine in the fridge (for months) if infused, but on the counter if it is just sugar and water.

simple syrup ratios

In general, the "weight" of the syrup refers to the ratio of sugar to water. All versions are made (in my home) in the same way—combine sugar and water, bring to a boil, make sure the sugar is dissolved, and done-zo. For most simple syrups, I use a medium syrup.

LIGHT SYRUP:
1 part sugar to
   2 parts water

MEDIUM (OR STANDARD) SYRUP:
1 part sugar to
   1 part water

HEAVY SYRUP:
2 parts sugar to
   1 part water

So, for heavy syrup, use 2 cups [400 g] of sugar in 1 cup [240 ml] of water; for light, use 1 cup [200 g] of sugar in 2 cups [480 ml] of water. For medium, use equal amounts sugar and water. Please feel encouraged to vary these ratios to your heart's content.

brandy syrup

I like a boozier brandy syrup and so use the following ratio and method. If you want it to be less strong, use less booze. If you want to cook out the heat of the brandy, add it with the water at the beginning of cooking. Sometimes I add slices of lemon or orange or warming spices, but that's really on a case-by-case basis.

1 cup [200 g] sugar   ½ cup [120 ml] brandy (or rum or whiskey, etc.)

In a medium saucepan over high heat, bring 1 cup [240 ml] of water and the sugar to a boil. Lower the heat to a simmer and cook until the sugar is fully dissolved, about 5 minutes. Remove from the heat and add the brandy.

citrus syrup

I like the combination of lemon, orange, and grapefruit together, but if you don't have all three, substitute a bit more of the other. Note that a syrup made entirely of orange tends to be too sweet and so will need some sort of acidity to perk it up—add a splash of champagne vinegar to balance.

1 lemon (1½ oz [45 ml])   1 grapefruit (5 oz [140 g])   2 cups [480 ml] Simple Syrup (page 109)

1 orange (3 oz [90 ml])

Peel the zest from the fruit in wide strips using a vegetable peeler, then combine the zest with the simple syrup in a small saucepan. Bring to a simmer and cook until the syrup reduces by 20 percent, about 5 minutes. Remove from the heat and let steep for 10 minutes. Strain the zest out and store the syrup in a jar in the fridge for months.

marigold syrup

Marigolds are one of my favorite botanicals to infuse into syrup because the flavor is so unique yet familiar—it tastes so clearly of tangerine, but is also herbaceous. Plus, a syrup is a good method to preserve the citrus flavor for use long after the plants have withered. If you don't have access to marigolds, substitute with Citrus Syrup (see facing page).

2 cups [480 ml] Simple
   Syrup (page 109)

10 marigold stems, leaves
   and flowers

In a saucepan, bring the simple syrup to a simmer. Add the marigolds, remove from the heat, let steep for at least 10 minutes, strain out the stems, and store the syrup in a clean jar for months.

PICKLE LIQUIDS

I love pickling stuff, and fruit is no exception. The problem I ran into when I started to pickle fruit is that while firm fruits can take a traditional pickle brine, the softer berries often need both more acidity and more sweetness. I ended up liking these soft fruits when pickled in a sugar-vinegar gastrique, which sounds fancy but is just making a caramel sauce, deglazing it in vinegar, and then pouring that over the fruit like a brine.

Additionally, the softer berries tend to mush when canned, so I often just pour the hot pickle liquid over the fruit and then refrigerate. If you have very soft fruit, I find freezing the berries and then pouring the hot liquid over the frozen fruit helps hold the structure intact as well. There are more detailed notes in each chapter's Preserved section.

basic fruit pickle brine

| 1 cup [200 g] sugar | 2 cups [480 ml] vinegar, any variety (I especially like balsamic or sherry) | 2 lb [910 g] fruit |

In a large, nonreactive saucepan over high heat, heat the sugar until it melts into a dark caramel. Avoid stirring the sugar as it melts; instead, swirl the pan to distribute and cook the caramel evenly (don't be surprised if it starts to smoke; you want to take it very dark).

Remove the caramel from the heat and add the vinegar. Beware as it will really spit, sputter, and the vinegary steam will probably make you cough.

Return the pan to medium heat and cook until the caramel is completely dissolved in the vinegar (feel free to stir with abandon now). When the caramel is fully dissolved, pour it over the fruit (be sure to have the fruit in a heat-safe container because this brine can be so hot it will melt regular plastic). Let the fruit stand for 10 minutes and then refrigerate.

Pickled fruit lasts for months in the fridge as long as the brine is covering the fruit.

Note: When all the pickled fruit is gone, don't pitch the liquid! It can be cut with soda water for a refreshing soda or used in the base for vinaigrettes.

traditional pickle liquid

This is my go-to pickle liquid ratio for vegetables as well as for firmer fruit such as apples, pears, and rhubarb.

2 cups [480 ml] vinegar, any variety except balsamic	¾ cup [150 g] sugar	¼ cup [50 g] salt

In a large saucepan, combine the vinegar, 2 cups [480 ml] of water, the sugar, and the salt. Over high heat, bring to a boil. Lower the heat to medium-low and simmer until the sugar and salt are dissolved. Pour over the vegetable or fruit you want to pickle.

Note: I add any other spices I'm using to the individual containers instead of the pickle liquid to make sure they distribute evenly. Pickles will store in the fridge for months as long as the pickled item is submerged in the brine.

fruits

My friend Laura Piskor screenshotted a tweet for me that said:

> Here's the problem with fruit: it's inconsistent. Some apples are delicious, some taste bad. Sometimes blueberries are great, sometimes they are disgusting. You know what's the same every time?
> Doritos.

It made me laugh. The tweeter isn't wrong. Fruit is an agricultural product subject to the whims of weather, soil, transport, and the farmer's care. Doritos are a manufactured product subject only to the whims of Cool Ranch or Flamin' Hot Nacho (I'm a Cool Ranch lady, myself).

Sometimes apples are delicious and want for little more than a piece of Cheddar to pair for a snack. Sometimes they taste bad and need to be cooked down into serious applesauce (see page 140) for salvation. Sometimes blueberries are great and can be eaten out of hand, no cookbook required. I guess I've never had one that tastes disgusting, so I don't have a solution at the ready, but I've certainly had less-than-stellar ones that come alive when roasted and turned into a pan sauce. The only way to know is to taste them and learn how to help along the ones that are languishing.

The following chapters are my guide for you. At the end of each one is a quick rundown on how to preserve the seasonal bounty of fresh fruit so that you'll have them on hand when the only thing on the grocery store shelves is twenty-four varieties of Doritos.

apples

Apples are a great illustration of the difference between farm scale and market. There are 7,500 apple varieties in the world, yet the average grocery store usually has about six varieties on hand year-round. Ironically, this always looks like a diverse array compared to the one type of banana, one type of peach, two types of melon, one type of strawberry, one type of blueberry, and so on. The reason, as far as I've learned, is an issue of scale, standardization, and market outlet.

Farms exist in all sizes: from the micro farms that grow on postage stamp–size plots of land in all environments—urban, suburban, and rural gardens—to the mega farms cultivating thousands of acres. Scale. Earl Butz, Nixon's Secretary of Agriculture, pushed the "get big or get out" mentality of American agriculture. It is believed (and supported by his legacy domestic agricultural policy) that the larger a farm is, the more efficient it is; the yields from 200 acres of apples are twice that of 100 acres but without a linear uptick in labor or expensive equipment infrastructure.

In order to achieve the economies of scale just described, a farmer can't grow 10 acres of twenty different crops; they need to stick with a handful to be efficient. Standardization.

Once they are growing 200 acres of apples, well, quite frankly, that's a lot of apples—too many to hand-sell at a farmers' market. The farmer needs a larger market. As Abby Schilling told me in the profile on page 281, there are effectively three different fruit markets: 1) the retail, grower-to-consumer, farmers' market–style market, 2) the larger, grower-to-retailer market supported by larger-scale distributors, and 3) the commodity, grower-to-processer, preserved fruit market. Market outlet.

As a rule of thumb, the grower-to-consumer market fetches the highest price per pound but also has the highest associated labor costs because the delicate fruit needs to be hand-harvested and hand-sold. It takes a lot of time to drive to, set up, and break down a farmers' market stand, so you better get top dollar—and the majority of that dollar needs to go to the grower. The grower-to-retailer market is in the middle, where the grower is outsourcing the labor and inventory costs to a distributor and retailer, and so is often getting a lower wholesale rate for their crops. The grower-to-processor market has the lowest price per pound for the fruit, but is large enough to handle tremendous volume. Michigan alone harvested 22.5 million bushels of apples at last count. Each bushel weighs on average 45 pounds [20 kg] so that's 1,012,500,000 pounds [459,262,274 kg] of apples. Even with our three hundred farmers' markets in the state, that's a lot of apples to move, so a good deal is sold to make baby food, canned applesauce, apple juice, and so on.

To handle that volume of apples and make consistent products, such as applesauce, that taste the same jar after jar, the processors will only take a handful of varieties of apples. Standardization.

Those few varieties are stable and can be handled successfully by grocery chains. Economy of scale.

And that's why those are the six or so varieties on display at any given grocery store, yet why it makes sense for a different grower to bring an array of weird old apple varieties to a farmers' market where customers can ask questions directly and are willing to pay top dollar for them.

HOW TO SELECT

Look for apples that are heavy in the hand and free of bruising or blemishes that have broken the skin. Such apples don't store as long and so, while they often have a good amount of edible fruit, they need to be eaten quickly.

SIGNS OF RIPENESS

Color is not a great way to tell ripeness because there are so many apples with different coloration. Some will always have green undertones, some will ripen to red, some have a red blush their whole lives. Apples are ready to pick from the tree when they come off easily. Take hold of the apple and lift in the opposite direction of the stem. If it comes free, the apple is ripe. If you have to really yank on it, it isn't. You can also tell by looking at the seeds. If they are dark brown, the apple is ripe; if they are white, they need more time. (Though you will have already sliced the apple in half and so should probably use the apple no matter what.)

HOW TO STORE

Apples store the longest in refrigeration or in a root cellar free from temperature swings. Avoid freezing, which damages the cells and leads to premature decomposition. Apples soften as they age, so use soft apples for cooking and firm apples for eating out of hand.

HOW TO CUT AN APPLE
(OR PEAR OR QUINCE)

CUT AROUND THE CORE

THIS IS THE FASTEST WAY TO GET PIECES GOOD FOR CUTTING INTO OTHER SHAPES LIKE SLICES OR A DICE.

REST THE APPLE WITH THE STEM SIDE FACING UP AND CUT JUST TO THE RIGHT OF THE CORE, LEAVING ABOUT A FINGER'S WIDTH BETWEEN YOUR CUT AND THE STEM.

PLACE THE CUT SIDE OF THE APPLE DOWN ON THE CUTTING BOARD AND CUT ON EITHER SIDE OF THE CORE.

ROTATE THE APPLE ONTO ONE OF THE WIDER CUT SIDES AND CUT THE FINAL PIECE AWAY FROM THE CORE.

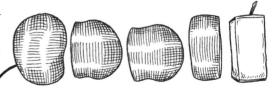

IN THE END, YOU WILL HAVE 4 PIECES OF APPLE—1 LARGE, 2 MEDIUM, AND 1 SMALL—AND THE CORE. CONTINUE TO CUT THE PIECES OF APPLE INTO ANY SHAPE YOU DESIRE.

USE AN APPLE CUTTER

REMOVE JUST THE SEEDS

THIS IS THE BEST WAY TO REMOVE THE CENTER OF THE APPLE WHILE LEAVING THE MAJORITY OF THE APPLE INTACT. I USE THIS FOR THE CRUMBLE-TOPPED QUINCE ON PAGE 356 OR TO FILL THE APPLES IN PAJAMAS ON PAGE 146. THIS IS ALSO THE EASIEST WAY TO REMOVE THE SEEDS FROM LEMON WEDGES.

PLACE THE APPLE ON ITS SIDE WITH THE CORE RUNNING NORTH-SOUTH. CUT THE APPLE IN HALF DIRECTLY THROUGH THE CORE.

FLIP THE APPLE ONTO ITS CUT SIDE AND REPEAT CUTTING THE APPLE INTO QUARTERS.

THIS IS THE FASTEST WAY TO GET WEDGES OF APPLE. THE TOOL IS A BIT OF A UNI-TASKER BUT I USE IT MORE OFTEN THAN I THOUGHT I WOULD.

REST THE APPLE WITH THE STEM SIDE FACING UP, THREADING THE STEM THROUGH THE CENTER OF THE APPLE CUTTER.

PRESS DOWN UNTIL THE CUTTER HAS CUT ALL THROUGH THE APPLE, LEAVING YOU WITH APPLE WEDGES AND THE CORE.

TAKE ONE QUARTER AND CUT AT A 45-DEGREE ANGLE, REMOVING THE CENTER OF THE APPLE BUT LEAVING THE BULK OF THE APPLE FLESH AS ONE PIECE.

REPEAT WITH THE OTHER QUARTERS.

AGATHA ACHINDU

A passionate advocate for food and health, Agatha Achindu had a vision that led her to innovate in the grocery sector. Starting in her home kitchen, she built the first nationally available brand of fresh-frozen organic baby and tots cuisine, Yummy Spoonfuls Organic Baby Food. She talked with me in the winter of 2021 about how the fresh fruit market works (or doesn't work) for a midsize producer.

Abra Berens: Can you tell me a bit about how Yummy Spoonfuls started and your motivation for bringing these products to market?

Agatha Achindu: What I tell people is that Yummy Spoonfuls found me. I was so frustrated with the food in my community, so I started teaching workshops on how to make fresh, whole foods for kids. Then I decided that just teaching these workshops wouldn't move the needle on the food that's available. I had to make it convenient for parents, so, in 2006, I decided to launch Yummy Spoonfuls to make fresh, organic food for babies and toddlers with no preservatives. That was the beginning of a great (and super-challenging) journey: Making fresh food in America isn't easy.

AB: Most Americans are not aware that there is an entire fruit market that exists outside of the fresh fruit market for grocery stores and farmers' markets. I imagine that even a midsize company like Yummy Spoonfuls is buying ingredients on that more-commodity market. When you went to scale, did that change how you sourced ingredients?

AA: When Yummy Spoonfuls was smaller, I would go to my farmers' market because we didn't need much. When we decided to scale up, our first challenge was getting enough fruits, vegetables, and herbs.

When we were small, I had a farmer friend from whom I would buy organic potatoes. When I wanted to buy in larger amounts, he said that he couldn't sell to me at wholesale because he was a small farm and needed to sell at retail prices. To buy wholesale, we needed to buy from larger growers. We would call producers and they said that all their product was already spoken for, that they were contracted out for three years unless someone breaks their contract. We were lucky because we hired a man who had wonderful relationships with growers, so the first year it was so expensive because we were buying at retail, but by the second year we were able to buy via contract with some new growers. I didn't even realize that was the system: You buy the crop from the ground.

AB: Contract growing is when you agree to purchase whatever they are able to grow. So, there's a time barrier to entry, needing to set up those contracts. Is there also a volume barrier to entry? In our area, Welches and Gerber have a large footprint, but those are multinational corporations. As a small business looking to grow to a midsize business, I would imagine that it is difficult to compete because of the volume difference.

AA: It is very difficult. That is another challenge facing small business owners in food manufacturing: You go in without thinking about all aspects of production. Even for us, when we were in Target nationally, we thought that was huge, but we couldn't compete with Gerber. In order to get people to work with us, we had to come up with a lot more capital. We knew we would have to contract for more food than we were able to funnel through the business, just so we could get access to the produce. It was more problematic for us because of the type of food we wanted to bring to market. We could get already frozen purées or not-so-fresh imported produce, but we wanted to use the highest-quality ingredients.

AB: That's a good point, that there's a market for "seconds" or damaged fruits. I don't know anything about that as a wholesale market. Is that an option for a business your size, or is that also difficult to gain access to?

AA: It is an option that is also difficult to get into. There are all of these different layers that people have already contracted for. Look at carrots. There are all of these different grades all the way down to the misfits. We didn't want the Grade B or Grade C because of what we do. But even if we did, it is already spoken for and under contract.

The first year, we operated at a loss because we were buying ingredients retail. The second year, we were able to put together that network of growers. Take pears, for example: By the second year, we were working with three growers because we couldn't buy enough to be the sole contract with one grower. We were able to get some from three different growers who had volume gaps in their contracts. We couldn't buy a lot, which is crazy when you realize that three truckloads isn't a lot. We had to do the legwork to get enough from a variety of producers.

AB: So if you are buying on contract and something terrible happens with the weather so the producer can't deliver on that contract, what happens with your business?

AA: We experienced this firsthand. There are two scenarios. The first was when there was an herb shortage. We have sixteen different SKUs [stock keeping units] with herbs that we needed to source. Luckily, for something like herbs, you're not using a lot, so we could go to the stores and buy retail to get enough and it isn't cost prohibitive. When we had this with pears, we had to take that SKU off the market. It was a PR nightmare because people loved the product and we couldn't restock.

AB: Can you talk about the other logistical hurdles that you navigated when growing the scale of your business and transitioning to a co-packer?

AA: If the first challenge was sourcing ingredients, the second challenge was equipment. When we needed to scale up to sell to Target, we couldn't find a co-packer [a third party who processes our recipes to our specs at volume] who would work with fresh food. We had to go to Rotterdam to buy our [processing] machines, and we had to buy them to put in a co-packer's plant to make our food, because they weren't standard machines.

We also had to organically certify the co-packer ourselves. To be certified organic, everything along the chain has to be organically certified, including the processing plant. The first man we worked with was a blessing because he was in the process of building an addition to his plant. He decided that he could dedicate that addition to our equipment and then we could get it certified, but he wasn't going to do it for his business. When we started out, we spoke to, I think, 150 co-packers and not one of them wanted to make our food because it was made from scratch ingredients and needed to be certified organic.

AB: *That's wild.*

AA: Yes, it is, but that's our food supply chain.

AB: *That's a good segue to my next question. If you could change our food system, what would you want to see?*

AA: I would want to change the system to prioritize health. A system that supported small farms and small food manufacturers would change what we eat. It would change our health care system, our environmental systems, it would change how we spend money. If we spoke to 150 co-packers and not one of them was willing to make fresh food, that means that they are making processed food. It should be flipped.

What I want someone who is reading your book to know is to go and find a local farmer in their community because that is where the change starts. Talk to them. People who do this backbreaking work don't lie. Find your local farmer and buy directly from them. That's the change we can bring in our own immediate community. For someone who sees Yummy Spoonfuls in Walmart, I want them to know the sheer amount of work that goes into making this food that isn't full of preservatives. It takes a lot to bring the food that I make in my home to market, and the system isn't set up for producers like me.

AB: *And because the system isn't set up for it, it is incumbent on consumers to place value on these options. Do you believe that if consumers make these changes it will change the system?*

AA: Yes, that's right. It is a supply and demand system. The reason manufacturers make crappy products is because consumers buy crappy products. For example, in 1995 when the Environmental Working Group identified the amount of arsenic in baby food, consumers stopped buying, and Gerber altered their recipe. When people don't buy, it pushes manufacturers to make that change. It's not any one body; it's all of us.

RAW

The number one concern about writing a fruit book is that no one needs the recipes because "you just eat fruit, right?" This may be no truer than for raw apples. They are the perfect food to eat out of hand. So, while yes, you can just eat an apple (though I always cut an apple because biting into it makes me feel like my gums are being pushed back from my teeth and it makes me shiver), there are more things you can do, mostly in the name of flavor combinations. They aren't complicated or life changing, but hopefully they encourage you to get that apple a day in a new way.

savory: apple "salad"

I need a new word for a dish that is more than a side but also not quite a meal unto itself. A salad evokes a big pile of greens. "Composed vegetable plate" doesn't mean anything to anyone. I make a lot of these sorts of dishes. This is one of them. My favorite lunches are one of these dishes with a glass of wine. My favorite dinners have two or three together in concert.

The chicories (radicchio, endive, frisée) provide bitterness against the sweet of the apples and the richness of the lentils and cheese. You could swap any of these for arugula or spinach. Swap any cooked grain for the lentils, and any hard cheese for the pecorino. The options are endless, but this is where I like to start.

Olive oil, for frying

½ cup [100 g] black or French green lentils

Salt

½ cup [120 ml] hard apple cider or white wine (optional)

1 head radicchio (about 6 oz [170 g]), sliced into ½ in [12 mm] petals

1 to 2 heads Belgian endive or radicchio (about 4 oz [115 g]), quartered lengthwise

¼ cup [60 ml] apple cider vinegar

½ cup [120 ml] olive oil

Freshly ground black pepper

2 tart apples (about 8 oz [230 g]), thinly sliced

2 oz [55 g] pecorino or other dry salty cheese, shaved into ribbons with a vegetable peeler

In a small saucepan, heat a glug of olive oil over medium heat. Add the lentils and a big pinch of salt and briefly fry, 30 seconds. Add the cider (if using) and cook until dry, about 1 minute. Add 1½ cups [375 ml] of water, bring to a boil, lower the heat to a simmer, and cook until the lentils are tender, about 20 minutes.

Just before serving, dress the greens with the vinegar, olive oil, and a big pinch of salt and black pepper.

Lay three-fourths of the greens out on a large, wide platter. Scatter the cooked lentils all over, followed by most of the apples and cheese. Top with the last of the greens, a few more shavings of cheese, and the remaining apples and serve.

sweet: # peanut butter apple stacks

In restaurants, I like a constructed dessert. One last plate of food to delight before the diners make their way into the night. At home, I like lazy desserts, ones where I can put out a couple of plates of sweet things and let guests build their own bites as we wind down a meal—some slices of apple, a stack of graham crackers, some sauce to bind them together. Something for my friends to linger over and stay a bit longer.

½ cup [120 ml] heavy cream

¼ cup [65 g] smooth, natural salted peanut butter

2 Tbsp powdered sugar

2 to 4 apples, variety of your choosing, doesn't matter the size

1 recipe Graham Crackers (page 49)

1 recipe salty pecans (see page 78)

In a medium bowl, whisk together the heavy cream and peanut butter until it starts to thicken, about 1 minute. Add the powdered sugar and continue whipping vigorously until the cream holds soft peaks.

Just before serving, cut the apples from the core and slice the large pieces into slices about ¼ in [6 mm] thick.

On a large platter, make a stack of graham crackers, a pile of apple slices, a bowl of the peanut butter whipped cream, and a smaller bowl of the salty pecans. Place in the middle of the table and encourage your guests to dip the apple slices in the whipped cream and eat with a graham cracker and sprinkle of pecans.

Alternatively, spoon some peanut butter whipped cream onto each graham cracker, top with a couple of apple slices, and finish with the pecans to serve as a platter of assembled bites.

Note: The apples should be cut just before serving to minimize browning. If you want to build the bites, do so just before serving or the whipped cream will deflate and make the crackers soggy (see why it is easier to let people build their own?).

ROASTED

The biggest hurdle to roasting most fruit is the amount of liquid released. When exposed to heat, the cells in fruit break, causing juice to rush forth. Apples are drier in texture than berries, so juicing is less of an issue. That said, a very hot pan will encourage the apples to brown more quickly, making it more likely that the texture will stay mostly intact. Get that pan very hot and then hold your nerve before stirring. Allow the apples to really sear and darken, even burn a touch.

savory:

aa++ salad

I'm a big fan of wide, flat platters of salad versus a deep bowl of salad. Building the salad in layers ensures equal distribution of the ingredients whether you're the first person served or the last. This salad can be made with any sort of crouton if you don't have pumpernickel, but I love how the dark brown crouton looks against the stark white of the goat cheese.

DRESSING

⅓ cup [80 ml] olive oil

¼ cup [60 ml] apple cider or red wine vinegar

1 small shallot (about 2 oz [55 g]), minced

2 Tbsp Dijon mustard

Salt

SALAD

4 slices Pumpernickel (page 39)

Neutral oil

Salt

2 Tbsp butter

2 apples (about 8 oz [230 g]), cut into large chunks

½ tsp ground black pepper

4 oz [115 g] arugula

4 oz [115 g] goat cheese

To make the dressing: In a small bowl, whisk together the olive oil, vinegar, shallot, mustard, and a pinch of salt.

To make the salad: Tear the slices of bread into irregularly shaped cubes. In a large frying pan, heat a large glug of neutral oil over medium heat until it shimmers. Add the bread with a big pinch of salt and fry until well toasted, about 3 minutes, stirring occasionally. Add the butter and let melt into the croutons, toasting for 1 minute more. Remove to a paper towel–lined plate, wipe out the pan, and heat another large glug of neutral oil over high heat. Add the apples, black pepper, and a big pinch of salt. Stir to coat, then leave undisturbed to brown, about 2 minutes. Stir and brown the other side of the apples. Remove from the heat.

In a large bowl, dress the arugula with half the dressing and a pinch of salt. Taste the greens and add more dressing as desired.

To serve, scatter half the greens on a large platter. Dot the greens with half of the roasted apples, half of the croutons, and half of the goat cheese. Repeat with the remaining greens, apples, croutons, and goat cheese.

sweet:

apple butterscotch pudding w/candied nuts

I often make desserts out of only a few components, but rely on different textures, temperatures, and flavors to make the dish feel complex. Here, the deeply flavored and sweet butterscotch pudding should be ice-cold in the pudding cup, the apples warm and buttery, and the candied nuts salty and spiced to contrast.

1 recipe Butterscotch Pudding (page 104)	2 apples (about 8 oz [230 g]), cut into a large dice	1 recipe Candied Nuts (page 75)
2 Tbsp butter		

Divvy the pudding among four cups, leaving at least 1 in [2.5 cm] of headroom between the pudding and the top of the cup. Cover (to prevent a skin from forming) and return to the fridge.

In a large frying pan, heat the butter over medium-high heat until foamy. Add the apples and stir to coat. Roast for 2 minutes. Stir and roast the other sides until equally browned.

To serve, spoon the warm apples over the pudding. Top with a handful of the candied nuts. Serve immediately as the warm apples will soften the pudding as it rests.

POACHED

Poached fruit can be made well in advance and then served rewarmed or fridge-cold. Because of this, I always make at least twice as many apples as I think I'll need. They keep for a long time (upwards of a week) in the fridge and go with just about everything. I've used sweet cider in all of these recipes because I like the flavor, but you could easily swap hard cider or dry white wine and stir in a ¼ cup [50 g] of sugar or a ¼ cup [85 g] of honey.

savory:

roast chicken w/rosemary-poached apples

One of the most underrated cuts of chicken is the leg quarter: a connected thigh and drumstick. This cut is often less expensive than the breast, always juicier, and looks good on a plate. You can also make this recipe with a whole chicken, spatchcocked and roasted, or with duck legs or with buttery white beans if you are not into meat.

continued

2 cups [480 ml] sweet apple cider

1 lemon (about 1½ oz [45 ml]), zest cut into wide strips and juiced

1 sprig rosemary

Salt

4 apples (about 1 lb [455 g]), peeled and cored

4 chicken leg quarters (about 9 oz [255 g] each) or duck legs (about 4 to 6 oz [115 to 170 g] each)

Freshly ground black pepper

4 Tbsp (2 oz [60 g]) butter

5 oz [140 g] salad greens

¼ cup [60 ml] apple cider or sherry vinegar

½ cup [120 ml] olive oil

In a medium saucepan, combine the cider, lemon zest and juice, rosemary, and a big pinch of salt. Bring to a simmer over medium heat. Add the apples, return to a boil, lower the heat to a simmer, and poach until tender but not falling apart, about 8 minutes. Allow to cool in the poaching liquid (if poaching ahead, store the cooled apples in the poaching liquid for up to 1 week). Reserve ½ cup [120 ml] of the poaching liquid.

Season the chicken legs or duck legs liberally with salt and black pepper. In a large frying pan, place the legs skin-side down and set over medium heat. Cook until the fat is rendered and the skin is crispy and deep golden brown, about 7 minutes. Flip over in the rendered fat and cook the chicken legs for another 7 to 10 minutes or the duck legs (if using) for 1 more minute to bring to medium doneness. Remove from the pan and let rest in a warm place for 5 minutes.

Add the reserved poaching liquid to the saucepan and bring to a boil. Add the butter and whisk to make a silky butter sauce. Remove from the heat.

Dress the salad greens with the vinegar, oil, a big pinch of salt, and couple of turns of black pepper.

Serve the chicken or duck with a poached apple on the side, a big spoonful of the butter sauce spooned over the top, and a giant pile of salad greens nearby.

sweet:

chilled poached apples + almond cookies

This is my favorite style of dessert: some fruit, something creamy, and something crunchy. As the apples are not all that sweet, I often pair them with some yogurt and nuts in the morning for breakfast or spoon them over a bowl of oatmeal.

2 cups [480 ml] sweet cider

¼ cup [85 g] honey

1 cinnamon stick

2 whole star anise

6 black or pink peppercorns

4 apples (about 1 lb [455 g]), peeled and cored or cut into quarters with seeds removed

1 cup [240 ml] heavy cream

1 recipe Almond Brutti ma Buoni (page 69)

In a medium saucepan, combine the cider, honey, cinnamon, star anise, and peppercorns. Bring to a simmer over medium heat. Slip the apples into the poaching liquid and cook until tender but not collapsing, about 8 minutes. Remove from the heat and let the apples cool in the cooking liquid to room temperature, then refrigerate until cool.

To serve, divide the cream among four serving bowls. Top with an apple and ¼ cup [60 ml] of the poaching liquid. Serve with a stack of almond cookies nearby.

STEWED

Stewed is different from poached in that the apples cook down until mushy and any excess moisture evaporates, which concentrates the flavor. It's basically applesauce.

savory: # snow melt stew

This is my favorite soup to make just after the holidays when I'm craving slightly more austere meals as an antidote to the decadence. The name started as a joke because no one would order Celery Root–Apple Soup at the restaurant, but "Snow Melt Stew? Well, I'll take two, please." A rose by any other name smells as sweet, but doesn't sell well in restaurants in January.

Olive oil

1 lb [455 g] yellow onions, thinly sliced

4 garlic cloves [28 g], thinly sliced

5 sprigs thyme

Salt and freshly ground black pepper

1 cup [240 ml] dry white wine or hard cider

4 lb [1.8 kg] celery root, peeled and cut into chunks

1 lb [455 g] tart apples, cored and cut into chunks

3 qt [2.8 L] water or stock

1 cup [240 ml] heavy cream

Chives or sage leaves (optional)

In a big soup pot, heat a glug of olive oil over medium heat. Add the onion, garlic, thyme, and a big pinch of salt and black pepper. Sweat until soft, about 7 minutes.

Add the wine and cook until dry, about 3 minutes. Add the celery root, apples, and water. Bring to a boil over high heat. Lower the heat to a simmer and cook until the celery root is soft when mashed with the back of a spoon.

Carefully transfer the mixture to a blender and process until very smooth (you can also use an immersion blender, but it won't be as silky smooth). Whisk in the cream, taste, and adjust the seasoning (it will probably need more salt).

Serve hot, topped with grinds of black pepper and a scattering of chopped herbs (if using) alongside a green salad and a thick slice of buttered toast for sopping.

sweet:

apple crepe cake w/sherry custard

If you're not into making this a crepe cake (which is literally just a bunch of crepes stacked on top of one another with a bit of filling between the layers), spoon a little of the applesauce into the center of the crepe, fold into a triangle, and bake to warm. I'd serve it either way for dessert or without the custard for a special breakfast. My friend Anne Pelloquin once referred to this applesauce as "Abra's Very Serious Applesauce" because it is very serious in flavor. Note that it can be made in large batches and freezes well, in case you have a lot of apples that are starting to go soft on you. I find this cake takes about 1 qt [960 ml] of applesauce if using already made sauce.

8 Tbsp (4 oz [120 g]) butter	Pinch of salt	1 recipe Crepes (page 44), cooked and cooled
3 lb [1.4 kg] apples, peeled and cut into chunks	½ tsp vanilla extract	1 recipe Sherry Custard (page 82)

In a large saucepan, heat the butter over medium heat until it starts to brown, about 4 minutes. Add the apples and salt, stir to coat, and then lower the heat to medium-low. Cook until the apples collapse and make a deeply golden-brown applesauce, about 20 minutes, stirring infrequently but thoroughly as it has a tendency to stick.

Add the vanilla, remove from the heat, and allow the mixture to cool to room temperature.

To build the cake, lay a crepe on a cake serving dish and spoon a layer of the applesauce all over. Repeat until all the crepes and applesauce have been used. Cover and refrigerate until firm, for at least 2 hours and up to 1 day. Pour the sherry custard over the top, cut into slices, and serve.

Note: This cake doesn't store that well, especaially after the custard is poured over. It will keep covered in the fridge for a day or two before the applesauce starts weeping and makes the crepes soggy.

BAKED

You can bake an apple? Who would have known?! (Insert eyeroll emoji.) The idea that an apple tastes good after it is baked is not, you know, revolutionary. That said, in Michigan we eat apples for approximately six out of twelve months, so eventually I want something besides apple pie. These are my favorites.

savory:

one-pan sunday roast

The English Sunday Roast is one of my favorite things: a hearty meal, usually a roasted joint of meat and vegetables, served in the late afternoon–early evening that straddles the line between fancy dinner and truly traditional, casual pub fare.

I bake the apples whole with just a slight scoring around the equator to encourage them to collapse in an organized fashion. I like how it looks and am not bothered by avoiding the seeds and stem as I eat. Apples swing savory like champs and can be paired with chickpeas, roast duck, goose, rabbit, venison, or even a fatty fish such as salmon or lake trout. In my house, pork is queen, and this combo, along with the crispy crackling, reigns supreme.

4½ lb [2 kg] rolled pork loin roast with skin

Salt

3 lb [1.4 kg] potatoes, cut into wedges or chunks

3 carrots (about 1 lb [455 g]), cut into chunks

1 large onion of any variety (about 8 oz [230 g]), cut into wide petals

1 tsp dried herbes de Provence or thyme

½ tsp caraway seeds

Neutral oil

Freshly ground black pepper

6 tart apples (about 1½ lb [680 g]), skins lightly scored around the equator

2 Tbsp all-purpose flour

½ cup [120 ml] hard cider or dry white wine

2 cups [480 ml] chicken or pork stock

2 Tbsp whole-grain mustard

2 Tbsp sherry or apple cider vinegar

¼ cup [60 ml] olive oil

6 oz [170 g] baby spinach

continued

Using a sharp knife, score the skin of the pork roast deep enough to cut through the skin but not so deep as to cut the muscle. Leave ¼ in [6 mm] between cuts: This allows the fat to render more completely, provides a natural place to carve the roast after cooking, and makes the crackling not too much to chew in any given bite. Rub the roast all over with 1 Tbsp of salt and let rest (ideally) for 2 hours or up to overnight.

Preheat the oven to 450°F [230°C].

In a large bowl, combine the potatoes, carrots, onion, herbs, and caraway seeds with a big glug of neutral oil, a big pinch of salt, and a couple grinds of black pepper. Transfer the mixture to a baking tray, roasting pan, or large cast-iron skillet. Nestle the pork roast, skin-side up, on the bed of vegetables.

Bake for 15 minutes, then lower the oven temperature to 325°F [165°C]. Add the apples to the side of the pan and continue to roast until the pork loin reaches an internal temperature of 140°F [60°C] and the skin is golden brown and crackled, about 2 hours. If the pork has reached the proper temperature but the skin hasn't crackled, increase the heat to 450°F [230°C] and roast until the skin has popped, checking every 5 minutes (this can also be done under a broiler with good success, though you will have to rotate the roast). Lift the pork from the tray, transfer to a platter, and lightly cover with aluminum foil. Let rest for 20 minutes. Transfer the roasted vegetables and apples to a serving platter.

Drain all but 2 Tbsp of the roasting fat from the tray (reserve the excess for another recipe or discard). Place the tray on a stovetop burner over medium heat. Add the flour and whisk to make a roux, cooking until golden brown and fragrant. Add the hard cider and scrape up any brown bits. Add the stock, whisking away any lumps, and bring to a boil. Cook until lightly thickened into a gravy, about 2 minutes.

In a small bowl, combine the mustard, sherry, and olive oil with a pinch of salt. Dress the spinach with half of the dressing and another pinch of salt and grind of black pepper. Taste and adjust the seasoning and add dressing as desired.

Slice the pork through the score lines and serve alongside the roasted vegetables, apples, a big pour of gravy, and the spinach salad on the side.

sweet:

apples in pajamas

I once met a pastry chef who said that she abhorred all baked apple desserts because they were just too obvious, a low-hanging crowd-pleaser. I am not a pastry chef, and I like pleasing a crowd (or, in this case, a "crowd" of six people). Find an apple that will hold its structure when it bakes, like a Greening, Granny Smith, Jonagold, Northern Spy, Pink Lady, or Braeburn.

6 apples, any size (or one per person)

6 oz [170 g] Almond Brutti ma Buoni cookie dough (page 69)

1 recipe Puff Pastry Dough (page 61)

½ cup [120 ml] egg wash (see page 30)

6 tsp SSS (page 78), or about 1 tsp per apple

Core the apples and stuff each with 1 oz [30 g] of the cookie dough.

Roll the puff pastry into a ¼ in [6 mm] thick sheet. Cut into six squares large enough to wrap around a single apple. Place an apple in the center of each square and bring up the corners to meet at the top. Gently press the seams together to lightly seal. Chill the apples for 30 minutes to set the pastry.

Preheat the oven to 350°F [180°C]. Line a baking sheet with a silicone mat or parchment paper.

Brush the pastry with the egg wash and sprinkle with the SSS. Place on the prepared baking sheet and bake until the pastry is golden brown and cooked through, 25 to 30 minutes. Transfer to a wire rack to cool. Serve warm or at room temperature. If serving warm, I like to serve each apple in a pool of ice-cold heavy cream.

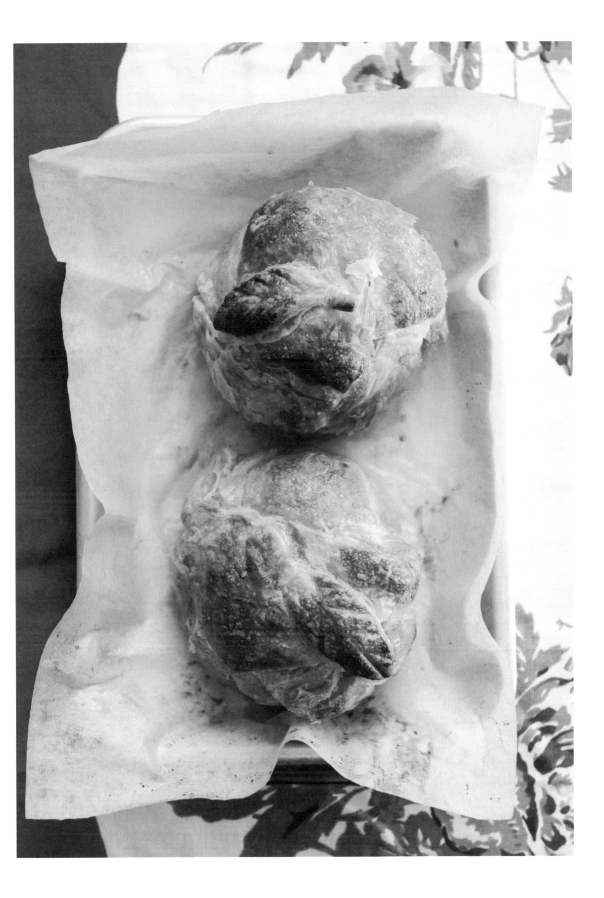

PRESERVED

Most apples will store well if kept in a cool, dark place with no swings in temperature. The texture will eventually suffer as their moisture evaporates through the skin. Different varieties store better; if you ever see Goldrush apples, those store the best in my experience, with taste and texture lasting months past harvest. Because of the inherent storage crop nature of apples, I don't spend too much time preserving them unless I have a bunch with blemishes or bruises. Imperfections shorten the shelf life of the apple itself as well as the others around it as it will emit more ethylene gas, which accelerates the ripening (and decomposition) of the surrounding fruit. It is best to remove the imperfect fruit, cut away the imperfection, and preserve what is still good.

APPLE BUTTER

Apple butter is effectively applesauce that has been cooked way, way down until it is deeply browned and as thick as a jam, usually about 1½ to 2 hours. You can add any of the warming spices if you want, but I like to use just apples. I also don't add sugar; I just keep cooking the apples until they concentrate their own sugar. All of this said, I don't make apple butter that often because I get irrationally angry when it sputters and spits on me during stirring. Some of the worst arm burns I've gotten have come from very hot, very sticky apple butter splatters. Because of that, I tend to cook it too fast and burn the bottom. A friend slow cooks it in the oven after the initial sauce making, but that can take up to 4 hours, and ugh, I don't know, I prefer to do other stuff with apples.

JELLY

Take 5 lb [2.3 kg] of apples, wash and quarter them, then stew over medium heat with 2½ lb [1.2 kg] of sugar and 2 qt [2 L] of water until the apples are mush. Strain the mixture, pour the liquid back into the pan, and cook until it reaches a set point of 210°F [100°C]. Feel free to flavor with mint to serve with lamb or use to thicken other fruit jams like strawberry.

VINEGAR

Soak any discarded apple skins or cores in white distilled vinegar with a spoonful of sugar for about a week to extract the apple flavor into the vinegar. It is not a true apple cider vinegar, which is made by making sweet cider, fermenting it into hard cider, and then acidulating it with a vinegar mother. The flavor achieved by this method tends to be lighter and more "apple-y."

PICKLED

I love a pickled apple! I use the Traditional Pickle Liquid (page 113) and pour it over cored and sliced apples. Pickled apples are great on a charcuterie platter, relish tray, or to garnish a richer cut of meat (such as pork, game, or fowl). They will keep for months in the fridge or canned.

SYRUP

Take any discarded cores or peels and cook down in a Simple Syrup (page 109) until golden brown. Strain the skins and cores and then reduce until the texture is about halfway between maple syrup and molasses. Use as a drizzle on yogurt, with a spritz of seltzer for a drink, or warmed and spooned over a slice of apple pie or galette.

DRIED

Dried apple snacks are one of my favorite bored-hungry treats—when you aren't really hungry but are craving something. They're slightly sweet, full of fiber, and easy to make. I have a food dehydrator, so that is my preferred route, though a low oven (200°F [95°C] or so) works well too; it just takes a long time, upwards of 4 to 8 hours. Inspired by my friend Nic Theisen, who is adept at removing unnecessary steps, I stopped peeling and coring the apples and now just slice as thinly as possible on a mandoline before laying out to dry. It is a lot easier and faster, and apple slices with the ribbon of skin and star pattern where the seeds were are lovely.

apricots

There is a phenomenon at cookbook events where an attendee will ask, "What's your favorite [insert relevant topic]?" If you wrote a book on pie, it will be "What's your favorite pie?" If you wrote a vegetable cookbook, it will be "What's your favorite vegetable?"

I find this recurrent episode strange. Why must there always be a favorite? In the spring, rhubarb is my favorite, but in the fall, it is grapes. It's not, as we say, apples to apples. And yet so often it feels like folks are trying to suss out the winner.

So here you go: If I had to choose one fruit to rule them all, it would be apricots. I like tart fruit, and apricots often are. I find the dryish texture beguiling. I like that I can fit four in my coat pocket easily, whereas I'm hard-pressed to fit in more than one peach at a time. Apricots are tough to grow in Michigan. They tend to bloom early and so are often nipped by frost, meaning that there won't be apricots come July. When it's a good year for apricots, it feels like a windfall. They are good eaten out of hand or baked into something, they swing sweet, they swing savory, apricot jam is the best and my most utilized, I can call them "Abra-cots" and people barely grimace.

So that's it. Apricots are the best and all other fruits are for suckers. If you ask me the "What's your favorite" question when we meet in person, I will know that you have not read my book in its entirety. I probably won't point it out; I'll just say "apricots," and move on.

HOW TO SELECT

Look for apricots that are heavy in the hand and have taut skin. The color will range from golden orange to almost a rosy red. Avoid apricots with green undertones. Watch out for apricots that are soft or rotten at the point where the stem meets the fruit; it is often an open space that can allow bacteria in, shortening the apricot's shelf life.

SIGNS OF RIPENESS

Like most fruit, apricots will deepen in color as they ripen. Similarly, they will smell more floral as they ripen, and the flesh will soften.

HOW TO STORE

Store at room temperature for a handful of days or wrapped in a plastic or paper bag in cold storage to keep for longer. Be sure to return to room temperature or warm in your hands before eating.

NOTES

Inside the pit of the apricot is the kernel—crack it open to see the difference. There are two varieties of apricot kernels—sweet and bitter— often identified on the package or at the market. Both are used to flavor cookies, jams, and custards despite containing an amount of cyanide that can be dangerous if consumed raw or in quantity. You'd have to eat a lot of them, but still good to know.

RAW

Raw apricots can be frustrating. Sometimes they are mealy or too soft. When that's the case, I cook them, but when they are glorious and juicy and make you scream with joy—eat them raw.

savory: ## shattering cheese + apricot salad

Shattering cheese is cheese wrapped in phyllo and baked until melting underneath a crackling crust. While just about any firm, melty cheese can be turned into shattering cheese, I like the Finnish bread cheese juustoleipä best. Halloumi, paneer, or even a Brie-style cheese can be used in its place.

continued

2 sheets Phyllo Dough
(page 58)

Olive oil

Salt and freshly ground
pepper

6 oz [170 g] slab bread
cheese (juustoleipä,
halloumi, paneer,
or Brie)

6 apricots (about 6 oz
[170 g]), pits removed,
each cut into six slices

1 lemon (about 1.5 oz
[45 ml]), zest and juice

¼ tsp chili flakes (or use
mild Aleppo or Urfa
flakes, if you can
find them)

¼ tsp ground cinnamon or
five-spice powder

10 sprigs parsley, roughly
chopped

1 to 2 sprigs mint, roughly
chopped (optional)

1 shallot (about 1 oz
[30 g]), minced

2 Tbsp red wine or sherry
vinegar

Preheat the oven to 375°F [190°C]. Line a baking sheet with a
silicone mat or parchment paper.

Lay the first sheet of phyllo dough on a cutting board or counter
so the long sides of the rectangle run left to right. Brush with olive
oil and season with a pinch of salt and pepper. Lay the next sheet
of phyllo on top of the first and press them together.

Brush the entire sheet with olive oil again and then lay the cheese
in the center of the narrow side of the phyllo rectangle and to the
left of the long side. Fold the top of the rectangle down over the
cheese. Fold the bottom of the rectangle up over the cheese and
brush any dry sides of the phyllo with oil. Wrap the cheese from
left to right in the phyllo, making a tidy package.

Transfer the phyllo-enrobed cheese to the prepared baking sheet.
Bake until the crust is golden brown and the cheese is melting,
12 to 15 minutes.

Meanwhile, in a medium bowl, combine the apricots, lemon zest
and juice, chili flakes, cinnamon, parsley, mint (if using), shallot,
vinegar, and 2 Tbsp of olive oil with a big pinch of salt and toss
to make a quick salad.

Serve the cheese immediately from the oven, topped with
the apricot salad.

sweet:

apricots, rosemary sabayon + almond brutti ma buoni

TBH you could skip the rosemary and the cookies and just serve a big bowl of apricots swaddled in honey sabayon, but it is those unexpected pops of flavor that pique my interest. Not flavors that will crane anyone's neck, but a little something to catch an eye and turn a sly smile.

1 recipe Sweet Sherry Sabayon (page 87)	1 sprig rosemary, needles picked and minced	Flake salt, such as Maldon or fleur de sel
¼ cup [85 g] honey	2 lb [910 g] apricots	4 Almond Brutti ma Buoni cookies (page 69)

When making the sabayon, replace the sugar with honey and add the chopped rosemary.

Halve the apricots and remove the pits. Cut the fruit into wedges.

Divvy half of the apricots among four serving bowls. Spoon the sabayon evenly over the apricots. Top with the rest of the apricots. Sprinkle each bowl with a pinch of flake salt. Crumble an almond brutti ma buoni cookie over each bowl and serve immediately.

GRILLED

Apricots have a drier flesh than some other stone fruits, making them a perfect candidate for grilling, as they don't get too sloppy when heated. Grilling also brings out the best in an imperfect fruit. If you buy a box of apricots and are not wowed by them when eaten out of hand, those are the best fruits for grilling or cooking.

savory:

grilled chicken w/apricots, red onion + basil

One of the first big meals I ever made with my friend and mentor Rodger Bowser was a dinner celebrating a local farm that raised incredible heritage chickens. While the chickens were the star, the apricot salad that went along with them was a scene stealer. This dish made its way into my mind and now it just seems intuitive to pair these flavors together. It wasn't until I made the same meal (or similar, bent through the lens of time) and a dinner guest asked, "Where do you come up with these combos?" that I realized I built my repertoire from years of cooking with others (and great ingredients). Thanks, Rodger.

1 whole chicken (4 to 5 lb [1.8 to 2.3 kg])

¼ cup [60 ml] neutral oil

3 garlic cloves [21 g], smashed

Salt

¼ tsp chili flakes

1 lemon (about 1.5 oz [45 ml]), zest and juice

1 orange (about 3 oz [90 ml]), zest and juice

1 red onion (about 4 oz [115 g])

Olive oil

Salt and freshly ground black pepper

2 lb [910 g] apricots, halved and pits removed

5 sprigs basil

Break down the chicken into quarters: Set the chicken, breast side-up with legs pointing at you. Cut between the leg and the bottom of the breast and start to separate the two. Flip the bird over and pop the hip joint of the chicken by lifting the leg quarter

continued

up until you hear the ball-socket joint break apart. Cut around the oyster meat (a.k.a. the chicken love handle) and remove the leg. Repeat on the other leg. Then return the now legless bird to breast-side up. Cut down the center of the breastbone (between the chicken cleavage) and, cutting as close to the bone as possible, lift the breast away from the rib cage. Cut around the base of the wing so that the wing and breast stay connected as you separate them from the center cavity. Repeat on the other side. Save the center carcass for making stock, etc.

Place the chicken quarters into a dish or sealable bag. Add the oil, garlic, 1 tsp of salt, chili flakes, and citrus zest to the bag and smoosh around to coat the chicken. Refrigerate and let marinate for at least an hour and up to 2 days.

Heat a charcoal or gas grill to medium. Remove the chicken from the marinade (squeezing off any excess oil). Grill skin-side down until the skin is golden brown, about 5 minutes. Flip the chicken to a cooler part of the grill and continue cooking until it is cooked through (internal temperature of 165°F [75°C]), about 15 minutes.

Meanwhile, cut the onion into 1 in [2.5 cm] wide petals and toss with a glug of olive oil and big pinch of salt and pepper. Grill over medium-high heat until soft and slightly singed. Remove the onions to a medium bowl.

Toss the apricot halves with a glug of olive oil and a big pinch of salt and black pepper. Grill, cut-side down, until the fruit is slightly soft and has good grill lines. Remove from the grill and add to the bowl of onions. Add the citrus juice along with another glug of olive oil. Let cool slightly.

Just before serving, tear the basil into large pieces and add to the onion-apricot mixture.

To serve, pile the salad on top of each piece of chicken. Looking for sides? Serve with a bowl of cooked lentils, boiled potatoes, roasted sweet potatoes, or steamed bulgur and green salad for a robust meal.

sweet: # brittle-topped grilled apricots

As I've said, I'm not a natural baker. I like lending my energies to elaborate desserts for special occasions, but it isn't what comes naturally to me, and elaborate desserts aren't what I crave to end most meals. This is my sort of dessert: dead simple and infinitely riffable. If you don't have pistachios, hazelnuts, pine nuts, or even sesame seeds would make good swaps. If you're not into honeycomb brittle, a crumble of dry meringue would work well too. Already have a bit of citrus syrup in the fridge? Use that instead of making the honey syrup. A scoop of vanilla ice cream or Greek yogurt underneath would be perfectly at home here.

2 Tbsp honey	2 to 3 lb [910 g to 1.4 kg] apricots or at least 2 apricots per person, halved and pits removed	Shards of Honeycomb Brittle (page 77)
2 tsp red wine or sherry vinegar		½ cup [70 g] pistachios, toasted and roughly chopped
	Olive oil	Pinch of salt

Whisk together the honey, 2 Tbsp of water, and the vinegar to make a light syrup.

Heat a gas or charcoal grill to medium-high. Toss the apricot halves with a glug of olive oil (or if you don't like the added flavor, use a neutral oil). Grill the apricots, cut-side down, until the fruit begins to soften and the cut side caramelizes, about 4 minutes. Remove to a shallow dish and pour the honey syrup over the apricots. Macerate at room temperature while dinner is consumed.

Crunch up the honeycomb brittle and combine with the chopped pistachios and the salt.

Scatter the mixture over the apricots and serve.

ROASTED

Like grilling, roasting minimizes the flaws of less-than-great apricots. The indirect heat of the oven versus the grill takes a bit longer to soften the fruit and concentrates the flavor through moisture evaporation rather than caramelization. Plus, if you combine roasting the apricots while something else roasts in the oven, you're maximizing energy efficiency and ease.

savory: leg of lamb w/apricot bulgur, herbs + toum

Toum is a Lebanese garlic sauce that never seems like it is going to work and then it does, just like magic. I use it on so many things— to dress a bowl of cut tomatoes and cucumbers, on sandwiches instead of mayo, to marinate tofu before roasting—which is good because it is hard to make in small batches. Follow the recipe listed here and plan on having a good amount left over. Thankfully, toum not only goes on a lot of things but also stores indefinitely in the fridge, though be warned that the garlic smell can sometimes become permanent in a plastic container, so use glass if you can.

TOUM

1 cup (about 4½ oz [130 g]) garlic cloves, peeled

2 tsp salt

¼ cup [60 ml] vinegar (any variety except balsamic)

3 cups [720 ml] neutral oil

LAMB

1 boneless leg of lamb, 4 to 5 lb [1.8 to 2.3 kg]

Salt and freshly ground black pepper

2 lb [910 g] apricots, left whole

Olive oil

1½ cups [240 g] dry, cracked bulgur

5 sprigs mint

2 sprigs basil

10 sprigs parsley

1 small shallot (about 1 oz [30 g]), minced

1 lemon (about 1.5 oz [45 ml]), zest and juice

To make the toum: In a food processor, blend the garlic and salt into a fine paste. In a separate container, combine the vinegar and ¼ cup [60 ml] of cold water. With the machine running, alternate drizzling in the water-vinegar mixture and neutral oil until a thick mayonnaise-like sauce is made. Continue to blend until fully smooth. Transfer to a storage container and refrigerate to cool; store for up to 3 months.

To make the lamb: Season the leg of lamb liberally with a big pinch of salt and black pepper and ¼ cup [60 ml] of the toum. Marinate for 30 minutes or up to 2 days.

Preheat the oven to 425° [220°C].

Place the leg of lamb in a roasting pan and roast for 20 minutes. Lower the heat to 350°F [180°C] and continue cooking until it reaches an internal temperature of 135°F [57°C], about 45 minutes. Remove from the oven, cover loosely with foil, and let rest for 20 minutes.

While the oven is hot, in a baking pan, toss the apricots in a big glug of olive oil and roast until they start to collapse, about 20 minutes.

While the apricots are roasting, rehydrate the bulgur by bringing 3 cups [720 ml] of water to a boil over high heat. Add the bulgur and a pinch of salt, return to a boil, lower the heat to a simmer, and cook until soft, about 12 minutes.

Roughly tear the herb leaves and combine with the shallot, lemon zest and juice, a big glug of olive oil, and a pinch of salt.

When ready to serve, slice the lamb thinly. Serve with a spoonful of bulgur, a big handful of the herb salad, a couple of roasted apricots, and a swish of toum over it all.

sweet: # torrijas caramelizadas w/apricots

In the same family as English bread pudding and French pain perdu, torrijas are the Spanish iteration of make-something-out-of-old-bread-so-it-doesn't-go-to-waste. Long story short, make a custard base, soak bread in it, thicken the custard, and fry the bread in olive oil. The caramelizada part comes from torching an extra layer of sugar on the outside of the fried bread to make a caramelly crust that shatters as you make your way to the rich, creamy center.

While I like this best with roasted apricots, you can substitute other roasted fruit (as a guideline: the tarter, the better).

2 lb [910 g] apricots, halved and pits removed

Olive oil

Pinch of salt

½ cup [100 g] sugar, plus a pinch

6 slices Milk Bread (page 37), cut 1 in [2.5 cm] thick

1½ cups [375 ml] whole milk

¼ tsp five-spice powder or ground cinnamon

½ tsp vanilla extract or paste

Zest of 1 orange

5 egg yolks

Preheat the oven to 375°F [190°C].

In a baking pan, toss the apricots with a big glug of olive oil, a pinch of salt, and a pinch of sugar and roast until the fruit has softened, about 20 minutes.

Cut each slice of bread in half and lightly toast on the rack of the oven until slightly dry on the outside (or just use stale bread and skip this step). Transfer the bread to a baking dish or rimmed baking sheet.

In a large saucepan, combine the milk, five-spice powder, vanilla, and orange zest. Bring to a simmer over medium heat.

continued

In a large bowl, whisk the egg yolks and half of the sugar together until fluffy and pale yellow, about 3 minutes. Temper in the hot milk mixture to the egg yolk mixture (see page 31). Pour the mixture over the bread and soak for 5 minutes or until fully saturated. Remove the slices from the custard base and set aside.

Pour the custard base through a fine-mesh sieve back into the saucepan (to remove any crumbs). Set over medium-low heat, stirring constantly to keep the eggs from curdling, until the mixture is thick enough to coat the back of a spoon (or 175°F [80°C]).

Strain the mixture again into a bowl (to remove any cooked egg bits), press a piece of plastic wrap or parchment paper to the surface, and refrigerate until cool .

In a large frying pan, heat ¼ cup [60 ml] of olive oil over medium heat until shimmery. Sprinkle half of the remaining sugar over the soaked bread slices. Place them sugar-side down in the pan and fry until golden brown and caramelized. Sprinkle the unbrowned side of the bread with the last of the sugar, flip, and fry until caramelized.

To serve, spoon a pool of cooled custard onto a plate, place the fried bread in the center, and spoon a bit more custard over the bread. Top with the roasted apricots and eat immediately.

POACHED

The firm flesh of apricots makes them well suited to poaching. Plus, like all poached fruit, they last for a long time after cooking; simply submerge in the poaching liquid and refrigerate. Similarly, if it is the dead of winter and there are no apricots to be found, both of these recipes work well with dried apricots.

savory:

ginger-poached apricots over salmon, choi + chili oil

I use the term "choy or choi" as a general catchall of the choi family, Chinese cabbages in the brassica family. This group includes bok choy, tatsoi, pak choi, and choy sum. All are cabbages that don't form heads and have broad leaves. As cool weather–loving brassicas, they tend to turn up at farmers' markets in the spring and fall. Should you not be able to find them, you can substitute other cabbages, such as napa or savoy. Wash carefully, paying special attention to the dirt that can collect at the base of the stem.

2 cups [480 ml] dry white wine

1 orange (about 3 oz [90 ml]), zest and juice

1 lemon (about 1.5 oz [45 ml]), zest and juice

2 in [5 cm] ginger, peeled

2 whole star anise pods

2 green cardamom pods

2 lb [910 g] apricots, halved and pits removed

¼ cup [60 ml] neutral oil

2 Tbsp chili flakes

4 salmon fillets (about 4 oz [120 g] each), skin removed

Salt

4 to 6 baby bok choy (about 1½ lb [680 g])

In a medium pot over medium heat, bring the wine, orange zest and juice, lemon zest and juice, ginger, star anise, and cardamom to a simmer. Add the apricots and poach until tender, about 4 minutes. Remove from the heat and let cool in the poaching liquid.

continued

In a small frying pan, heat the neutral oil over high heat for about 30 seconds. Remove from the heat and add the chili flakes. Steep for 10 minutes.

In a large pot fitted with a steamer basket, bring 3 in [7.5 cm] of water to a rapid boil. Season the salmon all over with salt. Transfer carefully to the steamer basket. Steam, covered, for 5 minutes. Add the bok choy and steam for 4 minutes more.

To serve, place a fillet of the fish on a plate next to a couple of bok choy. Top with a few poached apricot halves and drizzle all over with the chili oil.

sweet:

rosé-poached apricots + earl grey semifreddo

Normally I like the temperature difference between a cold and a hot fruit, but here I keep the fruit room temperature and the semifreddo cold. As always, you can substitute water for wine if you either aren't drinking or don't want to pour your wine in a pot instead of a glass. This recipe will make more semifreddo than is needed for four people, so either cut it in half or keep it in the freezer for subsequent meals.

2 cups [480 ml] heavy cream

3 Earl Grey tea bags or 1 Tbsp loose tea

1 recipe Custard (page 81)

¼ cup [85 g] honey

2 cups [480 ml] dry or semi-dry rosé wine

2 lb [910 g] apricots, halved and pits removed

1 Tbsp SSS (page 78)

In a large saucepan, scald (see page 31) the cream over medium heat. Add the tea bags and steep for 20 minutes. Remove the bags, discard, and chill the cream completely.

In a medium bowl or the bowl of a stand mixer, whip the now-cold cream to medium peaks. Add to the custard to make the semi-freddo base.

Line a loaf pan (or any vessel, really) with plastic wrap, pour the semifreddo base into the prepared dish, and freeze completely, at least 4 hours but preferably overnight.

In a medium frying pan, combine the honey and wine. Bring to a simmer over medium-low heat. Add the apricots, return to a simmer, and gently poach until tender, about 4 minutes depending on ripeness. Remove from the heat and let the apricots cool in the poaching syrup.

To serve, lift the semifreddo from the pan using the plastic. Cut into 1 in [2.5 cm] thick slabs and transfer to cold plates. Top with a few apricot halves and drizzle a bit of the poaching syrup over the semifreddo. Sprinkle with the SSS and serve immediately.

BAKED

A baked apricot works because it is naturally lower in juice than something as drippy as a peach, so you don't have to worry too much about moisture mitigation. Baking, like roasting, concentrates the flavor of an apricot without the additional caramelization.

---

savory:

apricot grilled cheese sandwich

I think the best grilled cheese sandwiches start in a pan and finish in the oven, yielding maximum textural complexity: crispy exterior and melty, melty interior. This sandwich is a study in contrasts, pairing the decadence of a fatty Brie, the austere graininess of true pumpernickel, and just enough apricot tutti-frutti to keep it festive. And as if that weren't enough, the color combo makes this sandwich a triple threat—visually appealing, contrasting textures, and tasty AF. Note: This makes one sandwich but can easily be scaled up.

MAKES 1 SANDWICH

2 Tbsp butter

2 slices dark Pumpernickel (page 39)

4 oz [115 g] Brie-style cheese (average grocery store brand is A-OK)

2 apricots, pitted and cut into ½ in [12 mm] wide wedges

Preheat the oven to 400°F [200°C].

In a medium, ovenproof frying pan, warm half of the butter over medium heat until melted and foamy. Place one slice of pumpernickel in the butter and fry for 30 seconds. Layer the Brie and sliced apricots evenly across the bread and top with a second slice of pumpernickel, pressing firmly to ensure good contact. Flip the sandwich over, add the rest of the butter to the pan, and swirl for about 30 seconds. Place the whole pan in the oven and bake until the Brie is melted, about 6 minutes. Remove from the oven, cut in half, and eat while warm.

sweet: burnt apricot tarts

Zingerman's Bakehouse used to make a tart like this and, on the off chance they didn't sell, employees (me) got to take them home. One such day I remarked to a coworker that, while it was a treat, day-old pastry didn't live up to the hype of the pastry. My more-skilled scavenger coworker told me to dust the tart with powdered sugar and then flash it under the broiler to both refresh the pastry and caramelize the sugar.

This was my first introduction to burnt sugar and the complexity it adds to any straightforward pastry. Now I do that even if the tarts are being eaten on the day they are baked, and so, too, can you. If you have a blowtorch, you can burn the pastry much more evenly than with the broiler, but if you don't (and don't want to run to the hardware store) a broiler works well too.

1 recipe Puff Pastry Dough (page 61)

1 recipe Pastry Cream (page 85)

2 apricots (about 2 oz [55 g]), halved and pits removed

Powdered sugar, for dusting

Roll the puff pastry into a ½ in [12 mm] thick square about 8 by 8 in [20 by 20 cm] and cut into four equal squares.

Spoon 2 Tbsp of pastry cream into the center of each square. Place one apricot half over the pastry cream. Bring the corners of the puff pastry up to meet in the center, leaving the apricots exposed. Pinch the corners together to seal. Chill for 30 minutes to set the butter in the dough.

Preheat the oven to 400°F [200°C]. Line a baking sheet with a silicone mat or parchment paper.

Place the tarts on the prepared baking sheet and bake until the pastry is cooked through, about 15 minutes. Remove from the oven and turn the oven to a high broil.

Dust each tart with powdered sugar and place under the broiler to burn, keeping a sharp eye and rotating the tray as needed. Remove from the oven and serve warm or at room temperature.

PRESERVED

Apricots, like most other stone fruit, make some of my favorite preserves.

JAM

Jam ratio: 60:40 fruit to sugar. I like a bit of tartness in my fruit preserves, so I add a splash of citrus or vinegar if the finished product tastes too sweet. But apricot jam tends toward tangy on its own, so it rarely needs much. Additionally, the skins of apricots are so thin that they blend right into the jam as the fruit cooks; no scaling, peeling, poking, or prodding required. I don't tend to add any other flavors to apricot jam, though vanilla, lemon herbs (such as verbena, balm, or thyme), ginger, or cardamom are perfectly at home. I do always add one of the apricot kernels to each jar.

apricot thumbprint cookies

Apricot jam is my favorite for any sort of cookie or bar featuring jam. I like the Almond Brutti ma Buoni cookies (page 69) as thumbprint cookies. Scoop a ball, push your thumb into it, bake halfway, then spoon some jam into the belly button and finish baking.

apricot glaze

Thin the apricot jam 50:50 with water (¼ cup [60 ml] of jam with ¼ cup [60 ml] of water) and then brush over fresh fruit tarts for a shine. Thin with buttermilk to glaze doughnuts, or brush a bit over roast chicken just as it finishes cooking for a deep amber hue.

DRIED

I have not had good luck drying my own apricots but always have a jar of store-bought on hand. They are great chopped into a cabbage salad with spicy chili oil (see page 215) and a lot of cilantro. They tenderize in savory stews like a Moroccan-inspired lamb stew with chickpeas and tomato. They also pickle well using the Basic Fruit Pickle Brine (page 112) to add an extra pop of sweet-sour to any salad or cheese plate.

apricot cordial

1 lb [455 g] fresh apricots, pits removed and roughly chopped

½ lb [230 g] dried apricots, roughly chopped

2 cups [480 ml] vodka or gin

⅓ cup [80 ml] Simple Syrup (page 109), flavored or plain

In a large jar with a lid, combine the chopped fresh and dried apricots and vodka.

Seal and let stand at room temperature for a week. Strain, pressing any fruit bits through the strainer that want to go (read: it doesn't have to be perfectly clear). Whisk in the syrup, taste, and adjust as desired. Store at room temperature for up to 2 months.

Uses: Combine 2 oz [60 ml] cordial with 6 oz [180 ml] soda water for a spritz.

Shake 2 oz [60 ml] cordial with 1 oz [15 ml] lemon juice over ice, strain, and serve up.

Spike a glass of iced tea with 2 oz [60 ml] cordial.

One of my favorite things to make in the summer are fruit spritzes. I blend 1 lb [455 g] apricots in a blender with 1 Tbsp sugar and then pour ¼ cup [60 ml] of the juice into 1 cup [240 ml] of soda water. You can use any sort of fruit juice (and I often use store-bought), but apricot is my number one favorite of all time.

blueberries

Blueberries are maybe the most agreeable fruit: They travel pretty well, are easy to eat, taste good cooked, and are a dream to preserve for post-season enjoyment. I prefer a tart berry, but even the sweetest blueberries don't cloy because their relatively thick skins have tannins similar to red grapes or tart cherries. These same compounds are good for cartilage development and joint protection. Blueberries don't ask a lot and are only a pain when cooked blueberry hits a white tablecloth or shirt, which often splatters and stains. There's not a whole lot else to say. Blueberries are like the golden retriever of the fruit world; they're just all-round pleasant company.

HOW TO SELECT

Look for blueberries that are even in texture (firmer than not), avoiding any boxes that have a lot of wrinkled or squished berries (some are inevitable, a lot are not). Freshly picked blueberries will often have a downy bloom on their skin; this is desirable and not a sign of anything gone wrong. I tend to prefer a smaller berry because they are often a bit tarter, but as the saying goes, size doesn't really matter.

SIGNS OF RIPENESS

The darker and warmer the color, the riper the berry. Underripe berries will have tinges of green in their undertone. Overripe berries tend to feel soft, like their cells are starting to break down under the skin.

HOW TO STORE

Blueberries taste best at room temperature but store longer in the fridge. I usually keep them out on the counter (out of direct sunlight) for a couple of days, and, if there are still some left, either refrigerate or freeze. If refrigerating, wrap in a paper or plastic bag. If freezing, lay out on a baking sheet and freeze, then transfer to a resealable bag to store until ready to use or until next blueberry season when you remember that you have frozen blueberries and need to eat them up before the fresh ones come 'round.

NOTES

Wild blueberries are teeny-tiny compared to their domesticated cousins. I have never found fresh wild blueberries, though they are more available dried or in the freezer section.

The skins of blueberries contain most of the nutrients and antioxident compounds that help in joint protection.

RAW

You don't need a cookbook to tell you to eat blueberries raw. They go from bush to bowl to hand to mouth without need for instruction. I can eat about 5 lb [2.3 kg] of blueberries with no adornment before I start looking around for something else to do with them, and that's where this book comes in—for what's next after you've grazed to boredom.

savory:

salad of oat groats, blueberries, chicories + buttermilk

Oat groats are the whole seed of the oat plant. They can be rolled or ground or milled into flour, but left whole and boiled, they make for a delightfully chewy grain salad. Should you not have oat groats around, wheat berries, buckwheat, or black lentils make a fine substitution. Similarly, should you not have any chicories on hand, feel free to use arugula, baby kale, or spinach. Finally, if you don't like the looks of the fresh blueberries on hand, frozen will work, too, though they will leak juice all over.

Olive oil

¼ cup [45 g] oat groats

Salt

2 cups [280 g] blueberries

1 head radicchio (about 3 oz [85 g]), endive, or frisée (or a mix), cut into large petals

¾ cup [180 ml] buttermilk

Freshly ground black pepper

In a medium saucepan, heat a glug of olive oil over high heat until it shimmers. Add the oat groats and a big pinch of salt and toast for 1 minute, stirring a couple of times. Add 2 cups [480 ml] of water, bring to a boil, lower the heat to a simmer, and cook until tender, 25 to 35 minutes.

Drain any excess water away, immediately dress the oat groats with a glug of olive oil, and let cool.

To serve, on a serving platter or individual plates, lay out half of the radicchio, scatter half of the oat groats and half of the blueberries, and then drizzle with half of the buttermilk and season with salt and pepper. Repeat with the remaining ingredients to complete the salad.

I like this on its own or served alongside seared fish or roast chicken. It pairs well with red meats too, but can be easily over-taken by something strong like elk or venison.

sweet: # blueberry puffies

"Puffies" is not a term taught in culinary schools. I made it up. Though in my defense, someone else made up all the terms that are taught in cooking schools, so it's really just a matter of time. Puffies are puff-dough sandwiches and one of my favorite what-on-Earth-will-I-make-for-dessert solutions. This one is filled with lemon curd and blueberries, but could also be made with pastry cream or whipped cream and any other fruit substituted for the blueberries.

1 recipe Puff Pastry Dough (page 61)

Olive oil

SSS (page 78)

1 recipe Lemon Curd (page 94)

2 cups [280 g] blueberries

¼ cup [60 ml] Marigold Syrup (page 111), or really any type of syrup, including maple

Preheat the oven to 375°F [190°C].

Cut the puff pastry into eight 4 by 4 in [10 by 10 cm] squares, brush with olive oil, and sprinkle with a pinch of SSS. Transfer to a baking sheet lined with a silicone mat or parchment paper and bake until golden brown and puffed, about 12 minutes.

In a medium bowl, lightly whip the lemon curd until fluffy, about 1 minute.

In a separate medium bowl, dress the blueberries in the syrup.

To serve, divvy the lemon curd among four of the eight puff pastry squares. Divide the blueberries evenly across the lemon curd–topped squares and top each with one of the remaining puff pastry squares to make sandwiches.

BAKED

Baking with fruit is all about juice management. Blueberries are some of the easiest fruit to bake with because they are small and have relatively dense flesh that won't turn everything into what Cardi B named WAP (wet-ass pastry).

savory: # roast chicken over blueberries, cornbread + lemon

I love chicken roasted over bread. I love blueberries and cornmeal together. Cornbread often dries out in short order after baking. Blueberries lack the acidity to cut through the richness of chicken over bread. Blueberries and lemon love each other. This is an exact transcription of my mental stream of consciousness that developed this dish. My creative process is often more practical than artistic.

1 whole chicken (4 to 5 lb [1.8 to 2.3 kg]), back removed, then cut into quarters

Salt

Neutral oil

1 loaf Cornbread Cake (page 65), cut or torn into chunks

½ tsp chili flakes (optional)

1 cup [140 g] blueberries, fresh or frozen

2 lemons (about 3 oz [85 g]), seeds removed and cut into smaller chunks

2 cups [480 ml] chicken stock

Preheat the oven to 400°F [200°C].

Blot the skin of the chicken dry, then season liberally with salt.

In a large, ovenproof frying pan, heat a glug of neutral oil over high heat. Sear the skin of the chicken until golden brown and crispy, about 6 minutes. Remove to a plate.

Add ¼ cup [60 ml] of water (or white wine or hard cider) to the frying pan to deglaze. Add the cornbread, chili flakes (if using), blueberries, and lemons. Pour the chicken stock into the pan, then place the chicken, skin-side up, over the cornbread. Bring the stock to a boil, then remove from the heat and transfer the pan to the oven. Roast until the chicken is cooked through, about 35 minutes.

Serve with a green salad on the side.

sweet:

blueberry spelt muffins

Spelt flour is becoming more widely available, so I've started swapping it for all-purpose flour in a lot of recipes. Spelt has a lower gluten content than wheat, making it easier for some to digest and harder to overwork if you're a naturally heavy-handed stirrer like me. I use either fresh or frozen blueberries for these muffins, but have taken to adding the blueberries directly to the muffins as opposed to the batter before scooping. It helps minimize batter bruising (see page 29).

MAKES 12 MUFFINS

1 recipe Muffin Batter made with spelt flour (page 46)

1 cup [140 g] blueberries

Sugar, for sprinkling

Preheat the oven to 375°F [190°C]. Grease a 12-cup muffin tin or line with baking papers.

Scoop the batter into the cups until about three-quarters of the way full. Add a handful of blueberries to each cup.

Sprinkle with sugar and bake until golden brown and set in the center, 12 to 17 minutes, rotating the pan halfway through.

Note: You can also bake this as a loaf or round cake; just swap the pan and then test using the knife test (see page 30) for doneness.

ROASTED

Cooked blueberries are the most beautiful color, a deep indigo that never fails to stop me dead in my tracks. I encourage you to take a moment between prepping and cleaning to run your finger through the blue-black schmear caused by the blending of their thick skins and pectin-filled juice. Stunning.

savory: ## venison (or lamb) w/parsnips + blueberry sauce

I grew up in a hunting family and venison was common on our table. The heady gaminess works with the sweet tannin of blue-berries. Should you not have any venison, lamb or goat is a fine substitution. I've also made this with pork and duck or simply skipped the meat and let a big pile of arugula take its place. This is one place where substituting mushrooms for a vegetarian option is not ideal.

3 lb [1.4 kg] parsnips, tipped and tailed, peeled, and cut into chunks

2 garlic cloves [14 g], peeled and smashed

Salt

½ cup [120 ml] heavy cream

2 or 3 venison chops (about 2 oz [55 g each]) per person

Neutral oil

1 sprig rosemary (optional)

½ cup [120 ml] red wine

2 cups [280 g] blueberries

2 Tbsp butter

In a medium pot, place the parsnips and garlic, cover with water, add a big pinch of salt, and bring to a boil over high heat. Lower the heat to a simmer and cook until tender, about 20 minutes, then drain, reserving ¼ cup [60 ml] of the cooking liquid.

In a medium bowl, combine the cooked parsnips, cream, and reserved parsnip cooking liquid and smash lightly to make a rustic paste. Set aside.

Season the chops all over with salt and then blot dry. In a large frying pan, heat a glug of neutral oil over high heat and sear the chops until browned on one side, about 4 minutes. Flip and sear the other side until medium rare, about 2 minutes depending on thickness. Remove the chops to a platter and cover with an aluminum foil tent to rest.

Add the rosemary sprig (if using) and wine to the frying pan to deglaze the pan over medium heat. When the wine is reduced by half, add the blueberries and cook until the berries begin to burst, about 3 minutes. Add the butter and swirl to enrich the sauce. Remove the rosemary sprig.

To serve, divvy the parsnip paste among four plates, add the chops, and spoon the blueberry pan sauce all over.

blueberries + griddled cake

You can substitute any sliced cake for the angel food cake in this recipe, but I like this combination. Perhaps unexpectedly, I make this the most in the winter with frozen blueberries, which I roast straight from frozen.

Butter

1 Angel Food Cake
(page 63), cut into 2 in
[5 cm] thick slices

2 cups [280 g] blueberries

¼ cup [60 ml] maple syrup

Olive oil

Salt

1 cup [240 g] sour cream

In a large frying pan, heat a knob or two of butter over medium heat until foamy. Pan fry the cake slices until golden brown and toasted, then flip and fry the other side.

Wipe out the frying pan and heat another knob of butter over medium heat until foamy.

Add the blueberries, maple syrup, and a glug of olive oil to the frying pan and roast in the now-melted butter. Cook until the blueberries burst and their liquid reduces by half, about 5 minutes. Remove from the heat and sprinkle with a pinch of salt.

In a medium bowl, whip the sour cream with a whisk until smooth and slightly fluffy.

To serve, top each slice of cake with a hefty dollop of sour cream and a big spoonful of the sticky roasted blueberries.

PRESERVED

JAM

Blueberries make great jam because they are so high in pectin. The jam sets up quickly, so it tastes fresh, especially with a squeeze of lemon added at the last minute. I use a 60:40 ratio of fruit to sugar.

PICKLED

I like blueberries pickled with the Basic Fruit Pickle Brine (page 112). This is one of the few times I'll use red wine or sherry vinegar in the pickle liquid. Uses: Pickled blueberries go well with any sort of game meat or higher-fat cheese. I really like rye bread (like the Pumpernickel on page 39) smeared with a triple cream bloomy rind cheese (like Brie or Saint André) and then topped with a spoonful of pickled blueberries.

VINEGAR

Blueberries turn a lovely purple when blended into vinegars, and make one of my favorite shrubs.

Combine 1 cup [200 g] brown sugar with 1½ cups [375 ml] apple cider vinegar and 1 cup [140 g] blueberries (fresh or frozen). Purée in a blender until smooth and pour through a fine-mesh sieve into a wide-mouth jar. Discard the pulp. Add two bay leaves and infuse for at least 10 minutes and up to 2 months.

Uses: Blueberry shrub makes a nice spritzer just with soda water or a really pretty gin gimlet. Just shake 2 oz [60 ml] gin with ½ oz [15 ml] blueberry shrub with ice and garnish with a lime wedge or wheel. It is also a great vinaigrette base, which I like most on spinach salads.

FREEZING

You can't ask for an easier fruit to preserve. Lay the blueberries out on a baking sheet to individually freeze. Once frozen, scoop up and package into a freezer bag and use at will.

cherries

Being a native Michigander, I'm legally required to love cherries. You're given a pound of dried cherries when you get a Michigan driver's license and every baby born in the mitten is outfitted with a cherry-shaped beanie. Just kidding, but we do grow a lot of cherries in the fruit belt—over 180 million pounds of tart cherries and about 62.5 million pounds of sweet cherries every year. Growing that many cherries means that you work them into many an unsuspecting recipe—cherry BBQ sauce, cherry salsa, cherry sausages—and it works, mostly.

I used to cook in the Grand Traverse area, which is responsible for about 80 percent of Michigan's cherry production (along with a lot of other tree fruits and berries). It was there that a diner at one of the farm dinners I hosted remarked, "You put fruit in a lot of stuff. I didn't think I would like it, but I do." That one little comment made me realize, I do, in fact, add fruit to a lot of savory dishes, which, with a bit of time, led to this cookbook. That comment also was the first time someone said something to the effect of, "That didn't sound good, but it was!" to me, which comes up more often than I'm really proud of. Shruggy shoulders. We all have to have our "thing."

So, cherries are where it all started. I hope this chapter encourages you to work fruit into an unexpected savory dish, even if it doesn't sound like it is something you will like. And if you just can't be bothered, you can be an honorary Michigander by never being too far away from a slice of cherry pie.

HOW TO SELECT

For sweet cherries: Look for firm, even fruit, avoiding any that have blue or brown mold around the stem or any cracks in the flesh of the fruit. The skin should be bright, shiny, and taut. Ideally the fruit will look like it is trying to burst through the skin. As it ages, the flesh loses moisture and the skin loosens.

For tart cherries: Look for bright coloring and taut skin, though the fruit will always feel softer in the interior because tart cherries contain more moisture in their cells than sweet cherries. Avoid the box if it contains cherries that are squished or have numerous brown spots.

SIGNS OF RIPENESS

Most cherries are picked ripe because the tree is picked all at once. This means when cherries are available, they are generally ripe.

HOW TO STORE

Keep sweet cherries at room temperature out of direct sunlight. If you need to keep for longer, pop them in the fridge.

Tart cherries should be stored in the fridge. They break down faster than sweet cherries because their flesh is so heavy with juice.

NOTES

Cherries come in a range of colors from pale yellow to deep dark burgundy. The darker the flesh, the richer the flavor because of the presence of betalains or anthocyanins. The darker flavor, like in a beet, makes the fruit taste more complex and sometimes earthier. The absence of those flavors makes the cherry taste sweeter because there are no other competing sensations.

There are a lot of devices on the market to help you pit a cherry. I still use my grandmother's contraption of a mini-piston that screws onto the top of a mason jar. The piston pushes the pit through the other side of the cherry and into the jar. There are also handheld versions. Should you not want to buy such a uni-tasker, my friend Kate Fiebing uses a rigid straw to push the pit out with ease.

NIKKI ROTHWELL

Dr. Nikki Rothwell, coordinator of the Northwest Michigan Horticulture Research Center, is an expert in Michigan tree fruit and the issues that affect the trees, the fruit, and the farmers who raise apples, cherries, plums, peaches, and pears. In addition to her tree and pest management work, she and her husband, Dan Young, own Tandem Ciders in Suttons Bay, Michigan.

Abra Berens: Years ago you told me that if someone isn't born into a cherry growing family, they basically can't become a cherry grower. Can you explain that?

Nikki Rothwell: Specialty crop farming requires a lot of initial invest-ment, particularly if you are new to the game (i.e., not born or married into a fruit farming family). Land prices in northwest Michigan are extremely high. Next, planting trees is expensive in terms of money and time. Right now, nurseries cannot keep up with demand. To plant dwarf apples in a high-density situation (which should always be done given all the research and economic work) is a two- to three-year wait. Once you have the trees, costs run $20,000 to $25,000 per acre. Tart cherries are much cheaper to plant, but we do not mechanically harvest those trees until they are physically big enough to "shake," which in most cases is six years—six years of spraying, pruning, mowing, etc., with no returns—time and money. A shaker runs about $180,000; to justify a specialized piece of equipment like that, you need a lot of acres. With the tart cherry industry at somewhat of a crossroads (between import pressure, invasive insects, climate change), everyone assumes grapes, or some other crop, will be better. However, transitions take money—grapes (the media darling as a cherry successor) are also $20,000 per acre to plant and take a few years to get into production. The other thing that people don't consider is that wine grapes are very similar to tart cherries . . . both are grown by growers, but are paid by processors at the amount they want to pay. Winemakers and cherry processors are the ones buying those commodities and basically setting the prices. If the grower is vertically integrated, that's another story, but that's more investment.

AB: And all of that takes time and know-how, which is only acquired one year at a time. What are the other pressures on growers in areas with booming populations and tourist industries?

NR: Urbanization, land prices, housing prices—the best lots for homes are also best for fruit production. Additionally, we have people moving here who love the agriculture of the region until they actually butt up against it—having a bird cannon boom in the vineyard nearby, growers spraying when winds are down at 3:00 a.m., potential drift from pesticide applications, tucking fruit on small roads, the smells from processing facilities. It is hard to reconcile those ag ways with newcomers who have no idea about real agriculture. It seems harder and harder to be a community (which is not unique here or in this political climate) with people drawing lines in the sand. I also worry about how to recruit, engage, and retain the next generation of growers. How do we keep them profitable and in business? Other pressures growers face are regulatory issues: labor audits, ever-changing safety rules, bookkeeping, spray record maintenance. Many new rules keep food and the environment safe, but for many growers it is not why they wanted to farm; that combined with the fact that many do not have the skill set to do these things online or electronically. I am sure I can think of others . . .

AB: How do you see markets for "value-added" agricultural products like hard cider or cherry products factoring into our farming future?

NR: I think there is still a future for value-added, especially in our region that is highly dependent on tourists, and because there are people willing to pay more for products when they know where they come from. I also see that value being extended into other markets where people have expendable income and are happy to pay for a product they identify with vacation, a fun experience, or wanting to "know their maker." I have personal issues with this kind of situation, as it increases the divide between the haves and have-nots. Those who cannot pay for "local" greenhouse-grown greens in February rely on places like the Dollar Store in some urban and rural food deserts. I would love efforts and funding to help add value to the food chain and be able to supply people without extra income with those healthy foods, but I digress.

As for my personal business, Tandem Ciders, we do depend on that value-added component to make it work. We are not the cheapest cider on the market, and we rely on quality to drive purchases because folks value that quality. There is probably a saturation point for alcoholic markets/businesses, limiting potential expansion of the industry. I also wonder about collaborations using commodity products like apples to increase regional sales of something like cider. There is little interaction, in the grand scheme, between commodity apple farmers and cider producers. We need to figure out how to grow and sell more apples and cider and to band Michigan together on both fresh eating and value-added fronts.

AB: *What do you wish the average consumer knew about growing fruit and the tree fruit industry?*

NR: I wish people understood what a complex business fruit farming is. It's a science, an art form, a way of life, with the end result that puts food on America's table. They don't understand why an apple costs X or a bottle of local wine Y. They have no idea what goes into producing these fruits, and there is little empathy for growers: "They have a new truck. They get handouts from the government. They are using pesticides all the time and poisoning the environment. They pay no taxes." I have heard it all. There is a tremendous amount of misunderstanding about agriculture and the processing of food in this country.

AB: *In the face of climate change, will the Grand Traverse region stay the cherry capital of the world?*

NR: It will perhaps be our downfall. Tart cherries are the most inherently variable crop from year to year. Climate change has played into that. Trees bloom early, then suffer from spring frost/freeze events.

We have also had milder winters and trees come out of dormancy earlier and faster with early spring warm-ups. And being Michigan, we are certainly not going to get through spring without dips below freezing. We see more hail events, which were pretty uncommon when I first started. Hail can devastate fruit but also vines and trees, which take a lot longer to recover.

Warmer and wetter conditions are the predictions of climatologists, both of which favor insect and disease development. The perfect and sad example is the spotted wing drosophila, an invasive insect really hurting cherry and blueberry growers in Michigan. Insects are temperature and humidity dependent, and favorable conditions yield more generations of insects building populations to millions; no grower can control those numbers. Mild winter also mean the cold does not knock down pest pressure as it did in the past.

Diseases are also favored by the climate predictions. The best example is fire blight of apple. We have seen more cases of fire blight in the last ten years in northern Michigan because our springs are warming. This bacterial disease loves warm weather at bloom when bacteria colonize the flower parts and are washed into the flower by rain or dew. The bacteria spread throughout the plant and can kill trees, especially those planted into modern orchard systems. In the past, our springs were too cool to favor the pathogen that causes fire blight, but as we warm, we have more outbreaks.

AB: How do you use fruit in your kitchen?

NR: As you can imagine, there is a lot of fruit in a lot of forms in our household. My gram wasn't much of a cook or a baker, but that didn't stop her from trying. My mom carried on with much better results, and I still love to bake to this day. All of those older recipes (cobblers, buckles, etc.) are perfect for capturing the fruit of the month in Michigan. Nothing beats a cherry pie . . . nothing. We can probably argue about top pies forever, but in northern Michigan, it's a Montmorency tart cherry pie with cherries pulled from a cooling pad, pitted with family on your patio, and baked with your gram's pie crust. Dan, being from the East Coast, always argues for apple but objects to the cinnamon and nutmeg I put in my apple pie compared to his mom's. But, I mean, they serve theirs with Cheddar cheese, so there's clearly no accounting for taste. We are big on apples and pork in the fall, especially with cider. We have a drunken pork recipe that is awesome every time.

RAW

This is the place for sweet cherries, which have a denser flesh than tart cherries, more akin to nectarines or cantaloupes. While I love both of these recipes, there is also good fun to be had simply eating sweet cherries out of hand and spitting the pits into the summer grass.

savory: ## brined cherries + salty snacks

Lupini beans are most widely known in the Mediterranean Basin and often eaten brined as a snack. I've only ever bought processed lupini beans because I read about how one needs to meticulously rinse them to remove the toxic alkaloids that give them a distinct bitterness not dissimilar to uncured olives, which got me to thinking about how I love olives and dark cherries together. Which, naturally, made me think about brining cherries to cure a bit like an olive. And now, here we are.

1 lb [455 g] sweet, black cherries, unpitted	1 lb [455 g] Castelvetrano olives	1 orange, peel cut into wide ribbons
1 Tbsp salt	1 tsp fennel seed	2 sprigs rosemary
One 16 oz [480 ml] jar lupini beans, rinsed	½ tsp chili flakes	½ cup [120 ml] olive oil

Pack the washed cherries in a clean jar. In a medium bowl, dissolve the salt in 2 cups [480 ml] of water to make a brine. Pour the brine over the cherries and let soak for at least an hour and up to a week. In a medium bowl, combine the beans and olives.

In a small frying pan, dry toast the fennel seed and chili flakes over high heat until fragrant, about 1 minute. Add to the beans along with the orange peel, rosemary, and olive oil. Toss to coat.

Just before serving, drain the cherries, add to the beans, and serve (preferably with a glass of vermouth).

sweet:

chocolate pudding w/coffee-soaked black cherries

Similar to brined cherries, these cherries benefit from a long soak in a coffee syrup to help marry the flavors of coffee, chocolate, and red fruit. Tossing the soaked cherries in the coffee rub ups the ante and gives a good textural difference with the silky pudding. If you don't have the time or inclination to soak the cherries, simply tossing in the coffee rub adds just that extra something to an already luxurious dessert.

1 recipe Chocolate Pudding (page 106)

1 lb [455 g] dark, sweet cherries, halved and pitted

1 cup [240 ml] brewed coffee, cold

¼ cup [50 g] granulated sugar

2 Tbsp ground coffee

1 tsp brown sugar

¼ tsp ground ginger

¼ tsp salt

Divide the pudding among four glasses, bowls, or jars and keep cold.

Pack the cherries into a jar.

In a medium bowl, dissolve the granulated sugar in the coffee and then pour over the cherries and let soak for an hour.

Just before serving, drain the cherries, keeping the liquid to serve as a sidecar (see page 31) if you like, and toss with the ground coffee, brown sugar, ginger, and salt in a medium bowl to coat. Divide the cherries evenly among the pudding cups and serve.

BAKED

This is the place for tart cherries. Tart cherries have a thicker skin and juicier interior than sweet cherries, much more like a grape than a nectarine. They benefit from a touch of sweetness even when paired with savory elements to balance the acidic punch that lifts even the richest of dishes.

savory: # cherry baked brie w/seedy crackers

Save your well-aged, high-quality Brie for another time. I like this recipe best with the most average grocery store Brie-style cheese because I can't taste the glory of a perfectly ripened cheese when it is melted in the oven and slathered in roasted cherry juice. And if I can't appreciate the nuance of the finest ingredient, there's no point in spending the money on it.

One 8 oz [225 g] Brie/ Camembert-style cheese

1 cup [160 g] tart cherries, pitted

¼ cup [60 ml] maple syrup

¼ cup [60 ml] bourbon or rum (or balsamic vinegar if you're not drinking)

1 recipe Seedy Crackers (page 48)

Preheat the oven to 375°F [190°C].

Cut the top of the rind off the Brie, leaving as much of the cheese intact as possible.

In a medium bowl, toss the cherries with the maple syrup and bourbon.

Place the Brie in an ovenproof baking dish. Top with the cherries (some will spill off) and bake until warm and melty, about 15 minutes.

Remove from the oven and spoon some of the cherry liquid back over the Brie. Serve with the seedy crackers (and maybe a big salad for a lunch).

sweet:

cherry pie

Hands down, this is my favorite pie. I love tart fruit. I love flaky pastry. I love making pie. I don't love pitting cherries, but I can often find already pitted frozen cherries and so problem solved. I like this pie warm with a big ball of melting ice cream. I also like it at room temperature for breakfast. I don't even mind it when it is too sweet, although it is better when it isn't.

½ recipe Pie Dough (page 60), or just make a whole recipe and only use one ball of dough

½ tsp almond extract (optional)

1 recipe Super Juicy Fruit Pie Filling (page 102)

Heavy cream or egg wash (see page 30), for brushing

2 Tbsp SSS (page 78)

Allow the pie dough to rest at room temperature for at least 10 minutes to make it easier to roll. On a floured surface, dust the ball of dough with flour and then bash with a rolling pin to make a flattened disc. Start rolling: I always roll in a north/south direction directly in front of me and then rotate the dough 90 degrees (and flip it over, adding more flour to the dough and rolling surface) to roll into a rough square. Then I rotate 45 degrees (flip and flour) to roll into a round. Final rotation is 180 degrees (flip and flour) and you should have roughly a circle and not something that looks like Australia (even though it doesn't matter what the final shape is as long as there aren't holes or cracks through the center).

Lay your 9 in [23 cm] pie pan in the center of the rolled dough and cut a circle 2 in [5 cm] wider than the pie pan (this will allow the dough to overhang the tin and give you plenty of dough to crimp the edges). Lay the cut round into the pie pan and pop in the fridge to chill for 30 minutes.

Gather the remaining dough and fold it over itself to make a smaller piece. (I fold instead of wad the scraps because it adds layers to the pastry, keeping it flaky even though it has already

continued

been rolled once.) Bash the dough again with the rolling pin and roll into a round that is at least as big as the pie pan to make sure the lattice stretches over the whole pie. Cut the dough into 1 in [2.5 cm] wide strips.

Add the almond extract (if using) to the cherry pie filling. Fill the pie pan with the fruit filling and thickened (but cooled) fruit goo.

Lay the first lattice strip running north-south on the left side of the pie. Lay the second lattice strip running east-west on the bottom of the pie. Continue laying lattice strips alternating north-south with east-west to make a chevron pattern. Trim any excessive lattice overhang.

Roll up the lattice ends in the overhanging pie dough and then press aggressively with a fork to seal. Pop into the freezer to chill for at least an hour to set the pastry.

Preheat the oven to 350°F [180°C].

Remove the pie from the freezer and brush with heavy cream or egg wash and sprinkle with a bit of SSS. Bake the pie until the center is set and the pastry is golden brown, about 50 minutes. Let cool completely before slicing.

GRILLED/ROASTED

Cherries show well with a hint of smoke, which is best achieved with a wood-burning grill or campfire. I don't have a wood-burning grill (yet), so I use my gas one or just pop cherries very close under the oven broiler. If using a grill, I still use a frying pan over the grill grates to prevent the cherries from falling through the cracks. Aluminum foil pouches also work well to keep the cherries corralled when grilling.

savory:

buttermilk pork tenderloin + grilled cherry salad

This buttermilk brine, which is equally at home on chicken or lamb, adds a tenderizing level of acidity, and the lactose in the milk encourages deep browning as the meat grills.

1 pork tenderloin (about 1 lb [455 g])

1 Tbsp brown sugar

Salt

1 cup [240 ml] buttermilk

4 sprigs thyme (optional)

Neutral oil

2 cups [320 g] sweet cherries, pitted and halved

Freshly ground black pepper

1 cup [160 g] bulgur or couscous, steamed according to the package instructions

10 sprigs parsley, leaves picked

¼ cup [60 ml] sherry or red wine vinegar

¼ cup [60 ml] olive oil

Rub the pork all over with the brown sugar and 1 tsp of salt, then place into a sealable container or bag. Add the buttermilk and thyme (if using) and squish it around to coat evenly. Let the pork cure in the fridge for at least 4 hours or overnight.

Heat a grill to medium. Grill the pork for 3 minutes on each side. When the internal temperature reaches 135°F [57°C], remove from the grill and let rest for 15 minutes (the temperature will increase the last 10 degrees as it rests).

While the pork grills, using a small frying pan on the other side of the grill, heat a glug of neutral oil and roast the cherries with a big pinch of salt and black pepper until the fruit softens, about 8 minutes.

In a medium bowl, combine the grilled cherries, bulgur, parsley, vinegar, and olive oil with another big pinch of salt and black pepper. Toss, taste, and adjust the seasoning as desired.

Slice the pork into ½ in [12 mm] thick medallions and serve with a big scoop of the cherry salad.

sweet: tart cherry syllabub + smashed almond brutti ma buoni

Syllabub is an easy, old-fashioned dessert that can be made in advance for a party. I make this with sweet vermouth, liking the bitterness, but sherry or sweet white wine are more traditional. Feel free to use any sort of cookie or crumble here, but since cherry pits are used to make almond extract, cherries and almonds are always a natural flavor combination.

2 cups [320 g] tart cherries, pitted

¼ cup [60 ml] maple syrup

1 recipe Syllabub (page 90)

4 Almond Brutti ma Buoni cookies (page 69)

Turn on the broiler.

In a medium bowl, toss the cherries with the maple syrup and transfer to an ovenproof dish or frying pan. Place the cherries under the broiler until they char and soften, about 4 minutes, then let cool.

To serve, layer the syllabub and cherries in four jars or glasses. Smash the almond cookies into a crumble and sprinkle on top of the syllabub.

PRESERVED

PICKLED

Pickled cherries add another layer of acidity anywhere they are strewn. I use the Basic Fruit Pickle Brine (page 112) and usually use balsamic vinegar, though red wine or sherry would be at home too. Uses: Pair with starchy vegetables such as parsnips, carrots, sweet potatoes, or squash, or soft cheeses and pâtés. A pot of Chicken Liver Mousse (page 218) with toast points and a pile of pickled cherries may be my favorite snacky dinner.

DRIED

Dried cherries are truly one of my favorite ingredients. I almost always buy dried tart cherries, but watch out because they often come sweetened, which doesn't make much sense to me. I use them just about anywhere I would raisins. Dried cherries also pickle well using the Basic Fruit Pickle Brine (page 112), but only pickle them for the flavor because there's no reason to preserve an already preserved product.

CANDIED

IMHO candied cherries should always be kept on hand to top ice cream, fold into sour cream for a quick dessert, or add sweet-tart to a pan sauce or cheese board. But I especially love to slip them into a cocktail or two.

candied cocktail cherries

I've made a variety of different cocktail cherries with different liquors and spices. But honestly, I like them best with sweet vermouth, which helps keep the sweetness and spices balanced with a bit of bitterness. If you swap another liquor (like bourbon, brandy, or rum), add some warming spices (cinnamon, star anise, nutmeg, clove) to the mix.

1 lb [455 g] cherries (I leave the pits in and just warn people, but I seem to be alone in this)

1 cup [240 ml] sweet vermouth

¼ cup [50 g] brown sugar

¼ cup [60 ml] water (or cherry juice, if you have it)

Pack the cherries into clean jars.

In a medium bowl, combine the vermouth, sugar, and water to make a syrup. Pour the syrup over the cherries and let steep at least overnight and for up to 2 months at room temperature.

FREEZING

Cherries are a breeze to freeze. I generally take the time to pit the cherries before freezing to save myself the headache later. Beyond that, just lay them out on a baking sheet to individually freeze before transferring to a resealable bag for later use. Large-scale fruit processors do a good job of pitting, individually freezing, bagging, and storing cherries so you don't have to. To be honest, I almost always use frozen cherries in place of fresh ones except in the raw recipes, so feel actively encouraged to do the same.

drupelet berries: raspberries, blackberries + mulberries

About a year ago, during the first week of August, I was commiserating with a farming friend, lamenting the ensuing frenetic pace that always peaks with the end of summer. I was bracing, as I always am that time of year, for the waves of visitors to our beach town, the urgency to wring the last bit of summer vacation from the days that are noticeably shortening, and the demands to be endured by those of us in the service industry. I ended my moaning with a simple declaration, "I hate August."

He responded, "Yeah, but at least it isn't July." For him, July is the bear because the days are so long and filled from sunup to sundown not only with harvesting, washing, packing, and selling, but also with planting, weeding, and starting seeds for fall crops, the start of the last crops running in tandem with the peak of the first. The two ends of the spectrum merge together like *A Wrinkle in Time*, and all that there is is more work that needs to be done.

Our third friend responded, "You two are crazy. Summer is the best!" We responded in unison, "Keep it. Give us February."

That's the problem with summer. It piles on. It's too much. Not only the work, but also sensory overload. How can one possibly enjoy the peak of cherry season when the raspberries also need attention? It's hard to take the time to savor a handful of mulberries from the tree in the yard when you're trying to get the grass mowed in the hour between sunset and actual darkness. I want to create meals to delight and celebrate each ingredient at its peak, but there's a limit to how much even I can eat in a given setting.

My solution is freezing. Holding out for the quiet hush of steps in snow as a salve to bawdy bare feet on summer grass, yes, but also, more practically, the actual freezer. I rarely eat a raspberry in the height of summer. I'll occasionally swipe a handful while running to the next thing, but mine are destined for cold storage where they will wait patiently for the pale shadow of long, dark nights and dinner parties that fill those luxuriously slow hours.

Raspberries, blackberries, and mulberries are all drupelet berries, a collection of individual drupes of fleshy fruit surrounding a single seed attached to a common carpel. The issue, most frequently, with freezing is mushy fruit devoid of its sweet juices. The water in the cells expands when frozen and breaks the cell walls as it pushes for somewhere to go. When the water contracts during thaw, it leaks through those fissures and collapses the texture of the fruit. Compared to the one big berry that is a king crimson strawberry, drupelets are a collection of tiny berries providing a measured structure even after thawed. It is not the same as fresh fruit certainly, but a better tasting option than "winter berries" on grocery shelves, which were harvested underripe, pumped with ethylene, and shipped across the globe in a refrigerated truck.

It is also true that my affection for freezing drupelets is in part because of the ease. They take no preparation except spreading out into a single layer on a baking sheet and sticking in the freezer. The next day, simply scoop the individually frozen fruits into a resealable bag and return to the freezer. Skipping this step will inevitably lead to a frozen log of berries, which is more difficult to use. Compared to the blanching, peeling, and removing the stones of other July fruits, drupelets require a miniscule amount of my stretched attention, for which I am always eternally grateful.

HOW TO SELECT

Look for berries that are even in color and texture. They are not pungent in their aroma, but if very ripe will have a heady, wine-like smell. Avoid berries that are collapsed, moldy, or variegated, which can indicate age and a shorter shelf life. Beware of berries that are sold in too deep a container. Drupelets are very delicate and easily crushed by the weight of other berries piled on top.

SIGNS OF RIPENESS

The color should be lively and not have signs of white or green in the undertone. The berries will be heavy with juice and pull from the plant easily.

HOW TO STORE

Don't! These berries are best eaten within a few days of harvest or purchase. Storing in the fridge will help extend their shelf life, but the cold will dampen the flavor. Be sure to bring back to room temperature before eating to reinvigorate the aromatics. All drupelets take well to freezing, so if you aren't sure you'll get to them, individually freeze for later.

NOTES

Sun scald shows up on drupelets during excessively sunny and hot summers and presents as bleached spots on otherwise good-looking fruit. There's nothing wrong with those berries, and so there is no harm in eating them, but sometimes the texture is a bit mealy.

The darker the fruit, the more bioflavonoids and antioxidants present, which are linked to anti-aging properties.

RAW

The ups and downs of berries are that sometimes they taste perfect—sweet and tangy, summer on the tongue—and sometimes they are, well, less titillating. When that's the case, a splash of acid (citrus or vinegar) or a pop of spice will often help the berries along. All of the following recipes work well with thawed frozen berries. The texture will be a bit different, but passable. If the berries were frozen individually and then bagged, consider using still-frozen berries for the next two recipes. Playing with an unexpected temperature in a dish can be as surprising as a unique flavor combo.

savory:

roasted carrots with raspberries, beet cream, chili oil + cacao nibs

I don't tend to repeat. I rarely watch movies or read books a second time, and I'm not sure I've ever made a menu the same a second time. This is one of the few dishes that has been featured on repeat at the farm dinners I host. It is visually stunning and a surprising combination of flavors.

1 small beet (3 oz [85 g])

Olive oil

1 cup [240 g] sour cream

Zest of 1 orange

3 lb [1.4 kg] carrots, washed and cut in half or left whole if small

Salt and freshly ground black pepper

1 tsp chili flakes

½ cup [120 ml] neutral oil

6 oz [170 g] raspberries

¼ cup [30 g] cacao nibs

5 sprigs parsley, leaves picked

2 sprigs mint, leaves picked

Preheat the oven to 400°F [200°C].

Wrap the beet in aluminum foil with a few drops of water and bake until completely tender, about 20 minutes, depending on the size of the beet. When the beet is tender, remove from the oven, rub the skins away, and blend in a food processor with a glug of olive oil until smooth.

Add the sour cream and orange zest and blend to make a hot pink cream, then chill until firm, about an hour.

In a large bowl, dress the carrots in a big glug of olive oil and season with salt and pepper, then transfer to a baking pan and roast until deeply caramelized and tender, about 35 minutes.

In a small saucepan, toast the chili flakes over high heat until fragrant and starting to darken, about 30 seconds. Remove from the heat, add the neutral oil, and let steep for a minimum of 10 minutes.

To serve, spoon the beet cream onto a large serving platter, top with the roasted carrots, drizzle liberally with the chili oil, scatter the raspberries and cacao nibs all over, and finish with a flurry of the herb leaves.

sweet:

lemon soufflé w/blackberries + olive oil

Oh dang, I love a frozen lemon dessert, especially paired with a thick pour of olive oil and jet-black blackberries. Frozen soufflés are not finicky the way hot ones can be because they require no urgency between their making and their serving. You can make them a day or two ahead with no trouble. If you are in the throes of midsummer frenzy, this flavor combination works equally well with lemon sorbet or vanilla ice cream topped with a hefty grating of lemon zest.

⅓ cup [80 ml] heavy cream

¾ cup [180 ml] Lemon Curd (page 94)

4 oz [115 g] blackberries

1 Tbsp sugar

¼ cup [60 ml] olive oil

Flake salt, such as Maldon or fleur de sel

Wrap four 6 oz [180 ml] dishes with parchment paper extending above the lip of the container by a few inches. Secure with tape or a rubber band and set aside.

In a medium bowl, whip the cream until stiff peaks form, 1 to 2 minutes. Add the cream to the lemon curd. Divide the mix among the prepared dishes and freeze until fully set, 8 hours or overnight.

In a medium bowl, mash the blackberries and sugar to release some juices.

To serve, remove the parchment collars, then top the frozen soufflés with the mashed blackberries, drizzle liberally with the olive oil, and scatter a pinch of the salt all over.

ROASTED

Hot and fast is the key to roasting drupelets. They don't, on average, contain as much juice as strawberries, so a good sear will keep the berry shape intact, though deflated, and quickly concentrate the juices.

savory:

chicken liver mousse, roasted raspberries + oatcakes

For those uncertain about liver, this mousse is a good gateway to the world of offal. The only technique to know is, like roasting berries, cook the livers hot and fast and remove them from the heat before they are gray-brown. The butter emulsifies into the hot liver, suspending the fat in the protein. Work quickly, and if it seems to curdle, simply warm the mixture and blend again.

6 oz [170 g] raspberries

1 lb [455 g] chicken livers, membranes or any green from the gallbladders removed

1 tsp salt

½ cup [120 ml] brandy

1 shallot (about 1 oz [30 g]), thinly sliced

5 sprigs thyme, leaves picked

1 lb [455 g] butter, at room temperature

1 recipe Oatcakes (page 50) or store-bought crackers or crostini

Heat a medium frying pan over high heat until smoking hot. Add the raspberries and sear quickly, 1 to 2 minutes. Shake to flip and remove from the heat. Set aside.

Return the pan to the heat and sear the livers, sprinkled with the salt, until golden brown, about 2 minutes. Flip the livers and sear the other side, then remove to the bowl of a food processor.

Add the brandy to the frying pan (watch out—it may flame up), and deglaze the pan. Add the shallot and thyme and lower the heat to medium, allowing the shallot to soften as the brandy reduces, about 4 minutes.

Add the brandy-shallot reduction to the food processor and blend until minced. Add the butter, one knob at a time, and blend until very smooth. Pass the mousse through a fine-mesh sieve, and transfer to ramekins or a serving dish, and then cool completely.

To serve, smear a good bit of the mousse on top of an oatcake. Top with a roasted raspberry and a drip or two of juice that collected after cooking.

sweet:

coconut tapioca pudding w/roasted mulberries + lime

I find mulberries the least interesting of the drupelets. Despite their beauty—large, uniform berries and a royal purple color—they often lack depth of flavor. Again, an acid perks them up, and here lime is my citrus of choice. It is a natural combination with the coconut pudding, but something as ubiquitous as lemon or as rarified as yuzu would be a treat. I've also made this with cow milk half-and-half instead of coconut milk and then dressed the mulberries with a bit of sherry vinegar with pleasing results. The tapioca pudding can be made several days in advance, though it will often get very thick as it sits. I like it on the looser side, and so I whip in some extra cream or coconut milk just before serving to soften.

6 oz [170 g] mulberries

1 lime (about 1 oz [30 ml]),
    zest and juice

Pinch of salt

1 recipe Tapioca Pudding
    (page 108), using
    full-fat coconut milk

Heat a medium frying pan over high heat until smoking. Add the mulberries and pan roast until caramelized and starting to release their juice, about 2 minutes. Remove the pan from the heat and add the lime zest and juice and salt, then let cool.

To serve, divide the pudding among four pudding cups and top with the roasted mulberries.

BAKED

Drupelet berries take very little time in the oven to soften and are better to bake than big berries such as blueberries or strawberries because they don't leak juice all over. I often combine them with a bit of citrus or vinegar to pep up the flavor if working with bland berries.

savory:

baked ricotta w/black pepper raspberries + a big salad

Another top ten favorite snacky dinner right here. Fast, filling, feels healthy, requires little planning, and can be eaten at a table, on a porch, or on a picnic blanket. The egg makes the baked ricotta extra fluffy but could be left out if need be. I like how spicy the chili flakes make the berries. If you aren't a hot head, feel free to reduce or omit them.

16 oz [455 g] ricotta

1 egg

Salt

6 oz [170 g] drupelet berries (blackberries, raspberries, etc.)

½ cup [120 ml] olive oil

½ tsp chili flakes

¼ tsp herbes de Provence

½ tsp coarsely ground black pepper

6 oz [170 g] salad greens

1 lemon (about 1.5 oz [45 ml]), zest and juice

Toast

Preheat the oven to 400°F [200°C].

Beat the ricotta and egg with a pinch of salt until well combined. Transfer to a baking dish and bake until the ricotta mixture is set, about 12 minutes.

While the cheese is baking, in a medium bowl, combine the berries, ¼ cup [60 ml] of the olive oil, chili flakes, herbes de Provence, black pepper, and a pinch of salt.

Remove the ricotta from the oven and top with the berry mixture, then return to the oven. Bake until the berries just start to burst, about 8 minutes. Remove from the oven and let rest for 5 to 10 minutes.

Dress the salad greens with the lemon zest and juice, the remaining ¼ cup [60 ml] of olive oil, and a pinch of salt.

Serve the baked ricotta with the toast and a big helping of the salad greens.

sweet: ### raspberry surprise crème brûlée

One of my first restaurant memories is the crème brûlée at Kiki's Bistro in Chicago. I can't remember why, but I took a cab there by myself to meet the rest of my family, so I was clearly feeling very grown-up indeed. I announced that I would eat my own dessert and not need to split one anymore. My parents, to their credit, always encouraged us to eat as adults and thus did not blink at the proclamation. The crème brûlée arrived and, in my memory, was the size of a bathtub. I used my spoon to crack through the perfect caramel glass surface, plunged it into the warm vanilla custard, and found a surprise layer of chocolate painted on the bottom of the bowl. It remains the standard-bearer for all-time great desserts.

Here, I've pulled on that same desired surprise by painting the bottom of the bowl with raspberries. I am a firm believer that nothing but caramel should garnish a crème brûlée. If you ever serve me an apple crumble crème brûlée, I will leave and take a cab straight to Kiki's for the proper version. I also find it perfectly acceptable to serve traditional vanilla crème brûlée with a dish of ice-cold raspberries on the side. Just don't sully the caramel glass by skittering them over the top. There are very few things I'm dogmatic about, but this is one of them.

1 cup [120 g] raspberries	1 Tbsp sugar, plus more for the caramel crust	1 recipe Crème Brûlée (page 79)
Zest of 1 orange	Pinch of salt	

Preheat the oven to 300°F [150°C].

In a medium bowl, combine the raspberries, orange zest, 1 Tbsp of sugar, and salt, and mash with a fork.

Divide the berry mixture evenly among four ramekins, terra-cotta dishes, or ovenproof jars and place into a high-sided roasting dish. Gently pour the crème brûlée mixture into the ramekins over the berry mixture.

Place the roasting dish in the oven, then fill the roasting dish with warm water until it reaches three-quarters of the way up the ramekins. Bake until the custard is just set with a bit of a wobble in the center, 45 to 60 minutes. Remove from the oven and the roasting dish and let cool in the fridge for at least 4 hours to fully set the custard.

Just before serving, sprinkle each ramekin with sugar. Using a blowtorch or the oven broiler, caramelize the sugar and swirl the ramekin to move the caramel evenly across the surface. Repeat a second time to fully coat, creating a true glass crust. Serve immediately.

PRESERVED

While I've made it clear that freezing is my default preservation technique for the drupelet berries, they do lend themselves to other methods as well.

JAM

Jam ratio: 60:40 fruit to sugar. Because mulberries tend to lack acidity, I generally add a splash of red wine or sherry vinegar to the jam at the end of cooking. I don't love the seeds of drupelet berries in jam, and so I often strain at least half out after cooking. I also often make the jam with frozen berries; just give a thaw and carry on.

- These jams tend to be brilliant in color and so I often spoon them over stark white items for contrast—cheese, meringue, ice cream, etc.
- Blend 50:50 jam and mustard for a vibrantly colored fruit mustard to go with charcuterie or on any old sandwich (page 243).
- I also like to blend drupelet berry jam with hot sauce or vinegar to make sweet and savory sauces, which are often good with poultry, fish, or the sweeter root vegetables.

PICKLED

Pickled raspberries were the first fruit I pickled with the Basic Fruit Pickle Brine (page 112). To keep the integrity of the drupelet berry shape during pickling, I always pour the hot liquid over frozen berries. The pickle liquid still penetrates the center of the fruit, but cools it more quickly, helping keep the shape intact.

What wouldn't I use these on? I spoon them over any sort of roasted vegetables, especially carrots, parsnips, squash, and sweet potatoes. I've used them as a base for a vinaigrette or a very piquant sauce when mounted with butter or cream. They are also extremely good spooned over ice cream or panna cotta. Oh! And add a spoonful to a glass of bubbly water and, donezo, no liquor required, but a splash of booze is welcome.

VINEGAR

Drupelets take well to infusing vinegar or shrubs. For the vinegar, simply soak a pint of berries in 1 cup [240 ml] of apple cider vinegar until flavorful. To make a shrub, combine a pint of berries with 1 cup [240 ml] of vinegar and 1 cup [200 g] of sugar.

The vinegar makes nice vinaigrettes or marinades. The shrub pairs well with gin, vodka, brandy, or bourbon. It also adds umph to a glass of fizzy water.

FREEZING

Easy enough to be done even when one hits peak summer grouchy. Simply dump a container on a baking sheet lined with parchment or a silicone mat and place in the freezer. When the berries are fully frozen, quickly transfer to a resealable bag and return to the freezer. If not individually frozen, they will become a big mass of drupelets, not individual berries.

grapes

When Erik and I first started dating, someone dismissively said, "He's great, just sort of vanilla." I, having just taken a class on spices that included comparing a variety of regional vanillas to synthetic vanillin, responded, "Oh, you're right! Incredibly complex masquerading as plain and everyday." The person rolled their eyes and chalked it up to young love. But I'm no puppy and really, they should have listened because Erik (and vanilla) is succulenté and both will make you delight. I guess it wasn't their fault for not understanding; we've been fed false, unnuanced, bad-boy narratives and flavors for years.

Blame the laboratories and the processed food companies that run them. In his book *Hooked*, Michael Moss details how multinational food corporations use "flavor houses," which run up and down the New Jersey coast, to decode the chemical compounds in foods that convey the scent and/or flavor of food without the pesky food attached, thereby "changing the nature of our food over the past 50 years because 80 percent of flavor is actually smell, not taste." While these flavor houses are driving to maximize smell, the most valuable thing they do for the processed food industry is lower the cost and increase the speed of production of their goods. Like all things mass produced, consistency and identifiability are paramount. By replacing the true, complex, and varied scents of vanilla with a flimsy stand-in, these food companies have essentially created a new, manufactured vanilla.

This process is cheaper than the real deal—no land to obtain, no farmers to pay, no perishable food to transport or preserve. Once you have the compound, it can be replicated to infinity and beyond despite agricultural labor shortages, inclement weather, or failing soil health. Our understanding of vanilla is completely divorced from the process of growing, harvesting, and drying of the actual beans. What we are left with is a flavor that is ubiquitous, easy to identify, and excruciatingly banal.

The same is true for grapes. Grapes are not the flavor of purple popsicles. Grapes range from bloomy, thick-skinned Concords to ethereal, green Lakemonts. There are table grapes, wine grapes, wild grapes, even sour grapes (though those are usually of our own making). Most of the grapes in grocery stores have been bred for uniformity: no discernable seeds, skins thick enough to travel but thin enough to be palatable to most people, and year-round consumption. Grocery store grapes are not my favorite, but I eat them regularly. They will always be better than eating grape candy or not eating grapes at all.

Grapes present great variety, depth of flavor, and an equally long history never to be supplanted by white lab coats. Life's too short. Delight in the fall bounty when selecting specialty varieties from the market. Pick up a bag of grocery store grapes when those varieties aren't there but you really want grapes. Buy real vanilla and keep dating that person if they make you happy, no matter what anyone says.

HOW TO SELECT

Look for grapes with tight skin and uniform fruit. There will occasionally be a stray damaged grape on the cluster, but avoid bunches that are missing grapes or where some are wrinkly. This is often a sign of age and that the grapes still attached to the cluster will not store well. Similarly, look for clusters with firm, green stems. Brown or loose stems are also an indication of age and that the grapes will not last as long. Freshly harvested grapes, like some blueberries, will often still show a waxy bloom on the fruit itself (a good thing, not something to be avoided).

SIGNS OF RIPENESS

Ripe grapes will be fragrant and heavy in the hand.

HOW TO STORE

Before you store grapes, give them a once-over and remove any damaged or brown fruit, which encourages rot in surrounding fruits. Store in the fridge wrapped in a protective layer.

Grapes emit a medium amount of ethylene, so leaving the bag slightly open will allow that gas to escape while protecting them from the circulating cool air of the fridge.

NOTES

Seedless grapes have been bred by growers to have inconsequential seeds in the center of their fruit. They are not considered GMO because that modification is the result of variety selection as opposed to gene modification. I happen to like a lot of varieties that are seedy. The best way I've found to remove the seeds is either to cut the fruit in half and flick the seed out with the tip of a knife or to use a bobby pin to fish the seed out through the hole where the stem attaches to the fruit. Or chomp through those seeds, which are rich in antioxidants and fiber.

PRODUCER PROFILE

MICHAEL + PETER LAING

Michael and Peter Laing are managing members of Mawby winery and the owners of bigLITTLE Winery in Suttons Bay, Michigan. Mawby, which specializes in sparkling wines, was the second winery founded in Leelanau County by Larry Mawby in the 1970s. Michael and Peter took up the helm at Mawby and in 2011 started bigLITTLE, which focuses on varietal-, vintage-, and location-specific table wines. They are second-generation winemakers who both grow their own fruit and work with the larger grape and wine market to produce diversified product lines for sale at their winery and distributed nationally.

Abra Berens: Mike and Pete, I wanted to talk with you today because during our recent cold snap, I heard you were out in the vineyards building fires to keep the air moving and prevent the frost from settling. That made me realize, I don't think that many people think of wine as an agricultural product subject to the same whims of nature as fruit at a farmers' market. Can you speak to what it takes to grow grapes for your wines?

Peter Laing: It's a full-time job for one person to manage about 10 acres of grapes. We manage about 30 acres of grapes. Our vineyard manager, Megan, is full-time, year-round, and then we hire a couple of folks on the H2A visa program, in collaboration with Bluestone [another area winery]. We have two, they have five, and together that's a picking crew to be to able pick at the rate necessary to run the press.

The thing I want people to know is simply how many times we touch each vine to make wine. We touch each vine at least seven times throughout the season, between pruning, harvesting, etc., by seven pairs of hands. If you go back to when Larry [Mawby, founder of Mawby Wines] was fifteen, they were hand picking all of the cherries in the region. You'd have 250,000 people up here from Appalachia or from South and Central America. People don't think about the hands that go into not only growing the fruit but also making and selling the wine.

AB: Do you think that's a disadvantage to making that change from hands to machines?

PL: Yes, I think it's a loss. With fewer people who have that direct contact, there's a loss of understanding of what goes into making food.

AB: Could you detail what all those touches are for both growing the grapes and making the wine?

PL: First, pruning and tying the canes down to the wire, which for efficiency's sake we do at the same time, but it is still two passes: rough prune and final prune with tying. But let's call that two touches. Then we go through and sucker, removing some of the growth for airflow and canopy management. Followed by tucking, keeping the growth up into the trellis. So that's four or five touches. Move onto leaf removal again for airflow or hedging if the plants become too tall and start shading, getting us to six or seven. Before picking, we drop fruit, pulling excess fruit off the vines to ensure the quality of what we pick to press.

Michael Laing: Then pick, press, ferment. On to tirage, putting the wine into bottles to double ferment. So we're to twelve. Then when the wine is ready, we riddle it, tipping and turning the wine to allow the yeast to settle into the neck of the bottle. Then, disgorging, when the yeast is removed and finished. On to labeling. So where are we? Fifteen touches before selling it.

Another story to tell is how long it takes to actually produce a bottle of sparkling wine. Let's say that you decided that you want to make bubbly in northern Michigan. OK, well, you've found the site, which obviously isn't easy, but say you're ready to plant. First, it takes a couple of years to get the vines you want because the nurseries need to grow what you're after. They need to graft them to root stocks. Then they propagate for a year, and then you receive it and plant it. Then you have three to four years until you get fruit. Pick the fruit, make the wine, and then it ages in the bottle for three years. Look at how much time that is. People don't understand the long game of growing fruit and the capital tied up in inventory. You plant a tree or vine and you want it to last. No one is going to plant a cherry tree let alone a grapevine on land they don't own unless they have a twenty- to thirty-year lease.

AB: And that feels like a shift away from the commodity market of cherries toward a more value-added market because all of those ingredients, except for maybe plums, have a clear path to wine, cider, and the tourist industry as people come up and want to visit wineries.

ML: Yes, I agree with that. Just like with cherries, you're not going to make money up here growing grapes. It is way more lucrative to make wine from your grapes and sell that wine.

AB: Even considering the overhead?

ML: Yes, for sure. We are starting to get some of those economies of scale as the infrastructure catches up between mechanical harvesting, mobile bottling lines, etc. It is still your own wine but with shared infrastructure. There's less capital outlay to get there. What's funny is that a lot more of our energy and resources goes into selling the wine than making it. Wine is such a brand-oriented business, and we rely on the connection to consumers in our tasting room to explain what goes into the wine.

AB: How do you all square the nature of farming—it's so risky, it's so weather dependent, the margins are so low—with what you want out of your business and your careers?

ML: That's why we maintain a diversity of sourcing for our grapes. Not only from different regions but within our own. The vineyards we work with on the peninsula are spread out, so if there's a hail event in one place, it may not ruin all the grapes we're counting on. We use a lot of fruit from Washington State and California.

AB: How do you connect with those growers?

PL: It's the same as here—relationships, shared values. The proactive relationships we have with growers on the West Coast are so important. We are able to get the fruit and the wine that we want, as opposed to scrambling to fill a gap if our grapes get wiped out. We are buying year after year, planning for growth, not just taking whatever is left.

AB: When you get fruit from the West Coast, are you getting it as fresh fruit or as pressed juice?

ML: We get it as wine because it is more stable. It has been hard over the past few years to get tanker trucks from Washington here quickly enough for juice. Wine is more stable because you don't want it to ferment on the highway. Then we take it and blend it and do the second fermentation here. So we work with the grower and with the bulk wine producer. In the case of our largest selling wine, SEX, we outsource the entire process, which helps keep the price low.

AB: I sort of knew there was a bulk wine market, which I assumed was the gallon jugs of Chardonnay that my mom drank. It didn't occur to me that that wine could also become something else. I guess it's a bit like cheesemakers getting milk from a dairy; not every cheese is a farmstead cheese, and that doesn't mean it is of lesser quality.

ML: Yes, for us it is again about diversity but now of our product mix. Our tank-fermented wines don't have a vintage, are not varietal specific, and are not appellation designated on purpose. We blend for consistency of the end wine. The flip side is our bigLITTLE lines, which are all vintage-, varietal-, and location-specific. Those things stay the same and the wine varies from year to year. That's a different vibe and story altogether. The other thing to mention is that for fruit, we get one shot per year. In my lifetime I only make one vintage per year. That's a big difference between wine and the brewing-distilling market.

AB: Final question—do you guys drink your own wine?

ML and PL: Yes.

ML: Though actually probably not enough. Mostly with food. I mean, that's the way wine is meant to be enjoyed. They are higher in acidity and lower in alcohol.

PL: We have a library of over ten years of bigLITTLE wines that we should be tasting more often.

AB: Great. I'll be right over!

RAW

More often than not, grapes are eaten raw, plucked from the cluster with one's teeth while chillaxing in a toga on a chaise lounge and being fanned by handmaidens. When I've tired of the Grecian same old, same old, I opt for something truly decadent, adding a fistful of grapes to any salad, cheese plate, or bowl of ice cream or sorbet.

savory:
butter lettuce, grape, fennel, walnut + buttermilk salad

I think of salads in two distinct camps: 1) the classic tossed salad, where everything is added to a deep bowl and moved around to evenly distribute, and 2) flat salads built in layers on a shallow platter. The latter is best when you have delicate greens (like butter lettuce) that won't take well to tossing. Building in layers also means that the construction of the servings will be roughly the same if you are the first person to be served or the last—no more lettuce-only bites for the last in line.

1 to 2 heads (about 1 lb [455 g]) butter or other wide-leaf lettuce, core removed and leaves left whole

Salt and freshly ground black pepper

1 cup [160 g] grapes, any variety, halved and seeds removed

1 cup [120 g] walnuts, toasted

1 head fennel (about 4 oz [115 g]), thinly shaved and stored in acidulated water (see page 29)

1 cup [240 ml] buttermilk

On a large serving platter or individual plates, lay out a single layer of lettuce leaves. Season with salt and black pepper. Scatter a handful of the grapes and walnuts evenly over the lettuce leaves. Add a few pieces of shaved fennel, patted dry if stored in water.

Drizzle a bit of the buttermilk all over.

Repeat until all of the ingredients are gone and serve.

sweet:

grape salad over lime sorbet

Full disclosure: When we made this for the photo shoot, we wanted the lime-green color of store-bought sorbet. You should also feel encouraged to buy the sorbet if you want to.

¼ cup [85 g] honey

¼ cup [60 ml] olive oil, plus more for drizzling

1 cup [160 g] grapes, halved and seeds removed

3 sprigs mint, leaves picked and torn

1 recipe Lime Sorbet (page 97)

Coarse salt like Maldon or fleur de sel

In a medium bowl, combine the honey, olive oil, and grapes and let sit for 10 minutes or so to encourage the grapes to give up their juice. Add the mint leaves.

Divide the lime sorbet among four dessert bowls, cups, or jars.

To serve, top the sorbet with the grape salad, a big pinch of salt, and an extra drizzle of olive oil to garnish each dish.

ROASTED

Whenever I envision a dish with roasted grapes, I always want to leave them on the stem for maximum presentation drama. In the end, I always remove them because they're otherwise a pain to eat. One either needs to get the grapes off the stem with a knife and fork or sully one's fingers and manners by picking them up, sauce and all. The dream lives on, but practicality rules the day.

savory:

pan-roasted parsnips w/grape sauce + pecans

Making a pan sauce is so simple, but feels so restaurant-y. I remember the first day I was taught to make it on the line at Vie, I felt like such a pro. A pan sauce is made when the roasting fond has been deglazed and then mounted with butter to make a silky, emulsified sauce. This recipe is a good guide. When in doubt, add a splash of water and a knob of butter and your sauce will come back together again. The cornstarch is not used on any restaurant line I've seen, but is a great addition for stability, especially in a recipe like this that lacks the gelatin of an animal stock.

Boiling the parsnips in advance serves two functions: 1) It ensures that they are cooked through so having a raw center and burnt outside is not a concern, and 2) it keeps the parsnips from drying out during the pan roast.

continued

3 lb [1.4 kg] parsnips, peeled and cut into chunks

Neutral oil

1 cup [160 g] grapes, seeds removed

¼ cup [60 ml] brandy

1 rosemary sprig, needles removed and minced

2 Tbsp butter

1 tsp cornstarch

½ cup [60 g] salty pecans (see page 78)

In a large pot, cover the parsnips with lightly salted water. Bring to a boil, then lower the heat to a simmer and cook until tender when pierced with a knife, about 20 minutes. Reserve a cup of the parsnip cooking water, then drain the parsnips and let dry either by air-drying or blotting with a paper towel (the drying keeps the parsnips from spitting when pan fried in the next step).

In a large frying pan, heat a glug of neutral oil over high heat until smoking. Add the now-dry parsnips and allow to caramelize before flipping, about 6 minutes. Flip and caramelize the other sides, an additional 4 to 6 minutes. Transfer the parsnips to a serving platter.

Add the grapes to the hot pan and roast over high heat until they start to collapse, about 2 minutes. Add the brandy to deglaze (be careful—it may flame if using a gas stove). Add the rosemary and scrape up any fond from the pan. When the brandy is almost entirely evaporated, add ¾ cup [180 ml] of the parsnip cooking liquid and bring to a boil.

In a small bowl, toss the butter in the cornstarch and add to the pan, whisking vigorously to melt the butter and emulsify into the sauce, adding more of the cooking water if needed. When the sauce has reduced and is creamy and smooth, about 1 to 2 minutes, pour over the parsnips, top with the salty pecans, and serve immediately.

sweet:

rice pudding w/sherry-roasted grapes

There's a wide variety of sherries out there, ranging from pale, dry fino sherries to the king of sherries, dark caramel Pedro Ximénez. Once derided as something for only gray-haired ladies to drink, sherry (and lots of other fortified aperitifs and digestifs) have, thankfully, come back into fashion. It turns out gray-haired ladies have excellent taste and should be listened to carefully.

1 recipe Rice Pudding (page 107)

Neutral oil

2 cups [320 g] grapes, seeds removed

½ cup [120 ml] Pedro Ximénez or cream sherry

Bring the rice pudding to room temperature or warm slightly in a pan on the stove or in the microwave.

In a medium frying pan, heat a glug of neutral oil over high heat. Add the grapes and roast until they burst and their liquid starts to reduce, about 4 minutes. Add the sherry to deglaze the pan and reduce the liquid by half, about 1 minute.

Spoon the sherry-roasted grapes over the rice pudding and serve.

BAKED

Baked grapes have a concentrated flavor and dark, luscious color. If any of your baked goods start to take on too dark a color, simply cover the darkened parts with aluminum foil to shield from direct heat. This is true of all baked things, not just grape baked things.

savory:

ham + butter sandwiches

Ham and butter sandwiches are a Midwestern church basement staple. I used to be embarrassed about how much I love them. Then I went to Paris and had ham and butter on a baguette and realized that it is classic and should never be disparaged. Usually I opt for quintessential minimalism, but the combo of grapes, sage, and ham adds shine to the austere classic. I use more butter than is called for, but you can use as much butter as you want. If you don't make the focaccia, use any bread and add a thick slather of grape mustard (page 246) to the sandwiches.

1 recipe Focaccia Dough (page 35)

½ cup [80 g] grapes, seeds removed

3 sprigs sage, leaves picked and cut into ribbons

4 oz [115 g] salted butter, at room temperature

4 oz [115 g] sliced ham

Mix the focaccia dough, adding the grapes and sage in the second proofing.

Preheat the oven to 450°F [225°C].

Allow the focaccia to proof completely, then bake and let cool completely.

Cut the focaccia into eight equal pieces, then split each piece in half like a hamburger bun. Slather the lower half liberally with the butter and then top with the ham. Replace the focaccia lid and serve.

sweet:

grape custard pie

I've made traditional Concord grape pie exactly once in my life, and while it was delicious, it was not (to my mind) worth the fiddle of peeling half of the grapes and seeding all of them. This pie, on the other hand, comes together quickly because you don't need to peel a single grape. If you don't have hazelnut meal, use almond flour, or substitute traditional rolled, flaky pie crust. I prefer using red grapes for this pie because the color shows and red grapes have a tannic flavor in their skin that pushes back against the sweet.

2 cups [320 g] red grapes, preferably Concord, seeds removed	1 recipe Hazelnut (page 52) or Pretzel Crust (page 53)	1 recipe Brown Butter Custard Batter (page 41)

Preheat the oven to 350°F [180°C].

Place the grapes in the par-baked crust. Pour the custard over the top and redistribute the grapes.

Bake until the custard is puffed and just set, about 60 minutes.

Remove from the oven and cool before serving. You can serve warm but it will be a bit runny. The custard needs to cool completely to set firmly.

PRESERVED

Grapes not only preserve well, but they also have perfect timing. Grapes, in the northern Midwest, become ripe right at the time when I can lift my head up from summer work and look toward preserving before everything is covered in buckets of snow.

JELLY

I mostly find making a lot of jam drudgery, but not so with grapes. They have a ton of pectin, and since I usually pass the cooked fruit through a food mill, there's no need to pick out the seeds. Jam ratio: 60:40, fruit to sugar.

MUSTARD

Grape mustard is common in most wine-producing regions because mustard is planted between the vineyard rows as a pest deterrent. The mustard seeds are then mixed with the pulp cast off from wine making and served anywhere you would find regular whole-grain mustard. I don't make my own wine, so I use 50 percent grape jelly and 50 percent whole-grain or Dijon mustard and put it with any sort of rich meal, especially duck, game of all kinds, and pork.

PICKLED

Grapes taste great pickled and hold their shape well. I have made them with both the Traditional Pickle Liquid (page 113) and the Basic Fruit Pickle Brine (page 112) with balsamic vinegar. The former tastes more of vinegar and is good with fatty meats like duck and pork. The latter is sweeter and goes better with cheeses or creamier vegetables such as parsnips and sweet potatoes. Scatter a few spoonfuls over a platter of roasted vegetables or roasted loin for your next weekend meal.

JUICE

While wine making is probably the most traditional grape preservation method, I have really taken to drinking unfermented grape juice as I've gotten on in age. The thick purple skins are rich in antioxidants, and mixing 1 part juice with 4 parts soda water is a real treat in the middle of winter when it's all apples all the time.

RAISINS

The most traditional way to preserve grapes is to dry them into raisins. Sadly, our September sun does not have the same drying quality as in southern Italy, so drying outside or on rooftops is pretty much out. Thankfully, laying them out on the racks of a dehydrator or a 200°F [95°C] oven works well too. Like all home-dried fruit, if you don't remove a critical mass of moisture, mold can grow, so I still store my dried fruits in the fridge or freezer to be safe.

FREEZING

Grapes freeze well. Their skins are firm enough to keep them separate, preventing them from needing to be frozen individually. But I still do, just to make sure I don't get a gallon-size lump of frozen grapes. When thawed, I use them in just about any of the aforementioned recipes except the raw ones. They also make great ice cubes for champagne cocktails or an added twist to a gin and tonic.

ground cherries (a.k.a. cape gooseberries)

The single best question you can ask a vendor at a market, a stockist at your local grocery store, or a server at a restaurant is "What are you most excited about?" This is how I learned about ground cherries. I had taken my standard cursory scan of the farmers' market table, pausing briefly at the little lantern-encased fruits, but I didn't know them. It wasn't until I asked the young lady building the display the million-dollar question, "Hey, what are you most excited to eat this week?" She responded by setting down her lug of tomatoes and walking to the stack of ground cherries I had just breezed by. "OMG, have you had one of these yet?" In a single elegant movement, she slid the papery husk away from the golden, speckled fruit, twisting it free, and handed it to me. As an act of encouragement, she repeated the gesture, freeing a second fruit, and popped it into her own mouth.

OK, bottoms up, I thought. I expected it to be astringent like the similarly husked tomatillo, or sour like the similarly shaped gooseberry. It was neither. The ground cherry burst open, sending flavors of honey, yellow tomato, and something akin to pineapple washing over my tongue.

It is rare for me to be so surprised by a flavor, to be so excited to bring something new home. I wouldn't have given the balsa boxes of ground cherries a second look without the guidance of the grower. As I paid for my groceries, including more than a reasonable amount of ground cherries, I thanked her for the sample and letting me in on the secret. She simply responded, "Thanks for asking."

The point is in the asking. As someone who has worked under a farmers' market tent, in a restaurant dining room, and behind the swinging doors in fluorescent-lit basement kitchens, I can assuredly say that my colleagues and I are skilled workers. We want you to be excited about your food, have a good time, and turn you on to something we're pumped about. It takes a lot of know-how to do that elegantly. We've interacted with this food the most and the most recently. We've seen what has come before it and know what is coming in after it: disappointing strawberries leading to perfect raspberries before we move on to the unending months of apples. We know that there's no excuse for not having an immediate response to that important question should you ask it. We also know you should distrust anyone who says, "Oh, you know, everything's good." If we are being straight with you, we will relay a clear-eyed assessment of the qualities of any given crop or dish on the menu. Put yourself in our capable, dirt-nailed hands.

HOW TO SELECT

Look for ground cherries with husks intact and pale, golden yellow in color. Too green generally means underripe; dusky yellow is overripe. Avoid ground cherries that have black marks at either end, as these are usually the entrance for pests. The cherries themselves should be full, firm, and heavy to the touch (as we should all hope to be).

SIGNS OF RIPENESS

Ground cherries are called that because when they are ripe, they fall from the plant to the ground. Beyond how the fruit is harvested, ground cherries will be fragrant but not overpowering like some other fruit.

HOW TO STORE

Ground cherries are best for about a week or so after harvest. If you're going to eat them within that time, store at room temperature out of direct sunlight. If you need to hang on to them for longer than a few days, store in the fridge or freeze. When freezing, freeze in the husk. It's easier to remove the husk from a frozen berry because you can dehull more aggressively and not bruise the soft fruit.

NOTES

Ground cherries are generally low in acid and so are best when pepped up with something tangy—a squeeze of lemon, a splash of vinegar. There is little to be done with the husks of the ground cherries, though they make a good starter to light a bonfire.

RAW

There's little more that needs to be done to eat a ground cherry besides peeling back the paper lantern. Then again, there's almost always something more that can be done—like pairing it with something spicy or acidic to showcase the flavor.

savory:

red cabbage salad w/ground cherries, cilantro, pepitas + lime

I started making this salad when ground cherries were available but then liked it so much that I kept making it well after their season had passed. Simply substitute cubes of very ripe melon, pineapple, dried apricots, dates, or chunks of apple for the ground cherries.

This salad wilts quickly after being dressed, so either dress it just before serving or expect it to be more slaw-like in texture. This salad is hearty enough on its own but also pairs well with seared fish, grilled meats, or fried tofu.

½ head red cabbage (1 lb [455 g]), thinly shaved

1 cup (4 oz [115 g]) ground cherries, husks removed

1 bunch or 15 sprigs cilantro, roughly chopped

1 cup [140 g] pepitas, toasted

1 in [2.5 cm] piece ginger, peeled and grated

2 limes (about 3 oz [90 ml]), zest and juice

1 Tbsp maple syrup

¼ tsp chili flakes (optional)

½ cup [120 ml] olive oil

Salt

In a large bowl, combine the cabbage, ground cherries, cilantro, and pepitas. In a smaller bowl or jar, combine the ginger, lime zest and juice, maple syrup, chili flakes (if using), olive oil, and a big pinch of salt. Whisk or shake to combine the dressing.

Spoon half the dressing over the salad, add a pinch of salt, and toss to coat. Taste and adjust, adding more salt or dressing as desired before serving.

sweet: ground cherry floats

Whimsical is an over- and often misused word to describe food, but this dessert is straight whimsy for me. Floats might just be my favorite dessert because they are ebullient, lighthearted, and easy to execute. This play on the classic float feels updated enough for a fancy dinner party without sacrificing any of the fun.

1 pint [480 ml] Buttermilk Sherbet (page 97)

1 cup (4 oz [115 g]) ground cherries, husks removed

½ cup [120 ml] Marigold (page 111) or Citrus Syrup (page 110)

1 qt [1 L] club soda

Divide the sherbet evenly among four tall, Collins-style glasses, adding a few ground cherries between each scoop of sherbet. Spoon 2 Tbsp of syrup into each glass and top with the club soda. Using a long spoon or straw, give the glasses a swirl and serve immediately.

ROASTED

Like most fruits, ground cherries benefit from being roasted hot and fast in a blazing pan with enough space to evaporate the released juices. They also break down into a syrupy sauce when roasted at a lower temperature to trap the steam. Not better or worse—just a different end result. For ease of preparation, both of the following recipes utilize an already hot oven to roast the fruit.

savory:

cashew cauliflower w/ground cherry glaze + toum

One of the biggest hurdles for those new to a vegetarian or vegan diet is feeling satisfied with meals that lack the meat-protein starring role. Enter a giant roast cauliflower. I'd be happy with nothing more than this and a pile of salad leaves nearby. It would also be lovely with a very small portion of meat or fish as supporting cast.

1 large cauliflower (2 to 3 lb [910 g to 1.4 kg]), outer leaves and core removed, head left intact

Olive oil

Salt

2 cups (8 oz [230 g]) ground cherries, husks removed

½ cup [70 g] raw cashews, roughly chopped

¼ cup [60 ml] apple cider vinegar

1 Tbsp Dijon mustard

5 sprigs parsley, roughly chopped

½ cup [120 g] Toum (page 160)

Preheat the oven to 400°F [200°C].

Drizzle the whole head of cauliflower with olive oil and several pinches of salt, then rub all over to coat evenly.

Place the ground cherries in the bottom of a large, ovenproof frying pan. Top with the cauliflower, cover with aluminum foil, and roast in the oven for 25 minutes.

Pull out of the oven and remove the foil. The ground cherries should be softened and have released a lot of liquid. Spoon that liquid over the entire head of cauliflower to glaze evenly. Scatter the cashews all over the cauliflower head. Return to the oven and roast, uncovered, for 15 to 20 minutes.

Lift the cauliflower from the pan and place on a serving platter.

Add the vinegar and mustard to the remaining liquid in the pan, whisking to dissolve. Spoon the resulting mixture over the cauliflower and garnish with the parsley.

Serve with the toum alongside for dipping.

sweet:

basque cheesecake w/roasted ground cherries + rosemary

This cheesecake bakes at a high temperature for a good, long time to get a burnished crust. This is the perfect opportunity to roast some ground cherries right alongside the cake for maximum efficiency. Note that the cheesecake takes a while to cool, so be sure to plan ahead or just be fine with slices that won't come out cleanly.

1 recipe Basque Cheese-
 cake (page 64)

Olive oil

2 cups (8 oz [230 g])
 ground cherries, husks
 removed

1 sprig rosemary

1 lemon (1.5 oz [45 ml]),
 zest and juice

While the cheesecake is baking, place a medium, ovenproof frying pan in the oven to preheat for 10 minutes.

Remove the pan from the oven and add a glug of olive oil. Add the ground cherries and rosemary and return to the oven. Roast the ground cherries until they burst and the liquid is reduced to a syrup, about 10 minutes.

Remove the pan from the oven and discard the rosemary stem. Add the lemon zest and juice and stir to combine.

Transfer the roasted ground cherries to a bowl.

Allow the cheesecake to cool completely before slicing. Garnish with a couple of spoonfuls of the roasted ground cherries before serving.

STEWED

On fancy tasting menus there is often a transition course, sometimes called a palate cleanser, signaling the movement from the savory mains to the sweet endings. Often this is simply a bit of sorbet, which is really more of a pre-dessert. Ground cherries straddle the line between savory and sweet, making them perfect for a true transition course.

savory:

super grilled cheese sandwiches w/ ground cherry chutney

You can use this chutney on any number of things, including on a regular grilled cheese sandwich, but the extra step of breading the bread is really next-level. You could also skip the entire grilled cheese sandwich process and serve the ground cherry chutney with a dish of whipped ricotta and Pat's Crackers (page 47).

1 cup (4 oz [115 g]) ground cherries, husks removed

1 shallot (about 1 oz [30 g]), minced

¼ cup [60 ml] sherry vinegar

2 Tbsp honey

3 sprigs thyme (optional)

Salt

8 oz [230 g] ricotta

Freshly ground black pepper

8 slices Milk Bread (page 37) or store-bought bread, crusts removed

1 lb [455 g] low-moisture mozzarella, cut into ¼ in [6 mm] thick pieces

2 eggs, beaten

1 cup [140 g] bread crumbs

1 garlic clove, grated or pressed

Neutral oil

continued

In a small saucepan, combine the ground cherries, shallot, vinegar, honey, thyme (if using), and a pinch of salt, and stew over medium heat until the ground cherries burst and their liquid releases, about 10 minutes. Simmer until the liquid is reduced by half, about 10 minutes more, and then let cool to room temperature.

In a medium bowl, combine the ricotta with a pinch of salt and several grinds of black pepper. Whip the ricotta with a whisk or paddle until lightened in texture, 1 to 2 minutes.

Lay out the slices of bread. Smear four of the bread slices with the ricotta and top with the mozzarella. Smear the remaining four bread slices with the ground cherry chutney. Press the pieces of bread together to make four sandwiches each with ricotta, mozzarella, and chutney inside. Press the edges together to lightly seal.

Pour the eggs into a shallow bowl.

In a separate shallow bowl, place the bread crumbs, minced garlic, and a big pinch of salt. Stir to combine.

In a large frying pan, heat a hefty pool of neutral oil over medium heat.

Dip each sandwich in the egg and then into the bread crumb mixture.

Pan fry two of the sandwiches at a time in the oil until crispy and golden brown. Flip the sandwiches and brown the other side. Repeat with the final two sandwiches and serve while warm.

sweet: # biscuits w/ground cherry butter

This combination is perfect either for breakfast or as an afternoon snack with a cup of coffee or tea. The slightly vegetal flavor of the ground cherries works well with earthier flours such as spelt or rye. Feel free to substitute 50 percent of either of those flours for 50 percent of the volume of all-purpose flour called for in the biscuit recipe. I also sometimes paddle the butter and stewed ground cherries together to make a fruit butter, if you don't want to be smearing and spooning.

1 cup (4 oz [115 g]) ground cherries, husks removed	2 star anise	Butter, at room temperature
¼ cup [50 g] sugar	Pinch of salt	Flake salt, such as Maldon or fleur de sel
½ cup [120 ml] dark rum	1 recipe Biscuits (page 59)	

In a medium saucepan, combine the ground cherries, sugar, rum, star anise, and salt over medium heat. Stew the ground cherries until they burst and their liquid reduces by half, about 10 minutes. Remove from the heat, discard the star anise, and let cool to not hot or else it will melt the butter in the next step.

When the biscuits are baked, let cool for 10 minutes, then split in half. Smear each half liberally with the softened butter and a pinch of the flake salt, then spoon the ground cherry mixture over the buttered halves and serve.

PRESERVED

Ground cherry season is relatively short, about three to four weeks toward the end of summer where I live. I rely heavily on preserving them to use beyond that month of availability.

PICKLED

Use the Basic Fruit Pickle Brine on page 112 and pour over the ground cherries. Then can or store in the fridge for several months, making sure they are submerged in the pickle liquid.

Uses: Pickled ground cherries can be the welcome acidic punch to a wintery spinach salad or scattered over a dish of roasted roots (carrots, parsnips, beets, etc.).

Ground Cherry Glaze: Blend 1 cup (4 oz [115 g]) of pickled ground cherries in their pickle liquid and use it to baste a roast chicken or seared piece of salmon for a sweet and sour crust.

ground cherry sweet and sour sauce

1 cup (4 oz [115 g]) pickled ground cherries

⅓ cup [80 ml] rice vinegar

3 Tbsp ketchup

2 Tbsp soy sauce

½ tsp chili flakes

1½ Tbsp cornstarch

In a small saucepan, bring everything except the cornstarch to a simmer over medium heat.

In a small bowl, combine the cornstarch and 2 Tbsp of water to make a slurry.

Whisk the cornstarch slurry into the sauce and cook until thickened, about 5 minutes. Blend with an immersion blender or food processor to make evenly chunky.

Let cool and store in the fridge for 2 weeks.

CANDIED

I also candy ground cherries to preserve them, but mostly to use either in cocktails or desserts like the float on page 253. To do so, make a heavy syrup (2 cups [400 g] sugar and 1 cup [240 ml] water) and then pour over the ground cherries. Refrigerate for upwards of 6 months. I often add ¼ cup [60 ml] of vinegar to the syrup just before pouring over the ground cherries to give a bit of acidity to the syrup and help cut the sweetness.

These lend themselves to two perfect cocktails. First, a Champagne Cocktail: Pour 1 Tbsp of ground cherry syrup into 4 oz [120 ml] of sparkling wine and lightly stir. Garnish with a couple of candied ground cherries.

- For a Michigan Manhattan: Combine 2 oz [60 ml] of rye whiskey with ½ oz [15 ml] of sweet vermouth, ½ oz [15 ml] of dry vermouth, and 2 dashes of angostura or orange bitters. Stir or shake with ice, depending on your preference, and garnish with 3 candied ground cherries.

FREEZING

Nine times out of ten I freeze ground cherries as my preservation method of choice. Simply transfer the whole lot, husk and all, into a sealable freezer bag and pop them in the back of the freezer. They don't need to be individually frozen because the husks keep them from sticking together. When you are ready to use them, simply remove from the freezer and remove the husks by squeezing the fruit from their paper lanterns. This is easier to do when they are frozen (versus fresh) because you can be more aggressive with your squeezing and not damage the fruit inside.

Uses: Simply replace any fresh ground cherry with frozen in these recipes and carry on.

melons

One of the most magical days I've ever experienced working in a restaurant kitchen was back in 2016. I can't remember all of the ins and outs, but we were slammed and we all should have been pissed off because [insert crazy thing] happened after [insert crazy thing], as they always do in restaurants. In the slightest of breaks between tickets, Lindsay came around the corner holding two large cantaloupes the only way one can walk holding two melons at one time. Allison looked up and said, "Hey Lindz, nice melons." Lindsay, never one to miss a beat, responded, "You bet your butt. Best melons in the patch." Becky laughed so hard she snorted and then plated a perfectly cooked egg. I took the plate and said, "I love you, ladies," as I ran the food to the table.

It was one of a million simple (often hilarious) exchanges on a team that deeply cared for and respected one another. I'm sure it was made easier because we were all women. It would be rare for me to share that same level of camaraderie with a male colleague who said "nice melons." It has happened, but it is rare, and is also the hallmark of a relationship built on respect and care. To be clear, working with women is not a panacea against abuse; women can be as awful to each other as any man.

I'm sure by now it will come as no surprise that women make up a disproportionately low percentage of leadership and ownership roles in the food world—be it farming, manufacturing, or cooking. Over 50 percent of culinary school graduates are women, though only 19 percent of executive chefs are. Only 27 percent of farms are female-owned. And of the 11.1 million businesses owned by women, 99.9 percent are small businesses. These numbers are worse for BIPOC and LGBTQIA+ women.

The food world is especially difficult for women who tend to be the primary caregivers in their families. The hours are long and physical, the pay is low, and there is rarely sick pay, let alone maternity leave. Of the December 2020 job losses in the United States brought on by the COVID-19 pandemic, 100 percent were women leaving the workforce. One. Hundred. Percent. The demands of caring for children or aging family members were reported as the number one reason why they quit their jobs.

Beyond all of those things, think for a minute about being pregnant and working in a kitchen. When I write a job description for a cook, part of the description is that they have to be able to stand for extended periods of time and lift 50 lb [22.5 kg] (the weight of an average sack of flour). The minute a woman gets pregnant, she is told by her doctor to not stand for long periods and not lift anything over 25 lb [11 kg]. Through no fault of her own, she can no longer safely perform part of the job she was hired for.

Then pile on the lack of mentorship on how to expand a brand, the lack of financial literacy in women who have been told for years that they aren't "good at math," and the sheer discrimination women (let alone BIPOC) face when seeking capital to start a business, and those stats don't seem all that surprising.

Our businesses are better with a diverse array of voices leading them. Our society is stronger when we support pregnant people of all classes as they bring life into the world and raise the next generation. I was lucky enough to work in the kitchens of gracious and kind men, but I hurt for every woman who has put a beautiful plate of food in the window and then been made to feel (at best) less than and (at worst) physically threatened. I don't have the answers to these long-standing and pernicious issues, but I am dedicated to creating a work environment that is committed to the advancement of women so we can get to equal. My ask of you is to think about how you can do the same in big ways and in small, in your industry or in mine.

HOW TO SELECT

The field spot is where the melon has been resting on the ground and therefore has seen no sunlight. That bleached spot should be yellow, not white or green. Similarly, the rind of a ripe melon will have a warm undertone—more yellow than white or blue. Melons should be heavy in the hand and very fragrant. Avoid melons with any gashes in the rind (or at least plan on eating them quickly if you do buy one) and that have any puckering or pocking in the skin, a sign the flesh is deteriorating underneath.

There's a lot said about thumping a melon. I find it sort of hit-or-miss. If you tap a melon and it sounds hollow, it's a good bet that it is ripe. Similar to tapping a loaf of bread to test for doneness—it should sound open and hollow, not dull and muffled.

SIGNS OF RIPENESS

Muskmelons will be very fragrant—almost too fragrant. If a melon smells sort of like garbage as you walk by, that's a good sign that the muskmelon is extremely ripe and ready to go. I use the term "muskmelon" as a catchall for any non-watermelon melon such as cantaloupe or honeydew. Watermelons come in a variety of shapes and colors and can be used in any of the following recipes; just skip the steps about removing the seeds. If you are harvesting your own melon, the tendril adjacent to the melon stem will be withered. The skin of muskmelons will also have a bit of give when pressed with a prodding finger. Sort of like an avocado, it shouldn't mush but just give gently.

HOW TO STORE

If the melon is ripe and you're going to eat it in the next couple of days, store at room temperature out of direct sunlight.

If you've bought an underripe melon, store in a brown paper bag (to trap the ethylene) at room temperature out of direct sunlight to facilitate ripening. Once fully ripe, store in the fridge to prevent over-ripening.

If the melon has been chilled, allow it to come back to room temperature before eating.

RAW

I cut melon three different ways depending on how I want to utilize the rind. If I don't want the rind on at all, I tip and tail (see page 31) the melon. Next, resting one of the cut ends on the cutting board, I use a sharp knife to cut away the rind in large strips. I try to walk the line between not leaving any green behind and not gouging the sweet flesh. Then I cut the melon in half, remove the seeds, and go forth cutting into wedges or cubes.

If I want the rind left on entirely, I cut the melon in half, remove seeds if needed, and then place cut-side down and cut into classic wedges that look like Cheshire Cat smiles.

If I want to present wedges of melon with a bit of rind in the center, I tip and tail the melon and cut away the rind, leaving a strip of rind around the equator of the melon. Then I cut the melon in half and cut into wedges. The rind equator is now at the center of the melon wedge, allowing one's fingers to remain mostly clean while eating big wedges of juicy, summer melon. If balling a melon, I simply cut the melon in half, remove the seeds, and scoop perfect spheres from the flesh.

savory:

melon, cucumber + chickpea salad

This is one of the rare times that I find it worth it to scoop melon into balls. The visual of the spherical melon, round cucumber, and little chickpea BBs is top-notch. The only downside is that it makes the salad a little hard to eat, especially for young ones at the table, so be warned.

2 lb [910 g] English-style cucumbers, tipped and tailed (see page 31)

2 lb [910 g] melon, any variety, scooped into balls or cut into chunks

2 cups [360 g] chickpeas, cooked (or one 15 oz [400 g] can)

Salt and freshly ground black pepper

¾ cup [180 ml] buttermilk

1 cup [20 g] fresh herbs (parsley, cilantro, mint, dill, hyssop, etc.), leaves picked from stems and roughly chopped

½ cup [60 g] slivered almonds, toasted

Olive oil

Using a wide knife, whack the cucumber with the side of the blade to smash the cucumber into irregular chunks.

On a serving platter, lay out two-thirds of the cucumber, two-thirds of the melon, and scatter two-thirds of the chickpeas evenly over the top. Season the whole platter with salt and black pepper and drizzle the buttermilk liberally all over. Sprinkle two-thirds of the herbs and almonds over that. Repeat with the last of the cucumbers, melon, and chickpeas. Season with salt and black pepper again. Finish with the last of the herbs and almonds, then drizzle with olive oil and serve.

sweet:

cantaloupe sundaes w/black pepper + olive oil

Growing up, summer desserts were simply a parade of different fruit served with vanilla ice cream. We lived a few miles away from the original Hudsonville Creamery and my mom would buy their ice cream in the three-gallon tubs normally reserved for ice cream shops to avoid running out. Our fruit + ice cream parade would start with strawberries in the early summer, then sweet cherries, then peaches, all simply cut up, tossed with a bit of sugar, and spooned over a big scoop of ice cream. My favorite was melon with ice cream because the presentation was inverted. The melon became the bowl for the ice cream, and I felt like Willy Wonka (Gene Wilder, not Johnny Depp) when he crunches the candy cup that, up until that point, held the sweet treat.

As an adult, I like to make these sundaes as soon as the Minnesota Midget melon is available. It is a cantaloupe bred to be smaller and intensely flavorful. Leave the rind intact, cut in half, scoop out the seeds, and then fill with vanilla ice cream. The black pepper and olive oil are also adult updates from my childhood version; feel free to take it or leave it as you see fit.

1 cantaloupe (about 2 lb [910 g]), cut into quarters (or 2 small melons cut in half), seeds removed	Coarse salt 1 qt [1 L] Ice Cream Base (page 96), churned and frozen	Olive oil (optional) Freshly ground black pepper (optional)

Place the melon in a large bowl and sprinkle lightly with coarse salt.

Place a scoop of ice cream onto the melon, using the melon as a bowl.

Drizzle liberally with olive oil (if using) and a couple grinds of black pepper (if using) and serve.

GRILLED

The dense flesh of melon allows it to take some heat on the grill without falling apart. Even the moisture-rich watermelon can take a good sear—just make sure that your grill (or frying pan, if not grilling) is ripping hot. You want to sear the fruit quickly before the flesh of the melon is cooked through.

savory:

grilled melon w/tahini, chili oil + sesame seeds

Salt and melon are a classic combination—prosciutto-wrapped melon for example. Cream and melon is just as classic. This combination draws on each of those combinations for something new. Most of my summer dinners are a smattering of simple small plates that come together well. I would pair this dish with some grilled fish, a tomato-mozzarella salad, and something green, maybe arugula with lemon and some garlic bread crumbs. Or I'd just eat it on its own and be pretty happy too. Black sesame seeds are a bit hard to find, but make this dish extra easy on the eyes.

½ cup [110 g] tahini

1 muskmelon (see page 267) (2 lb [910 g]), rind removed and cut into 2 in [5 cm] wide wedges

Olive oil

¼ cup [60 ml] chili oil (see page 215)

Salt

2 Tbsp sesame seeds, toasted

In a small bowl, whisk the tahini with a couple tablespoons of hot water until smooth, light, and fluffy, about 2 minutes.

Drizzle the melon with olive oil.

On a hot grill, sear the flat side of the melon until charred, about 2 minutes. Flip and sear the other side. Remove the melon to a serving platter.

To serve, spoon the whipped tahini all over the melon, drizzle with the chili oil, sprinkle with salt, and scatter the sesame seeds all over.

sweet:

grilled melon w/grape sherbet + candied fennel seeds

Concord grape juice makes this sherbet extra purple and visually appealing. If you are avoiding dairy, either make a grape sorbet or use coconut milk for the sherbet. The candied fennel seeds are optional, but the licorice flavor helps keep the whole thing from being too sweet and adds a pleasant crunch to the dish. If you're up for it, cut the melon into rings to hold the scoops of grape sherbet in the center. It's a bit fiddly but helps keep the whole thing from sliding around into a mess.

1 melon (about 2 lb [910 g]), rind removed	1 qt [1 L] Fruit Sherbet (page 98) using Concord grape juice	¼ cup [60 g] Candied Fennel Seeds (page 74)
Olive oil		6 sprigs mint, leaves removed (optional)

Lay the peeled melon on its side (so the tip and tail are facing right and left). Cut the melon into 1½ in [4 cm] thick rounds. Remove the seeds from the center of the rings.

Drizzle the melon with olive oil.

On a hot grill, sear the wide side of the melon until charred, about 2 minutes. Flip and sear the other side.

To serve, place the melon rings on a serving plate and fill the centers with the grape sherbet. Scatter the candied fennel seeds all over. Tear the mint leaves (if using) and toss over the top.

PRESERVED

JAM

Paul Virant, the "Jar Star" chef of Chicago (and one of my mentors), taught me that you can do more than just freeze melon to preserve it beyond its short season. He also taught me to think about preserves as ratios instead of strict recipes to adapt the recipe to the amount of fruit we had on hand. I usually use 60 percent fruit to 40 percent sugar. The melon jam and pickled watermelon rind recipes are adaptations of the recipes he taught so many of us in the Vie kitchen. Thanks, PV.

vanilla cantaloupe jam

5 lb [2.3 kg] cantaloupe, peeled, seeded, and diced

8 oz [230 g] honey

1 vanilla bean or 1 tsp vanilla paste (the visible seeds add to this recipe)

1 oz [30 ml] lemon juice

In a large pot, combine the cantaloupe and honey and bring to a simmer over medium heat. Split the vanilla bean and scrape the seeds, then add both the bean and the seeds to the pot.

Simmer for 1 minute, then remove from the heat and cool and chill in the fridge overnight (this helps keep the large pieces of cantaloupe intact in the final jam).

The next day, return the cantaloupe mixture to the heat and simmer over medium-high heat until it reaches 220°F [105°C]. Add the lemon juice, remove the vanilla bean, and then jar.

PICKLED

Melon pairs well with the Basic Fruit Pickle Brine (page 112). For muskmelon (see page 267), use apple cider or white wine vinegar. For watermelon, I like to use balsamic vinegar.

Uses: I really like pairing pickled melon with any sort of fatty fish or cut of pork. Consider trying:

Tuna Tartare w/Pickled Melon: Dice the tuna finely, dice the melon finely, dress the whole thing with a spoonful of mayo and some chopped parsley or cilantro, then pile on top of crackers.

Grilled Pork Chops w/Pickled Melon + Cucumber salad: Grill the pork chops. Combine equal parts diced pickled melon with diced cucumber, dress with a big glug of olive oil, and spoon over the pork chop.

pickled watermelon rind

3 lb [1.4 kg] watermelon rind, flesh reserved to use in a different recipe

¼ cup [90 g] salt

2 cups [400 g] sugar

1½ cups [375 ml] apple cider vinegar

2 lemons, thinly sliced and seeds removed

2 cinnamon sticks

1 tsp allspice berries

1½ tsp whole cloves

Cut the tough outer skin off of the watermelon, being careful not to cut away the rind. Then cut the rind away from the pink flesh of the watermelon and dice the rind into cubes.

Dissolve the salt in 3 cups [720 ml] of water, pour it over the rind, cover, and refrigerate for at least 4 hours or overnight. Drain and rinse the rind and transfer to a large pot.

In a medium saucepan, combine the sugar, vinegar, lemon slices, and spices and simmer over medium heat until the sugar is dissolved, 10 minutes. Strain the sugar mixture and discard the spices.

Pour the sugar mixture over the watermelon rind and simmer over medium heat until the rind is translucent, 30 to 40 minutes. Store in the fridge or can to make shelf-stable.

FREEZING

Melon freezes very well. Simply peel, remove the seeds from the muskmelon, and cut into a large dice. Lay the melon on a baking sheet to individually freeze and, when fully frozen, bag up for storage for up to 6 months.

• My favorite thing to do with frozen melon is to blend it with a bit of simple syrup to make sorbet. It takes less syrup than the Sorbet recipe (page 96) because melon is often very sweet. For every 1 lb [455 g] of frozen fruit add ¼ cup [60 ml] of Simple Syrup (page 109) and a squeeze of lemon or lime, then blend in a blender to make a creamy sorbet.

nectarines + peaches

When I think of peaches, I think of two things.

The first is picking peaches with my grandfather in South Haven, Michigan. We'd go early in the morning and pick bushel basket after bushel basket, only to wrap up the day sitting on the tailgate as he sliced a sun-warmed fruit with his pocket knife, juice dripping down my chin, and my heart wrapped in the gauzy, golden light of future nostalgia.

The second is an image of the Joad family in *The Grapes of Wrath*. Parents and children alike harvesting peaches as fast as possible in the hard light of Depression-era Salinas Valley. Harvesting food and having none to eat themselves; the youngest child gorging on so many unsaleable peaches that he gives himself what his brother calls "the skitters."

These are the two ends of the agricultural spectrum for me—nourishing to cruel. We can wax poetic. We can talk statistics. One 2016 study says 63 percent of seasonal and migrant farmworkers live below the poverty line and struggle with food insecurity while harvesting fresh food for others. We can talk action plans. Support growers who look after their workers, know the source, care, advocate. All of that has to start with recognizing the difference between the quaintness of dipping into agriculture on a weekend and the grind of earning a living from it.

HOW TO SELECT

Look for fruits that are heavy in the hand and have tight skin. Wrinkly skin means that the cells underneath have started to deteriorate and collapse. Peaches should still have their fuzzy skin; nectarines never will. The fruit will have a pleasant aroma, but color is a stronger indicator of ripeness than aroma.

SIGNS OF RIPENESS

The color of the fruit should have warm undertones. Even white peaches and nectarines will have a subtle warmth to their look. Green tones indicate they are underripe. Both peaches and nectarines will start to give when pressed gently with the thumb along the suture (the line running from stem to tip). I'm always hesitant to encourage fruit squeezing. It can easily damage the fruit, and if you don't buy it, someone else will (or they won't, and the farmer gets stuck with what are now bruised seconds). Because of this, I buy peaches and nectarines that are a touch on the firm side but have warm-colored undertones. Then I squeeze them at home when I think they are just about perfect ripeness.

HOW TO STORE

Store at room temperature, out of direct sunlight, in a paper bag if well underripe, lined up on the counter if close but not quite there. Don't let the fruit touch one another or they are more likely to mold. Once the fruit is ripe, move to the fridge and eat within a few days.

NOTES

Peaches and nectarines are genetically the same except for one gene—the one that makes the skin fuzzy. Despite their similarities, I feel like nectarines have a denser flesh that is less susceptible to bruising but often lacks the sparkle of a peach. White peaches and nectarines tend to taste sweeter because they lack some of the earthier flavor that comes with darker pigmentation. This is not a warning against or advocation for either one, just information.

ABBY SCHILLING

Abby Schilling is a third-generation fruit and vegetable grower in Saint Joseph, Michigan. Abby's father, Mick Klug, expanded the farm he grew up on from 40 to 120 acres and returned the production to the diversified agriculture he saw as a child. Abby farms over 150 acres, providing fresh fruits and vegetables directly to consumers via a CSA program and farmers' markets presence.

Abra Berens: I wanted to talk with you, not only because you grow incredible fruit, but because you sell on the fresh market directly to consumers. Can you explain a bit about what that means and how it affects your business?

Abby Schilling: Yes, you can kind of separate fruit sales into three different markets. One, the commodity market, where fruit is grown in huge quantities and sold to a processor who turns it into a product: dried cherries, cherry juice concentrate, cocktail cherries, etc. Two, the fresh fruit wholesale market, where fruit is sold to a distributor to be consumed fresh by customers—the fruit that is in grocery stores, for example. Three, what I do, which is primarily the fresh retail market. I sell directly to consumers at farmers' markets or to chefs at restaurants—and a little bit to distributors.

AB: How does that change what you grow?

AS: It means I grow smaller quantities of a greater number of things that I can sell at a higher price point because there is no middleman. If I were growing a million pounds of cherries, I couldn't move them all myself and so I'd have to sell at a lower price point to someone who could take them all. By selling a greater variety of items, I spread my workload out over the whole season, making it easier to staff efficiently. Plus, that means that I have fresh food for families all year-round, as I freeze any surplus berries and cherries not sold fresh.

When my grandparents were farming, they grew a variety of different crops, with a focus on peaches, tomatoes, and cherries. After my dad, Mick, explored different avenues of farming such as large acreage of grain and juice grapes, he eventually moved the farm back to what he saw growing up: lots of different things growing together. He started going to the Chicago farmers' markets back in the late 1980s and was a founding member of Chicago's Green City Market. The access to the Chicago retail market revolutionized our farm. Now I attend farmers' markets four days a week, and sell to nearly a hundred restaurants.

AB: What do you wish non-farmers knew about your work?

AS: I wish people knew how many jobs farmers actually do. I am a landlord because I provide housing to workers. I am a website developer. I am a delivery driver. I am HR, customer service, accountant, meteorologist, public speaker, book keeper, marketer, sales manager, mechanic, and on and on. All of that is before I go home for the night. There is nothing about farming that is standard 9 to 5.

I also really want folks to know how important what they buy is to us. Clearly it takes a ton of work to get this food to market. I am there when it rains and when it is sunny. I need folks to really commit to attending markets and buying this food when I have it. You can get peaches at the grocery store, but I can tell you exactly how mine are tasting and know that everyone who worked to get them to you was paid a fair wage. I could grow everything cheaper if I didn't pay people right or treat the land right. If people value those things, they have to show up and support them.

AB: If you could change one thing about our food system, what would it be?

AS: Expanding and supporting a more local food system by reducing the importation of food from foreign countries, especially when US-grown food is in season. Many other countries from which the United States imports food do not pay fair wages, nor follow the same food safety and sustainability guidelines that US family farms do. It is also very concerning to me that small family farms continue to struggle with the rising costs of inputs, regulations, and labor. There will soon be a time that many can't sustain their businesses.

AB: Final question—do you eat what you grow?

AS: Absolutely! In all honesty, I love fruit in its simplest form: ripe off the tree. (Although I would never turn down a fruit pie of any kind and am a huge fan of any kind of pickled or preserved vegetable.)

RAW

In her book *How to Eat a Peach*, English cookery writer Diana Henry describes being served a bowl of halved peaches and a glass of Moscato d'Asti for dessert. Her fellow diners cut the peaches and slipped them into the sweet wine, letting them bob around for a bit, then ate the peaches dripping with sweet bubbly wine and drank the wine now perfumed with the peaches. I think of her every time I slide a few wedges of a perfect peach into a glass of late-harvest Riesling (we don't grow Moscato in the mitten). I think of her every time I barely handle fruit before presenting it to a table. I try to remember that serving fruit often requires very little from me at all, which makes the glass of wine studded with fruit that much sweeter.

savory: spicy, sweet, salty summer salad

A little bit of spice and a little bit of salt lift the sometimes one-note sweetness of fruit. Nectarines (or use peaches) often have an acidity and tannin that becomes more pronounced when paired with savory flavors. If you know me, you know I love a cabbage salad, often filled with some sort of legume. It is inexpensive, filling, and lasts for leftovers. I like this salad on its own or paired with any sort of grilled meat or fish, stewed white beans, or slabs of fried tofu.

Neutral oil

1 cup [200 g] black or French green lentils

½ cup [120 ml] hard apple cider or white wine

Salt

½ cup [120 ml] olive oil

½ tsp chili flakes

1 tsp herbes de Provence

1 garlic clove, minced

¼ cup [60 ml] red wine vinegar

2 lb [910 g] nectarines, halved and pits removed

1 lb [455 g] cabbage, thinly shaved

10 sprigs parsley, roughly chopped

continued

In a medium saucepan over medium heat, heat a glug of neutral oil until it shimmers, then add the lentils and briefly fry, 1 minute. Add the hard cider and cook until evaporated, 2 minutes.

Add 2 cups [480 ml] of water and a big pinch of salt, bring to a boil, then lower the heat to a simmer and cook until the lentils are tender, about 20 minutes.

Meanwhile, in a small frying pan, heat the olive oil over low heat until it is warm, 1 minute.

Add the chili flakes, herbes de Provence, and garlic. Let fry for 30 seconds, then remove from the heat and allow to steep for 10 minutes.

Pour the red wine vinegar into a small jar or other sealable container. Add the steeped oil and a big pinch of salt and shake to combine.

Cut the nectarines—if they are very hard, slice paper-thin; if they are very soft, cut into wide wedges; and if they are perfectly ripe, cut into bite-size pieces.

In a large bowl, combine the lentils (warm or cooled, up to you), nectarines, cabbage, and parsley, then dress with half the vinaigrette. Taste and adjust the seasoning, adding more vinaigrette as desired before serving.

sweet: # peaches + cream w/ginger thins

I have bemoaned that restaurant desserts are too fussy for me, that all I want at the end of a meal is some fruit and cream and maybe a cookie. Well, here you go. Now that I'm writing it, it feels too simple, but I'm sticking with the courage of my convictions. Don't try this with subpar peaches—make something else in the chapter. The salt makes the dish, so don't skip it. The cookies are optional, but ginger and peaches love each other, and it makes me feel like I tried a little more. I also go out of my way to warm the peaches a bit. Ideally, they sit in the sun throughout the meal or are resting on the top of the stove after all the cooking is done, absorbing that last little bit of radiant heat. The cream should be ice-cold for contrast. I've never served this without someone at the table crumbling their cookies over the bowl. I don't, preferring to dunk in the last dredge of cream, but I can see the rationale.

1 peach per person, warmed, cut into halves or wedges, pits removed

¼ to ½ cup [60 to 120 ml] heavy cream per person

Coarse sea salt

1 recipe Ginger Thins (page 70), or 3 cookies per person

Place the peaches in a serving bowl. Pour the cream over the peaches. Sprinkle the coarse salt all over.

Serve with a sidecar of cookies.

GRILLED

The best stone fruit to grill are firm ones. If the fruit is too soft, it will mush and juice all over. Like searing all fruit, hot and fast is your best bet. Peaches and nectarines are my favorite fruit to grill because they have a relatively large surface area and so are easier to manage. Brushing the cut side with some neutral oil before grilling will help them sear and not stick to the grate. As always, you can roast in a screaming hot frying pan or place under the broiler and achieve similar results.

savory:

grilled peach + ricotta toasts

I like the heady (not spicy) flavor of Marash or Aleppo pepper over these toasts, but those peppers are sometimes hard to find, so I often substitute smoked paprika. It is a bit spicier but still works. Similarly, you could substitute mashed avocado for the ricotta if you're avoiding dairy.

8 oz [230 g] ricotta

1 lemon (about 1.5 oz [45 ml]), zest and juice

Olive oil

Salt

2 to 4 firm peaches, halved and pits removed

Neutral oil

Marash or Aleppo pepper flakes, or smoked paprika

1 Tbsp balsamic vinegar

4 thick slices of sourdough

1 garlic clove

2 oz [55 g] arugula or other tender green

Freshly ground black pepper

In a small bowl, combine the ricotta, lemon zest and juice, a glug of olive oil, and a pinch of salt.

Brush the cut side of the peaches lightly with neutral oil, then sprinkle with the pepper flakes or paprika.

Grill the peaches, cut-side down, over medium-high heat until they have good grill marks but are not falling apart, about 3 minutes. Transfer the peaches from the grill to a bowl and toss with the balsamic vinegar, then let rest for a minimum of 10 minutes.

Grill the bread over medium heat until toasted and starting to char, about 1 minute. Flip and grill the other side, another 1 to 2 minutes. Rub the grilled bread all over with the garlic clove.

Slice the peaches into ½ in [12 mm] thick slices.

In a large bowl, dress the arugula with a glug of olive oil, a pinch of salt, and black pepper.

To serve, smear the garlic bread with the ricotta mixture, and top with the peach slices and a pile of the arugula.

sweet:

cream scones w/grilled nectarine + goat cheese sabayon

When I worked for Allie Levitt, one of the most under-lauded pastry chefs in Chicago, she made a strawberry shortcake with whipped goat cheese mascarpone filling. It opened my eyes to how goat cheese can easily swing sweet with the right fruit. I also once did an event with her chef-turned-butcher husband, Rob. The oven at the space was broken, so we jimmy-rigged the grill to function as an oven. We got it to 350°F [180°C] and then placed the baking sheet (with the biscuits on it) inside a tall aluminum foil pouch and baked over indirect heat (fire only lit on one side of the grill and biscuits on the other). I don't know why you would do this if your oven works, but some prefer to do everything on the grill so have at. I learned a lot from Allie and Rob over the years and thank them for their years of inspiration and friendship.

4 Cream Scones (page 56)	Neutral oil	1 recipe Goat Cheese Sabayon (page 87)
2 nectarines, halved and pits removed	¼ tsp vanilla paste or extract	

Preheat the oven to 350°F [180°C]. Bake the cream scones until lightly browned and cooked through, about 20 minutes.

Brush the cut side of the nectarines lightly with neutral oil. Grill the nectarines, cut-side down, over medium-high heat until they have good grill marks but are not falling apart, about 3 minutes. Transfer the nectarines from the grill to a bowl and toss with the vanilla, then let rest for a minimum of 10 minutes.

Slice the nectarines into ½ in [12 mm] thick slices.

Make the sabayon.

To serve, split the baked cream scones in half and pile the nectarine slices on the cut side of the scone bottom. Spoon the sabayon liberally over the top, then place the scone lid on top.

BAKED

While I grill peaches that are too hard, I tend to bake peaches that have gone a bit soft. Grilling benefits from the structure of an underripe peach. Baking renders peaches tender to the point of a quiver. That said, you will always have to account for the juiciness. Both of these recipes involve a dough that can handle a good amount of peach nectar. If you are making something like a pie that can become soggy with too much juice, be sure to add a thickener like cornstarch or go the way of the Pie Filling (page 102) to remove and reduce the liquid separately.

savory:

coconut milk shrimp w/jalapeño-peach cornbread

It's not that often that I cook with shrimp. They are hard to get fresh in my area and it's hard to tell in the freezer section where the shrimp came from, how they were harvested, and most importantly, how the people working to fish and peel the shrimp were treated. The international shrimping industry is rife with stories of forced labor and inhumane practices. Traditionally, shrimp from the Gulf Coast is subject to stronger labor regulation, and so that's a good place to start. There is also a growing shrimp aquaponic industry that raises shrimp well inland from our salty shores. Consider seeking out those growers. The prices are higher, but enslaved labor allows for artificially cheap prices on the backs of desperate people.

continued

1 recipe Cornbread Cake
Batter (page 65)

1 jalapeño, cut into thin
rings or strips (seeds
removed, if you want to
limit the spice)

2 Tbsp butter

2 lb [910 g] peaches, pits
removed, skins left on,
and cut into a large dice

Neutral oil

4 garlic cloves [30 g],
minced

½ in [12 mm] ginger,
peeled and diced

½ tsp chili flakes (optional)

Pinch of salt

2 lb [910 g] shrimp, shells
and tails removed

One 13.5 oz [405 ml] can
coconut milk

2 limes (about 2 oz
[60 ml]), zest and juice

8 sprigs cilantro

2 sprigs mint (optional)

2 sprigs basil (optional)

Preheat the oven to 375°F [190°C]. Place a 10 in [25 cm] ovenproof frying pan into the oven to preheat for a minimum of 10 minutes.

Make the cornbread, adding the jalapeño to the cornbread batter.

Remove the frying pan from the oven and add the butter to melt. Pour the cornbread batter into the pan and press to the edges. Scatter the peaches all over the top and return to the oven. Bake until the cornbread is golden brown, and the knife test (see page 30) comes out clean, about 20 minutes.

Meanwhile, in a large frying pan, heat a glug of neutral oil over medium heat. Add the garlic, ginger, chili flakes (if using), and salt and fry until it is fragrant, about 1 minute, lowering the heat as needed to keep the garlic from browning. Add the shrimp and quickly sauté until the shrimp are starting to turn pink, about 3 minutes. Add the coconut milk, bring to a simmer, and cook until the shrimp are cooked through, about 6 minutes. Add the lime zest and juice to the shrimp, taste, and adjust the seasoning.

Remove the cornbread from the oven and let cool for 10 minutes.

To serve, cut wedges of the cornbread and place in the bottom of a shallow bowl or plate with a rim, then ladle the coconut milk shrimp over the top. Scatter a pile of herbs on top.

sweet:

peach-berry cobbler w/whipped sour cream

My friend Kelsey Coday, an incredible baker, once referred to this as the "cuppa whatever cake": It's a cup of flour, cup of milk, cup of sugar, and then whatever fruit you've got around, and I think of her every time I make it. Peach blueberry is my favorite combo but I have made cobbler with every iteration of fruit I can think of. Kelsey also told me once that it is technically not a cobbler but a dump cake. I refuse to use that term because it makes me think of, ahem, other things, and so cobbler it will always be.

4 lb [1.8 kg] peaches, pits removed and cut into wedges or diced, skins left on

2 lb [910 g] blueberries

¼ cup [50 g] sugar

2 Tbsp all-purpose flour

Pinch of salt

1 recipe Cobbler Batter (page 43)

2 cups [480 g] sour cream

Preheat the oven to 350°F [180°C] and grease a 9 by 13 in [23 by 33 cm] baking dish.

In a large bowl, toss the peaches, blueberries, sugar, flour, and salt together to coat.

Tip the fruit into the prepared baking dish, then pour the cobbler batter on top. Dot the butter all over the top of the cobbler focusing on the corners. Place in the oven to bake until cooked through and deeply brown, about 45 minutes.

Whip the sour cream until it is fluffy.

To serve, dish some of the cobbler onto a plate (I'll take the corner) and top with a healthy dollop of whipped sour cream.

PRESERVED

JAM

Peach and/or nectarine jam is one of my favorites. I like to add a little bit of ginger or vanilla to the mix, but honestly, I often leave it plain. The 60:40 fruit to sugar ratio works for me. I rarely peel the peaches in advance and instead just pass the pulp through a food mill to remove the skins after they have softened. The only potential pitfall of peach or nectarine jam is that it can sometimes be too sweet if the fruit is very ripe. When that's the case, I add a splash of sherry vinegar just before jarring.

Uses: My favorite way to use peach or nectarine jam (besides on toast or scones) is to thin and use as a glaze over roast chicken or pork loin. I usually thin ¼ cup [60 ml] of jam with 2 Tbsp of water and 2 Tbsp of apple cider vinegar. Then, just before the chicken or pork is finished roasting, simply brush the glaze all over and return to the oven to caramelize.

PEACH PIT VINEGAR

The pits of peaches and nectarines have a flavor reminiscent of bitter almond. Soak the pits (especially those that still have flesh clinging to them) in apple cider vinegar to impart that flavor, then use anywhere you would vinegar, but I like it best as a shrub. Take ½ cup [120 ml] of peach pit vinegar and ½ cup [100 g] of brown sugar, shake to dissolve, then use as the base for a spritz, either with just soda water or soda water and bourbon. Thanks to Emily Spurlin for teaching me so much and especially for this technique.

PICKLED

Peaches and nectarines pickle well with the Basic Fruit Pickle Brine (page 112). Uses: I use the pickled fruit in salads, to garnish cheese, or chopped up with a bunch of herbs and olive oil for a fast, tangy relish.

CANNED

My grandmother would put peaches in heavy syrup and can them in a water bath. It certainly works. I find them almost too sweet and not better than what is available at the grocery store, so I let the big processors do that and I focus on other preserves.

FREEZING

Peaches and nectarines both freeze well. This is the one place where I take the time to peel the peaches first. If the fruit is very firm, you can peel with a vegetable peeler. If it is soft, blanch the whole fruit in salted boiling water for 30 seconds and then shock in cold water. The fruit should slip right out of their skins. Simply cut the fruit into whatever size you like and lay out on a baking sheet lined with parchment or a silcone mat to individually freeze.

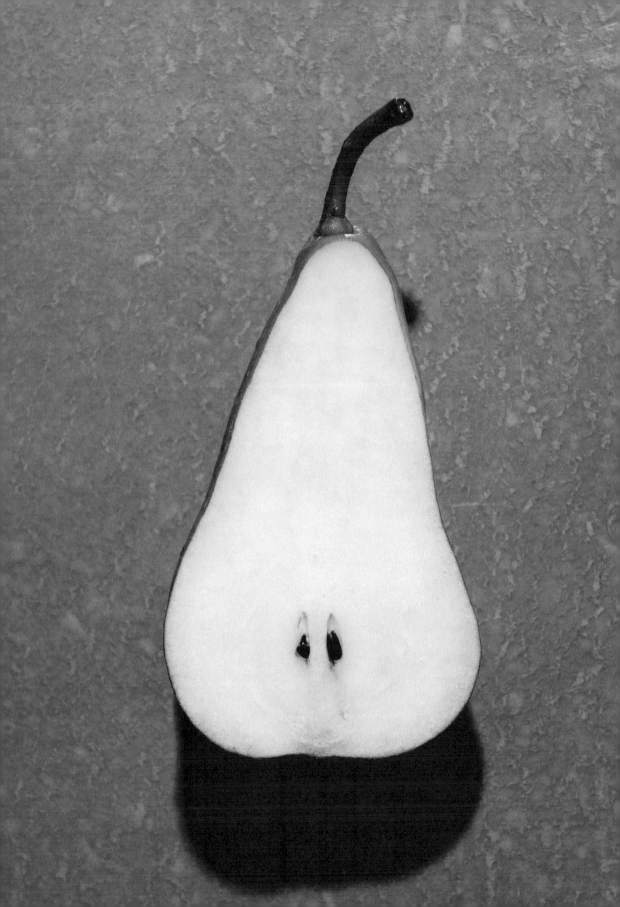

pears

My favorite thing about working in restaurants is the camaraderie among colleagues built upon the unending hours spent together. You quickly see someone's mettle tested by the daily stress, but it is the far-ranging and often banal conversations in the calmer times that deepen relationships.

My favorite example of this is the "either or" game. This game is played by simply asking someone if they prefer either A or B— either carrots or parsnips, either shrimp or scallops, either iceberg or romaine. As I write this I can't believe that we would spend hours asking each other these silly questions, but, alas, there were hours to be had and only so many topics to be covered. Plus, it does tell you a remarkable amount about a person if they choose potatoes over rice.

One day, this game led to an argument lasting multiple days between me and my chef and mentor Rodger Bowser. He asked, "Perfectly ripe peach or perfectly ripe pear?" I, of course, answered, "Peach."

"Wrong!" he scoffed.

"Wrong? There's no wrong in this game!"

"Nope, wrong. A perfectly ripe pear is vastly superior to any peach."

This normally laconic man then went on to wax poetic about pears. How the russet skin of a pear produces a tactile pleasure in the hand. How the flesh dissolves like sugared rice paper on the tongue, the flavors subtle and complex, unlike the lurid peach. And a pear would never embarrass anyone by dripping juice down one's chin the way a smutty peach will.

I interrupted this sonnet to admit I'd never had a perfectly ripe pear, which seemed apropos of the issue at hand. Rodger walked away, not in a huff, but because as is the way with kitchen conversations, dialogue was abruptly ended by customers or work.

For the next two days, every time I saw him, he would recite a new list of reasons why pears are the cream of the crop. To which I would respond with an eye roll and the insistence that while that very well may be, the fact remains, I've yet to ever taste a perfectly ripe pear. Unicorns are the most magnificent creatures ever to behold, but much like a perfectly ripe pear, they also don't seem to exist.

In an attempt to prove his point, Rodger took the time to baby two pears all the way to perfect ripeness. He called me over to his prep table and we sunk our teeth into them. The rough, golden skin yielded to tender flesh tasting of honey, vanilla, and the best Muscat you can imagine. It was a delight and rivaled even the best peach just pulled from the tree and eaten out of hand with juices spilling down the wrist.

"This is quite something; I still prefer a peach."

"You're fired."

I wasn't actually. To this day it is still those sorts of moments that made the years of laboring in tiny basement prep kitchens so fun.

HOW TO SELECT

Look for pears free of bruises or gashes that have punctured the skin. The firmer the flesh, the less ripe the pear. Buy harder pears if you won't be eating them quickly.

SIGNS OF RIPENESS

The color of ripe pears is warm in tone with yellow or red undertones. Ripe pears will dent easily when pressed with your finger. Pears don't generally have a strong aroma, but the riper the pear, the more fragrant it will be.

HOW TO STORE

Store at room temperature unless very ripe, then move to the fridge. Pears ripen quickly in the presence of ethylene. To speed along the ripening process, store multiple pears in a paper bag to trap the gas; to slow, wrap individual pears in paper to inhibit absorption. To really see the impact of ethylene, wrap half the pear in paper and store in a bag with another pear. The exposed section of the pear will ripen while the wrapped section will not. It's wild.

NOTES

There are over 3,000 different pear cultivars.

RAW

Ralph Waldo Emerson said, "There are only ten minutes in the life of a pear when it is perfect to eat." Thankfully, shaving raw pears is best done with underripe pears so they hold their shape. When slicing a raw pear, cut it in half longitudinally and then, using a melon baller or teaspoon, remove the blossom end, seedy core, and fibrous stem threads. Then place flat-side down on the cutting board and cut into the desired shape. Alternatively, slice the whole thing, stem and seeds included, on a mandoline into paper-thin cross sections. The fibrous parts will be so thin that they will be palatable.

savory: ## chicory salad w/shaved pears, walnuts + pecorino

This salad is pure autumn, when pears and chicories are at their finest. I like to cut the pear into long, wafer-thin layers and then match the thickness with the pecorino ribbons, relying on the walnuts for crunch and the greens for volume and a tinge of bitterness. If you don't have pecorino, Cheddar, Parmesan, Manchego, or ricotta salata would work well in its stead. You're really just looking for dry texture and a hit of acidity and salt. For the chicories, I like a mix of colors and so will often combine leaves of radicchio, Treviso, endive, and frisée.

1 pear, seeds and stem removed

4 to 6 oz [115 to 170 g] chicory leaves, left in large pieces

2 Tbsp sherry vinegar

2 Tbsp olive oil

Pinch of salt

1 cup [120 g] walnuts, toasted

2 oz [55 g] pecorino, shaved into thin ribbons

Freshly ground black pepper

Shave or cut the pears into thin pieces.

In a large bowl, dress the chicory leaves with the vinegar, olive oil, and salt.

Fan half of the leaves out on a large serving platter. Scatter half of the pears, walnuts, and pecorino on top of the leaves and finish with several grinds of black pepper. Repeat with the second half of the ingredients and serve.

sweet:

sliced pears w/salted caramel + crumbles

One of my favorite chef's treats is snacking on the crumble topping that falls off a pie and bakes on the sheet alongside the pie in the oven. This dessert idea came to me after attending a dinner party where the appetizer was pita bread dipped in olive oil, and then dipped in dukkha. The gist is the same here, a dip-as-you-go dessert where the caramel sauce binds the firm fruit with the salty crunch of crumble topping. If communal dipping isn't appropriate for your party, build individual plates by fanning the slices of pear out, dressing with caramel sauce, and garnishing each slice with a big pinch of crumble. This recipe is for one person, but it scales for a crowd.

¼ cup [30 g] Crumble Topping (page 76) per person	1 pear per person	2 oz [60 ml] Salted Caramel Sauce (page 88) per person

Preheat the oven to 350°F [180°C].

Scoop the appropriate amount of crumble topping for your party onto a baking sheet lined with parchment or a silicone mat. Bake until golden brown and crunchy, about 10 minutes, then allow to cool completely.

Remove the seeds and stem from the pear and slice into wide pieces.

Warm the caramel sauce gently.

To serve, place a pile of pears next to a bowl of the warmed caramel sauce and another bowl, or pile, of the crumble topping.

POACHED

Poaching pears has many benefits. It softens rock-hard fruit. It cooks them gently enough that they won't fall apart (unless they are already soft). It lightly preserves them, so if you find yourself with a big bushel, poaching can give you some time to enjoy all the fruit. It is a good way to batch cook for the week. Poached pears can be sweet or savory. The poaching liquid makes a delicious homemade soda when blended with soda water or a lovely holiday punch when spiked with bourbon.

savory:

red wine–poached pears w/goat cheese sabayon, pumpernickel + pine nuts

I like this as a replacement for a traditional cheese course or as the first course of a meal. As mentioned earlier, poaching can be done in large or small batches. If you want to get ahead or simply need to move a lot of pears, the volume of pears called for can be doubled or tripled, just make sure that the pears are fully submerged in the cooking liquid.

4 pears, peeled and cut in half, seeds and stem removed

2 cups [480 ml] dry red wine

1 Tbsp honey

½ tsp salt

4 slices pumpernickel bread, cut into cubes

Olive oil

Salt and freshly ground black pepper

1 sprig rosemary, needles picked and minced

¼ cup [30 g] pine nuts, toasted

1 recipe Goat Cheese Sabayon (page 87)

2 oz [55 g] spinach

continued

In a small saucepan, arrange the pear halves so they fit snuggly. Add the wine, honey, and salt, topping it up with as much wine as needed to just cover. Cut a piece of parchment paper or butter paper into a cartouche (see page 29), then press the cartouche over the pears to help keep them beneath the level of the liquid. Place the saucepan over high heat to bring the liquid to a simmer, then lower the heat to low to gently poach the pears until they are tender, about 12 minutes.

Remove from the heat and let cool in the liquid.

In a large bowl, toss the bread with a big glug of olive oil and a pinch of salt, then toast in a large frying pan over medium heat or in a moderate oven to make croutons.

In a small bowl, combine the rosemary, pine nuts, a pinch of salt, and glug of olive oil, then set aside.

In a medium saucepan, bring 2 in [5 cm] of water to a boil. Place a metal bowl over the water, not touching it, and warm the sabayon in the bowl.

Lift the pears from the poaching liquid and cut into thick slices.

In a large bowl, dress the spinach with a glug of olive oil, a pinch of salt, and a grind of black pepper.

To serve, spoon the sabayon evenly into the center of each plate followed by a handful of the spinach. Top with the croutons and slices of pear, then garnish with the rosemary pine nuts. Alternatively, leave the pears in complete halves and rest cut-side up on a bed of spinach and croutons, spoon the sabayon in the center of each pear, and garnish with the rosemary pine nuts.

sweet:

chilled poached pears + pecan sandies

Truth be told, I almost never eat these pears with cookies. I eat them whole, cutting bites with my spoon and slurping up the poaching liquid. I call these "Elizabeth David Moments" because legendary food writer Elizabeth David wasn't one to mince words and taught me the beauty of austere meals. I imagine a cold poached pear would conclude her famous "omelet and glass of wine" dinner.

4 pears (1½ lb [675 g]), peeled, halved, seeds and stem removed

One 750 ml bottle white wine

½ cup [100 g] brown sugar

2 Tbsp honey

1 cinnamon stick

4 star anise

4 whole cloves

½ in [12 mm] ginger, peeled and smashed with the back of a knife to soften

2 cups [480 ml] heavy cream

8 to 12 Pecan Sandies (page 72)

In a medium pot, arrange the pears to fit snuggly.

In a large bowl, whisk the wine, sugar, and honey together until dissolved, then pour over the pears. Add the spices, then cover with a cartouche (see page 29). Bring to a boil over high heat, then lower the heat to barely a simmer and poach the pears until they are tender, 10 to 12 minutes.

When the pears are tender, remove from the heat, let cool, and then chill for a minimum of 1 hour.

Divide the pears among four serving dishes and pour ½ cup [120 ml] of the poaching liquid over each pear. Serve with a sidecar of the heavy cream for guests to pour over the pears as they desire and a plate of the cookies.

BAKED

Pears bake beautifully because they don't tend to get soggy the same way moisture-dense berries or melon will. I tend to bake with the firmest fruit I can find to help keep the structure intact. That said, even fairly soft pears tend to hold their shape in the oven, so just use what you have on hand.

savory:

pear, bacon + onion tart

I always forget about puff pastry. It seems antiquated or passé, but lately it has had a renaissance in my kitchen. Making puff pastry is a long, tedious, and somewhat rewarding affair. Making ruff puff (see page 61) is faster and yields great results. Buying a good brand of store-bought puff pastry is also perfectly reasonable. No matter your puff piece, having stray sheets around is extremely practical, especially to pull together a stunner like this for a light dinner or fancy lunch.

½ lb [230 g] bacon, cut into ½ in [12 mm] wide lardons or strips

1 lb [455 g] onion, thinly sliced

5 sprigs thyme, leaves picked

Salt

½ cup [120 ml] hard cider or white wine

1 pear, halved, seeds and stem removed

1 recipe Puff Pastry Dough (page 61)

Egg wash (see page 30)

4 oz [115 g] Gruyère or Cheddar cheese, grated

Place the bacon in a large frying pan and then turn on the heat to medium-low. Cook the bacon slowly to render the fat and eventually crisp the bacon pieces, about 6 minutes. Remove the bacon to a paper towel–lined plate to drain.

Add the onion and thyme to the bacon fat in the frying pan. Then add a big pinch of salt and caramelize over medium heat, 15 to 20 minutes, stirring regularly.

continued

Deglaze the frying pan with the cider and allow the liquid to reduce completely, 5 minutes. Remove from the heat and let cool.

Slice the pears into ¼ in [6 mm] thick pieces.

Lay out one sheet of pastry on a baking sheet lined with parchment. Cut the other sheet of pastry into ¼ in [6 mm] wide strips down the long side of the sheet. Brush the edges of the uncut puff pastry sheet with the egg wash and lay the strips of puff pastry along the edges to build a border. Brush egg wash on top of the border pieces. Prick the interior of the tart all over with a fork to keep from puffing excessively.

Sprinkle the grated cheese all over. Scatter the caramelized onion mixture over the cheese base, followed by the bacon bits all over and finish with slices of pear. Chill the tart for 30 minutes.

While the tart chills, preheat the oven to 375°F [190°C]. Bake the chilled tart until the puff pastry is cooked through and lightly browned, about 25 minutes, rotating halfway through.

Serve warm or at room temperature with a big green salad on the side (if you want).

sweet:

ginger honey cake w/pears + whipped sour cream

There is nothing revolutionary about this combination of spiced molasses cake and pears, but the combination doesn't suffer from its ubiquity. Cranberries, apples, or even pineapple make good substitutes for pears in a pinch.

3 pears, peeled, halved, seeds and stems removed	1 recipe Ginger Honey Cake Batter (page 66)	2 cups [480 g] sour cream

Preheat the oven to 325°F [165°C].

Line the bottom of a 9 in [23 cm] cake pan with a round of parchment. Lay the pears cut-side down evenly inside the cake pan, stem end pointing toward the center. Pour the cake batter over the pears gently so as to not disturb them. Bake until the knife test (see page 30) comes out clean when tested from the center of the cake, 60 to 90 minutes. Let the cake cool for 30 minutes, then remove from the pan by loosening the edges with a butter knife and inverting the cake over a serving platter. Lift the parchment paper away, replacing any pears that may have dislodged.

Just before serving, place the sour cream in a medium bowl and beat with a whisk until light and fluffy.

To serve, slice the cake into six wedges and top with a hefty dollop of the whipped sour cream.

The cake can be made upwards of 3 days in advance if wrapped tightly and stored in the fridge. This cake doesn't store well at room temperature because the pears will start to mold. Be sure to bring back to room temperature before eating.

PRESERVED

JAM

Pear butter is a lovely way to use up a couple of random pears before they go off, or make it in giant batches to preserve the season and gobble up throughout the winter. The only problem is, like apple butter, pear butter tends to stick, requiring regular stirring, which leads it to splatter and really burning the arm that stirs it. My friend and former coworker Meghan Stone developed a system where you tape a kitchen towel all around your arm above an oven mitt, limiting the exposed skin that can be burned. It looks ridiculous but, like most things Meghan devises, works brilliantly.

Jam ratio: 60:40 fruit to sugar ratio is my go-to. Sometimes pears lack acidity and so I'll finish the butter with a splash of vinegar (usually sherry or apple cider). I also like to add vanilla, ginger, lavender, and/or cardamom, but sparingly.

Uses: Smear on toast, over yogurt and granola, on top of oatmeal, or as the base of a jam tart.

PICKLED

Pickled pears add a nice tang of acidity to normally rich fall and winter foods. Make the Basic Fruit Pickle Brine (page 112) using apple cider vinegar and pour over sliced or diced pears. I usually leave the skins on to maintain the integrity of the pear. I find it best to use slightly underripe pears for pickles. Thankfully those aren't hard to find.

Uses: Scatter a spoonful over dishes for a pop of acidity—roasted carrots w/pecans + pickled pears, spinach salad w/pickled pears + goat cheese, parsnip risotto w/pickled pears + walnuts.

SYRUP

I learned to never throw away the scraps of pears from my friend Deborah Rieth, who made this syrup every fall to top her family's pancakes all winter long. Simply gather the skins and core, add a simple syrup (50:50 water:sugar), then boil down until it's the viscosity of maple syrup. Strain the skins and cores out and store in the fridge forever or until it starts to mold.

plums

I'm a bit slow to poetry. I like reading some of it, but I have never made a habit of it like my more erudite friends. I like memorizing poems because it is hard for me. I like the austerity of the language because I tend to be long-winded. I wish I could write poetry without feeling like I'm trying too hard. I like poems that take a simple everyday occurrence and organize it into stanzas to make it shine with the heart-wrenching beauty or humor I feel in the simple moments of life.

To my mind, no poem does this better than "This Is Just to Say" by William Carlos Williams, which I always picture as a note left on the fridge for his unnamed roommates, alerting them to the fact that he has eaten the plums that were not his.

Yet, I do not find that this is the problem we most often have with fruit—that someone ate it up before we had the chance. It is often the opposite—that we buy fruit out of excitement and then it languishes in the back of the fridge. So, I've rewritten the poem (see page 344) in hope that it will inspire you to cook your roommates' forgotten fruits into compote, which is delicious, unendingly riff-able depending on what's in said fridge, and the best way to prevent the waste of forgotten fruit.

HOW TO SELECT

Look for plums that have tight skins and no obvious signs of wrinkling. Avoid plums that have gashes, damage, or rotten spots. If a plum has healed over earlier damage, it should be fine on the inside. Don't be turned off by dusty or bloomed skin; this is a natural coating on some plums and is a sign that they were picked recently and handled minimally.

SIGNS OF RIPENESS

Plums should smell fragrant and any undertones of green will have faded. They should feel heavy in the hand. The firmer the plum, generally, the less ripe. Choose a harder plum if you don't have plans to eat it within a couple of days. A ripe plum will be firm but give slightly when pushed gently with a probing thumb.

HOW TO STORE

Store at room temperature out of direct sunlight until fully ripe; storing in a paper bag to trap the naturally emitted ethylene gas will speed ripening. Once ripe, store covered in the fridge, or, ideally, eat.

NOTES

Plums range in color from pale yellow to dark, dark purple. The darker the color, the more tannic the flavor. Tarter plums are best for cooking. Supersweet plums are best for eating with no accompaniment.

RAW

As an Anglophile, I think there is nothing more romantic than taking a walk down a country lane, plucking a pocketful of plums from the hedgerow, snacking on a few in the moment, and the rest making their way back to the kitchen to be handled lightly.

savory:

buckwheat salad w/plums, cauliflower, mustard dressing + arugula

Both plums and cauliflower will weep moisture as soon as they are cut and come in contact with salt. For that reason, this is a salad best tossed together just before eating to keep the disparate textures intact. That said, the resulting pool of liquid at the bottom of the bowl—sweet plum juice and piquant mustard—is a real treat and should not be overlooked. I like this salad on its own, especially for lunch, or paired with a seared piece of fish or meat for a fancier dinner. Note: I've made this salad with fennel, kohlrabi, even jicama to replace the cauliflower, so know you have options.

½ cup [90 g] buckwheat groats

¼ cup [60 g] Dijon or whole-grain mustard

1 shallot, minced

2 Tbsp apple cider vinegar

½ cup [120 ml] olive oil

Salt and freshly ground black pepper

1 lb [455 g] plums, pits removed and cut into quarters or sixths

¼ head cauliflower (about 5 oz [140 g]), thinly shaved

4 oz [115 g] arugula

continued

Bring a medium pot of salted water to a boil over high heat. Whisk in the buckwheat groats, return to a boil, lower the heat to a simmer, and cook until tender, 12 to 15 minutes, then drain.

In a small bowl, combine the mustard, shallot, vinegar, olive oil, and a big pinch of salt and whisk to make the dressing.

Just before serving, combine all the ingredients and toss lightly with a pinch of salt and a couple grinds of black pepper. Taste and adjust the seasoning and serve immediately.

sweet:

maple pudding cake topped w/sugared plums

If plums smack of merry old England, maple pudding cake is nothing if not North American. This cake is a touch on the sweet side, so tarter plums provide a pleasing contrast. Note that the longer the plums sit with the sugar, the juicier the mixture will become, so if you like the juice, let it all hang out for at least 10 minutes. If you want firmer fruit, toss just before serving. I usually make this in individual ramekins for dinner guests, but baking in one big baking dish and scooping out portions is A-OK too. Do whatever works best for you and certainly don't not make it just because you don't have a bunch of cute ramekins.

1 lb [455 g] plums, pits removed and cut into quarters or sixths

2 Tbsp sugar

¼ tsp coarse salt

1 green cardamom pod, cracked open and seeds removed

¼ vanilla bean, thinly sliced

4 ramekins of Maple Pudding Cake (page 67), ideally still warm

1½ cups [375 ml] heavy cream, whipped

Place the plums in a large bowl.

In a small bowl, combine the sugar, salt, cardamom seeds, and vanilla bean. With your fingers, rub the sugar and spices together to bind the spice oils to the sugar/salt mixture.

Add the sugar mixture to the plums. Toss to coat and set aside.

Just before serving, top the individual maple cakes with a hefty dollop of whipped cream, then spoon the plums and some of their liquid over the whole lot. Serve immediately.

STEWED

Poaching and stewing are birds of a feather—poaching cooks the fruit in a liquid; stewing cooks the fruit in the fruit's own juices. Certainly a poached plum would be perfectly welcome in the following pleasant prescriptions.

savory:

stewed plums atop oatcakes w/ricotta

Oatcakes are the UK version of graham crackers: sweet, but not overly so, and somehow linked to good health even though they are essentially a cookie-cracker hybrid. This recipe similarly toes the line between sweet and savory, making it perfect to start a party, transition from dinner to dessert, or round out an afternoon cuppa tea or coffee.

2 lb [910 g] plums, pits removed and cut into quarters

¼ cup [60 ml] red wine

¼ cup [85 g] honey

½ tsp lavender buds

½ tsp chili flakes

Pinch of salt

4 oz [115 g] ricotta

Zest of 1 lemon

Freshly ground black pepper

12 to 24 Oatcakes (page 50)

In a medium pot, combine the plums, red wine, honey, lavender, chili flakes, and salt and cook over medium heat. Bring to a simmer, and then lower the heat to low. Stew until the plums start to fall apart, about 15 minutes. Remove from the heat.

In a medium bowl, combine the ricotta with the lemon zest and a couple grinds of black pepper.

To serve, smear the oatcakes with some ricotta and then top with the stewed plums.

sweet:

plums for breakfast: stewed plums over rice porridge + pine nuts

Rice overcooked in milk with a bit of cinnamon and raisins was my grandfather's favorite breakfast. I find it similarly pleasant. It's the sort of breakfast that feels decadent and cozy but isn't so sweet that it makes you feel gross for the rest of the day. In Michigan, my favorite plums, the very tart ones, come into season right as the mornings begin to cool way down. It's the perfect time for returning to warm breakfasts. Feel free to substitute oat or nut milk for cow dairy and preserved plums for fresh, if they are no longer in season.

4 cups [960 ml] milk

½ cup [100 g] rice

2 lb [910 g] plums, pits removed and cut into quarters

¼ cup [50 g] brown sugar

½ tsp ground ginger

1 tsp ground cinnamon

1 lemon (about 1.5 oz [45 ml]), zest and juice

Pinch of salt

¼ cup [30 g] pine nuts, toasted

In a medium pot, bring the milk and 2 cups [480 ml] of water to a scald (see page 31) over medium-high heat, then whisk in the rice. Bring to a boil, lower the heat to a simmer, and cook until the rice is overcooked and breaking down, thickening the porridge, 20 to 30 minutes.

In a separate pot, combine the plums, brown sugar, ginger, cinnamon, lemon juice and zest, and salt. Bring to a simmer over medium heat and stew until the plums start to break down, about 15 minutes.

To serve, dish the rice porridge into bowls and top with the stewed plums and a spoonful of the toasted pine nuts.

ROASTED

Plums have a more Jello-y interior than some other stone fruits like peaches and nectarines, so they will release more juice when roasted and the skins will often slip off from the flesh entirely. Either lean into that and let them get really saucy, or cut them into larger pieces and sear them cut-side down in a ripping-hot pan for less time (taking only a minute or two) to keep the fruit more intact.

savory:

ginger-plum-glazed ribs w/rye spaetzle + greens

I've taken to roasting just about everything in a big frying pan, making it easier to move from stovetop to oven and eliminating the extra dishes generated by searing and then transferring to a roasting dish. Here the frying pan does triple duty: roasting the ribs, then the plums, and finally crisping the spaetzle. The combination of fresh and candied ginger adds depth to this simple sauce, but feel free to use twice as much of one if you don't have the other.

4 to 8 pork baby back ribs depending on size (about 3 lb [1.4 kg] total)

Salt

Neutral oil

½ cup [120 ml] hard cider, or red or white wine

2 lb [910 g] tart plums, pits removed and cut into quarters

1 in [2.5 cm] fresh ginger, peeled and grated

¼ cup [30 g] candied ginger, thinly sliced

4 Tbsp (2 oz [60 g]) butter

4 cups [800 g] cooked Spaetzle (page 377)

6 oz [170 g] salad greens

1 lemon (about 1.5 oz [45 ml]), zest and juice

¼ cup [60 ml] olive oil

Freshly ground black pepper

continued

Preheat the oven to 300°F [150°C].

Season the ribs all over with salt.

In a large, ovenproof frying pan, heat a glug of neutral oil over high heat until just about smoking. Blot the pork ribs dry and sear until deeply caramelized on one side, about 5 minutes.

Flip and sear the other side, then transfer to the oven to cook until fall-apart tender, 35 to 40 minutes. When the ribs are tender, remove from the oven, transfer to a serving platter, and keep warm.

Return the frying pan to the stove top and deglaze with the hard cider over high heat, then allow the liquid to reduce by half, about 7 minutes. Pour that liquid into a bowl to reserve, then wipe the pan clean with a towel (no need to wash it yet).

Heat a glug of neutral oil in the pan over medium-high heat, then add the plums to roast. Avoid stirring until the plums have cooked a bit and are starting to release their juice, then give a good stir, flipping all the plums. Add the gingers and reserved liquid and bring to a boil. Lower to a simmer, then add the butter and stir to emulsify. Transfer the plum sauce to a bowl and reserve.

Wipe the pan out again and heat a couple of glugs of neutral oil over high heat. Add the spaetzle and pan fry until golden brown.

In a large bowl, dress the salad greens with the lemon zest and juice, olive oil, a pinch of salt, and several grinds of black pepper.

To serve, place a pork rib (or two) on each plate with a spoonful of the crisped spaetzle and a hefty ladle of the plum sauce accompanied by a pile of the greens on the side.

sweet:

blintzes w/roasted plums + hazelnuts

This is one of my favorite desserts not only because I love a tender crepe filled with sweet ricotta balanced by tart, cooked plums and the crunch of slightly bitter hazelnuts, but also because it can be made well in advance and reheated at the last minute for maximum ease.

4 oz [115 g] ricotta

1 egg

1 Tbsp sugar

Zest of 1 orange

4 Crepes (page 44)

1 lb [455 g] plums, halved and pits removed

Coarse salt

½ cup [60 g] hazelnuts, toasted, skins half removed, and roughly chopped

In a medium bowl, combine the ricotta, egg, sugar, and zest and stir to mix thoroughly.

Lay out the crepes and divide the ricotta mixture evenly among them, placing the ricotta in the center of each crepe. Fold the right and left sides of the crepe toward the center, then bring the bottom of the crepe (where the filling is) toward the top, making a little parcel. Place the crepes in a baking dish.

Turn on the broiler.

In a large, ovenproof pan, arrange the plums cut-side up and sprinkle with a hefty pinch of sugar. Broil the plums until they've taken on some color and started to soften, 4 minutes, but keep a sharp eye on them. Place the crepes in the oven on the lower shelf to warm while the plums broil.

To serve, place a warmed crepe on a plate, and then top with several broiled plums, a pinch of coarse salt, and a scattering of chopped hazelnuts.

BAKED

Plums of all varieties take well to baking. The sweet ones, lacking in sharp bite or tannic skins, gain depth as they cook with other flavors. The tart ones, with thick sour skins, mellow and lift up richer flavors that could cloy without their aid.

savory:

plum cream–baked pork shoulder w/turnip mash

This dish melds the traditional French entrée porc aux pruneaux with the classic northern Italian milk-braised pork for a deeply savory meal perfect to offset the snapping chill at the start of autumn and the end of fresh plum season. Should you want to make this and not have fresh plums, feel free to substitute prunes. It will be different, but very delicious. The only thing to note is that pork shoulders often come in a range of sizes. I find 3 lb [1.4 kg] roasts most commonly, but would be just as happy making this with a larger roast should I have one. For portioning, I assume about 8 oz [230 g] of raw meat per person, so this will reasonably serve six people or four heroically.

Neutral oil

3 lb [1.4 kg] boneless pork shoulder

Salt

¼ cup [35 g] flour

½ cup [120 ml] brandy or 1 cup [240 ml] hard cider

1 onion, thinly sliced

4 garlic cloves [30 g], minced

1 lb [455 g] plums, pits removed and cut into quarters

10 sage leaves, thinly sliced

Chili flakes (optional)

1 cup [240 ml] heavy cream

1 cup [240 ml] stock (chicken, pork, or vegetable)

1 lb [455 g] Yukon gold potatoes, cut into chunks

1 lb [455 g] turnips, cut into chunks

1 cup [240 ml] milk

4 Tbsp (2 oz [60 g]) butter

Freshly ground black pepper

Preheat the oven to 325°F [165°C].

In a large Dutch oven with a lid, heat a glug of neutral oil over medium-high heat. Season the pork all over with salt and then dredge in the flour. Sear the pork on all sides, allowing it to brown evenly, 8 to 10 minutes per side. When well browned, remove the pork from the Dutch oven and allow to rest on a plate or platter.

Deglaze the Dutch oven with the brandy over medium-low heat (beware, it might flame up). Add the onion and garlic with a pinch of salt and let soften, 7 minutes. Add the plums, sage, a pinch of chili flakes (if using), cream, and stock and stir to combine. Bring to a simmer, then return the pork (and any collected juices) to the Dutch oven. Cover and bake until the pork is fall-apart tender, upwards of 1 to 2 hours.

Meanwhile, in a large pot, boil the potatoes and turnips in salted water over medium heat until soft.

In a small saucepan, heat the milk and butter over medium-low heat.

Drain the potatoes and turnips, add the warm milk-butter mixture along with a big pinch of salt and black pepper, then mash into a coarse paste. Taste for salt and adjust as desired.

When the pork is tender, remove the pan from the oven, gently lift the pork from the pan, and let rest for 5 to 10 minutes to make it easier to handle. With an immersion blender, blend the sauce to smooth and thicken.

To serve, slice the pork into 1 in [2.5 cm] thick pieces, then either return to the sauce to serve with the potato mash on the side or divvy the potato mash among the serving plates and top with a slice of pork and a generous ladle of sauce.

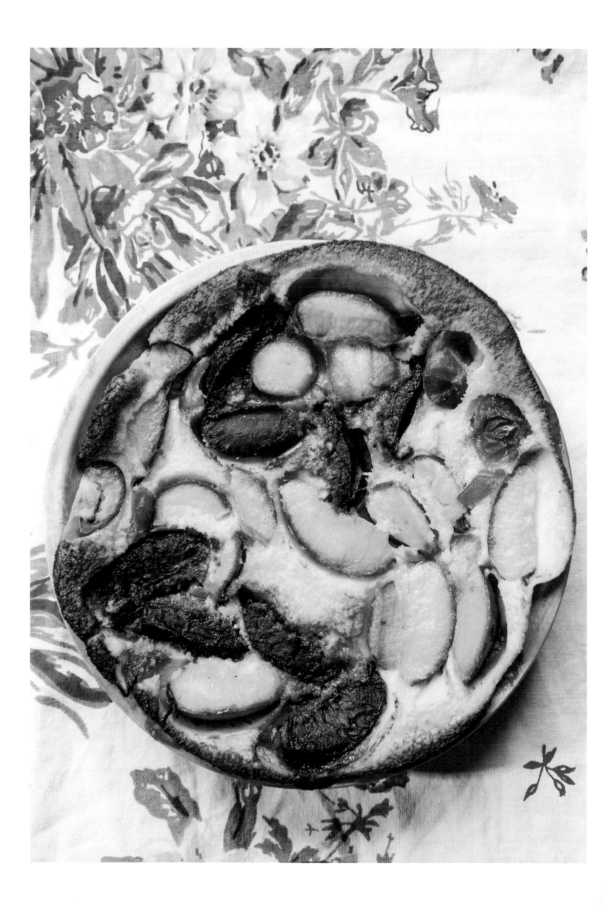

sweet: # rum-plum clafoutis

David Lebovitz introduced me to plum flaugnarde, a traditional French dessert that walks the line between custard and cake. Sandra Holl of Floriole Cafe and Bakery in Chicago opened my eyes to the idea that clafoutis could be made with more than just the traditional cherry. This dish is the happy marriage of those two inspirations.

1 lb [455 g] plums, halved and pits removed	1 recipe Clafoutis Batter (page 42), with rum replacing the brandy	2 cups [480 ml] Boozy Whipped Cream (page 91), made with rum

Preheat the oven to 400°F [200°C].

Grease an 8 in [20 cm] pie or baking tin and place the plums in it. Pour the clafoutis batter over the plums. Turn the oven down to 350°F [180°C] and bake until the batter is fully set, about 25 minutes. Allow to cool to room temperature.

To serve, slice the clafloutis and top with a heavy dollop of rum whipped cream.

PRESERVED

Plums, like most other stone fruits, preserve well. My default is plum sauce, oftentimes laden with ginger.

JAM

Jam ratio: 60:40 fruit to sugar. Find the tartest plums you can. I love Simka, Castleton, Stanley, Empress, or Damsons because of their striking dark color. Simply combine the fruit, pits removed but skins included, with the sugar and stew until the fruit is completely broken down. For a smoother jam, blend or food mill the skins; otherwise, leave chunky. Because plums have a good amount of pectin, the jam will firm up nicely when cooled.

- What isn't plum jam good on? I can't think of anything. Naturally, spread on toast slathered heavily with butter, top panna cotta, swirl into homemade ice cream, or place at the bottom of a dish of crème brûleé before baking the custard. Plums also love pork of any kind, so spoon a bit over just-roasted pork loin or grilled pork chops.

SALTED PLUMS

Like making preserved lemons, simply halve or quarter the plums, remove the pits, and then stack in a sterilized jar, sprinkling salt between each layer with enough salt to cover the plums. The salt will leach juice from the fruit, making a brine. Let the plums sit in the brine for at least a week at room temperature, shaking the jar occasionally to make sure the plums are well covered.

- Remove the plums from the brine and slice a little bit off. If it is too salty for your taste, rinse the plums, then slice thinly and add to salads or alongside seared meats and fish.

PICKLED

Choose a firmer-flesh plum for pickling, or the fruit will certainly go mushy. Use the Basic Fruit Pickle Brine (page 112) and pour over plums cut into halves or quarters and pits removed.

- Toss just-roasted parsnips with minced rosemary and transfer to a serving platter. Then dot the whole mixture with pickled plums and a drizzle of the pickling liquid.
- Add a few pickled plums to any fruit salad to give an extra layer of flavor.
- Top oatmeal with a few pickled plums and a heavy pour of maple syrup.

DRIED

Prunes get a bad rap, probably because most people think of them as a way for those of us of a certain age to get enough fiber, ensuring regularity. If you haven't eaten prunes in a while, give them a try, but just a couple. I think you'll be delighted. When I dry my own, I leave the pits in until the fruit is leathery and then pop the pits out.

- Cognac-soaked prunes are a perfect and elegant use of the fruit: Soak 1 cup [180 g] of prunes in ½ cup [120 ml] of cognac for an hour or so and then use to garnish panna cotta, ice cream, or something else creamy.
- Stuff prunes with walnuts and serve alongside blue cheese.

FREEZING

Should you want to freeze plums, I'd remove the pits but not bother peeling, and then individually freeze before transferring to a resealable bag.

just sayin'

I've stewed
the plums
that were forgotten in
the back of the icebox

and which
you had good intention of
saving
for breakfast

No need to thank me
they were imperfect
yet, not wasted

Fruit compote
such sweet
kitchen gold

quince

Quince defines the term *specialty crop* for me. It is not commonly seen at the market and I've never seen it at a grocery store. Quince is a little finicky to use. It cannot be eaten raw (it's too astringent to be palatable) and it requires long, slow cooking to render it from a tannic, rock-hard fruit into a sweet and yielding delight.

In the same family as pears and apples, quince originated in the rocky terrain of Western Asia—modern-day Armenia and Azerbaijan—but grows just about everywhere from as far north as Scotland to the hot plains of the Mediterranean. It is an old crop. The Romans wrote about it. Quince showed up on the supper tables of the members of the Ottoman Empire. Most of today's quince is grown in Turkey. In the United States, I don't know of a single farmer who grows quince at scale, though there are about 180 acres grown in California's San Joaquin Valley.

Scale is an important thing to know about when you're trying to understand a farm or agriculture as a whole. For simplicity's sake, I think of farms in three categories. Small: often less than 10 acres of cultivated land and usually selling straight to customers via farmers' markets or direct sales. Medium: anywhere from 10 to 500 acres, depending on the crop, and growing enough volume to benefit from a distributor to connect the product to the consumer. These farms often need to sell food on the lower-priced commodity market, but don't grow enough to translate volume into a meaningful income, instead relying on the specialty food market to bring in a higher price for their crops. Specialty markets are food processors such as baby food makers, juice producers, jam and jelly companies, or large distributors that can move a lot of fresh product through fresh fruit sellers like national chain grocery stores. Large: over 500 acres where crops are sold on the publicly traded commodity market and have little to no connection between the consumers and producers.

For large growers, it is all about scale. You have to be able to grow enough to make the lower per-unit price translate into financial stability. Midsize growers are the most rapidly shrinking size of American farms according to the 2017 farm census. They are often too big, growing more than the local market can support, but too small to capitalize on volume to pay the bills. Some midsize growers, like my friend and neighbor Gene Garthe (see page 350), rely on diversification to earn enough from a variety of crops to make their size work to their advantage. It's a hard row to hoe but can be done. In Gene's case, the result is a few acres of quince on a midsize tree fruit farm in Northport, Michigan, which add delicious diversity to not only his farm but also to the region as a whole.

HOW TO SELECT

Quince should be free of deep bruises or gashes and hard as a rock. A soft quince is a rotten quince.

Skin should be tight and even and will often be covered in a downy fuzz.

SIGNS OF RIPENESS

A ripe quince will be a golden yellow color, the fuzz will have dropped from the skin, and the aroma will be strong and floral.

HOW TO STORE

Store at room temperature out of direct sunlight until ripe. Store loosely and individually wrapped in cold storage to keep from ripening.

NOTES

I find quince unpalatable raw and so always plan on cooking them first. It is also full of pectin and so can be stewed down into a jelly and added to stiffen the jam or sauce of lower pectin fruit like berries. The color of cooked quince darkens the longer it is cooked—lightly poached quince will be a pale blush; long-cooked a burnished, sensual maroon.

Quince oxidize quickly after cutting, so if you need to dally between cutting and cooking, store in acidulated water (see page 29) to prevent browning.

Quince can also be interchanged with apples and pears in most baked goods. Sliding a few pieces into pies and crumbles perfumes the finished dish.

GENE GARTHE

Gene Garthe is a legacy fruit grower in Northport, Michigan. He is a poet's farmer who thinks deeply about the world and the agricultural system, including puzzling out issues of scale and diversity. I was lucky enough to be the neighbor of Gene and his wife, Kathy, when I was farming at Bare Knuckle. Together we experimented with running hogs through his fruit orchards, yielding some of the best-tasting pork I've ever had. (It helped that Kathy is an incredible cook and they both are tremendous conversationalists as hosts.) Gene also tends several acres of quince for Justin Rashid of American Spoon, a small-batch preserves company out of Petoskey, Michigan. Gene took a couple of hours to talk with me one Saturday in March of 2021.

Abra Berens: What I find so fascinating about your farm is that you are diversified not only in fruit crops but also in scale—the apples and cherries versus the quince.

Gene Garthe: Scale is critical. We just bought the Nelson Farm and so now we own 360 acres, which is a significant amount.

AB: And my understanding is that that is a midsize farm, is that correct?

GG: Yes, when I look at farm finances, we're always just about average. To operate at scale, you need to have about 100 acres. You can do it smaller, with older equipment or all hand harvesting, but that's a tough deal.

AB: And what's the breakdown of acreage by crop?

GG: Everyone asks me that; I have to think about it a second. Total acres in trees is about 170 acres. We have about 20-plus acres of apples, 8 acres of pears, 0.1 acre of quince. Wait. Did you get quince this year?

---

*AB: Yeah! I've never been able to get it before because you always sell it all to American Spoon! So when you called, I drove right over! *laughs**

GG: *laughs* Well, they are their trees! I have to sell them to them. Ha. Then about 30 acres of Balaton cherries and about 50 acres each of dark sweet and tart cherries.

AB: And how did you start growing the quince for American Spoon?

GG: Since the land is so variable, has so many different microclimates, we've found that it is best suited to different crops, and not just fruit but potentially maple syrup, cattle, and so on. The quince is a small part of our business, but when Justin couldn't find quince anywhere, he proposed that he'd buy the trees if I would grow them for him. Because the land is so expensive, unless you are producing a very high-value crop, you can't afford it. For our scale, we try to find niches in the market where we can expand the per-pound amount.

AB: When you are looking for those niche markets, is that a year-to-year decision or are you deciding and committing to it for decades at a time?

GG: Well, we have a few people that we do business with regularly—five or six products that go to the same people. But then you have to keep your mind open to new opportunities. Like a few years ago, we were doing organic. We went into it because a couple of different companies came to us looking for organic. We didn't do it because we just wanted to; you need to have a market to sell to. Suddenly we did. For organic tart cherries, it has been difficult because the company that buys them only wants them when they need them. That's not how trees work. Now this year has been different. The price for conventional tart cherries in 2019 was $0.19/lb and in 2020 was $0.50/lb, just because the demand for cherry pie filling was there. COVID actually benefited the canning companies because everyone was cooking at home. As soon as he called and said, "I'll take all of your tart cherries at $0.50/lb," I immediately took all of my tart cherries out of organic. I had a market at a good price. So that was a year-to-year decision.

AB: *And why take them out of organic? Is taking them out of organic less expensive?*

GG: It isn't so much that it is less expensive, but it is less risky. We have a really hard time producing a worm-free crop organically. The factors in the decision were 1) the risk, and 2) the fact that I didn't have a market for organic. So it was a no-brainer. Whereas organic had been a pretty good deal for us for quite a few years because we had someone buying. Montmorency tart cherries are traditionally a losing crop—always losing money. That has changed some with the use of tart cherry juice concentrate as a pharmaceutical add. When we grew them organically, the flavor was night and day better, in my opinion.

AB: *Why don't you grow apricots or peaches?*

GG: We did grow apricots. Our thinking was that we could shake them and sell them for baby food. But we couldn't get them to ripen at the same time, so that was that. Then we made the conscious decision to not go to fresh fruit. I didn't have the market and the other major part of the decision is that they come ripe right in the middle of cherry harvest, so there's a conflict there. Plus, for fresh fruit you need a whole different infrastructure—coolers, packing pads, etc. I've avoided that and decided to focus on commercial crops that can be harvested mechanically, except of course for the apples and pears.

AB: *So you were trying to leverage a big piece of equipment across different crops. How much does a cherry shaker cost?*

GG: A new one is about a quarter of a million dollars.

AB: *The costs are land, infrastructure, and time investment. What's the timeline trajectory for putting in an orchard?*

GG: Right now I'm trying to plant an old sweet cherry variety, but I'm having a hard time finding them, so I had to have them custom budded. To do that I have to commit to 1,000 trees at $10 per tree, and that will plant about 8 acres. I ordered them now, but they won't be ready for another two years. We're planting 150 trees to the acre with standard spacing, so we can harvest with a machine shaker. Before you get any kind of significant crop it will be at least five years, probably six years, from the time that they go into the ground. The pome fruits (apples, pears, and quince) are different with the transition to high-density planting—1,000 to 2,000 trees to the acre and expecting to get a crop by the third leaf.

AB: And once a tree comes into production, how long can you harvest?

GG: I have some blocks that are forty years old. That's not normal. I would say twenty-five to thirty years. It depends on how much damage you get from shaking. The older shakers were harder on the trees, so the orchards last longer with better equipment.

AB: Is the same true for pears and apples?

GG: Pears, the blocks of pears we have, I helped my dad plant when I was five years old, so that was sixty-five years ago. Then when I took over, I planted between those trees to increase the density. And we have some apple trees that are just as old.

AB: We've talked about this a bit with the quince, but how useful is that diversity in your operation—between sweet cherries, tart cherries, apples, pears, etc.?

GG: It has been a real valuable business decision. For our topography, in the low valleys, we can't plant cherries because of the frost, but the apples have done well there. The other big thing is that instead of spreading geographically, which can give us a two-week difference in harvest time, we've spread out cropwise because it gives us different outlets. We aren't dependent on one crop or one piece of equipment, or liable to breakdowns and bad timing.

AB: How do you feel about the evolution of farming in our area, when we talk about tart cherries as a loser crop—there's no market, they're hard to grow, it's labor and capital intensive? If farmers in our area transition to grapes because the wine market isn't going to decrease the way the cherry pie market has, is that a bother to you? On an emotional level?

GG: I'm not sad if the tart cherry thing goes away; I don't care if we're the cherry capital or the Riesling capital of the world. You can't justify it—I can grow them for $0.25 a pound, but I'm not making any money on them. This has been the history of the business. You know at the heart of it, I'm a capitalist. I still think Elizabeth Warren should be our president for her economic policies, but in the end, if I can't make money on a crop, it isn't worth it to grow.

BAKED

Quince, like the other pome fruits, do well baked. They are a bit drier than apples or pears and so won't release quite as much juice along the way.

savory:

midwinter pork bake

Quince comes ready between the end of bounty season, when there is so much food one can barely decide what to eat next, and the lean season, when one has to head scratch on how to make something else with the same root vegetables that have been available for months. This dish satisfies because, being a one-pot meal, it is easy enough to soothe winter fatigue but surprising enough in flavor to pique somewhat dulled interest. Note: The ingredients are infinitely swappable. Should you not have quince, use apples or pears. No rutabaga? Potatoes will fill in.

1 Tbsp salt, plus more as needed

1 Tbsp brown sugar

¼ tsp chili flakes (optional)

1 boneless pork loin roast (about 4 lb [1.8 kg])

2 lb [910 g] parsnips, peeled and cut into large chunks

2 lb [910 g] rutabaga, peeled and cut into large chunks

2 lb [910 g] quince, peeled, cored, and cut into large chunks

1 onion of any variety, cut into wide petals

1 lemon, cut into wedges and seeds removed

2 sprigs rosemary or sage (optional)

Olive oil

Freshly ground black pepper

½ cup [120 ml] brandy or whiskey

In a small bowl, combine the salt, sugar, and chili flakes (if using). Rub the pork loin all over with the salt mixture and let cure in the fridge for at least 1 hour or overnight.

Preheat the oven to 350°F [180°C].

In a large bowl, toss the parsnips, rutabaga, quince, onion, lemon, and rosemary (if using) in a big glug of olive oil, a pinch of salt, and several grinds of black pepper. Transfer to a baking dish.

Pour the brandy and a ½ cup [120 ml] of water into the baking dish and nestle the pork loin on top. Bake, uncovered, until the pork reaches an internal temperature of 140°F [60°C] and the parsnips, rutabaga, and quince are tender when pierced with a knife, 60 to 80 minutes.

Remove from the oven and let rest for at least 15 minutes, then lift the pork loin from the baking dish and slice into ¼ to ½ in [6 to 12 mm] pieces.

Discard the herb stems and serve alongside a big green salad with a very tart dressing, if you like.

sweet: crumble-topped quince

Lindsay Zamora is a truly wonderful cook with whom I was fortunate enough to work for a few years. One of my favorite things she ever made were oatmeal baked apples, which she described dryly as "an apple cut in half and topped with raw granola that you then bake." She undervalued their deliciousness. This is my version of Lindsay's dish, which, if given the chance, I'm sure she would make better than I do because she glides. Come to think of it, quince is a bit like Lindsay—its mere presence enhances just about any baked good.

2 to 4 quince (allow for half a quince per person, but since the oven is on, bake some extra for leftovers)	1 Tbsp butter per quince half 1 Tbsp honey	¼ cup [30 g] Crumble Topping (page 76) per quince half ¼ cup [60 g] sour cream per quince half

Preheat the oven to 350°F [180°C].

Halve the fruit by cutting around the equator (as opposed to from tip to tail) and scoop out the seeds. Place the fruit, cut-side up, in a baking dish and top with the butter and honey. Fill the dish with enough water to reach ½ in [12 mm] up the side of the baking dish, cover with aluminum foil, and bake until the quince is soft and golden, about 1 hour. Remove from the oven, drain away any excess water, then top with the crumble topping and return to the oven to bake, uncovered, until the topping is golden brown and crunchy, about 20 minutes.

Serve with a dollop of cold sour cream on top.

STEWED

As already stated, quince requires a long cook time to make it at all pleasant to eat. Enter slow cooking, the amiable alchemy of time and heat along with other ingredients that requires some patience to come into their best selves.

savory:

quince + lamb tagine

Quince, chickpeas, and lamb shanks are staples of North African, specifically Moroccan, cuisine, and benefit from long, slow cooking. So here they are, all together, for a low-labor, high-flavor meal. I've also made this skipping the lamb shanks altogether with good result.

Neutral oil

4 lamb shanks (about 6 lb [2.7 kg])

Salt

½ tsp ground ginger

1 tsp ground cinnamon

3 whole star anise

2 green cardamom pods

1 Tbsp sweet paprika

1 onion, thinly sliced

4 garlic cloves [30 g], peeled and smashed

1 cup [180 g] dried chickpeas, soaked overnight

2 quince, cored and cut into chunks

1 orange, cut into chunks

5 sprigs parsley, roughly chopped

1 lemon (about 1.5 oz [45 ml]), zest and juice

¼ cup [60 ml] olive oil

Preheat the oven to 300°F [150°C].

In a large, ovenproof Dutch oven, heat a glug of neutral oil over medium heat. Season the lamb shanks all over with salt, then sear until deeply browned on all sides, lowering the heat as needed, about 5 minutes per side. Remove the shanks from the pot and lower the heat to low, add the spices, and briefly fry in the lamb fat until fragrant, about 30 minutes. Add the onion and garlic with a big pinch of salt and sweat until starting to soften, about 4 minutes. Add the chickpeas, quince, and orange and stir to combine.

continued

Return the shanks to the Dutch oven and nestle into the other ingredients. Add 4 cups [960 ml] of water, increase the heat to bring to a boil, then remove from the heat, cover, and place in the oven. Braise until the lamb, chickpeas, and quince are all tender, about 2 hours.

Meanwhile, in a small bowl, combine the parsley, lemon zest and juice, olive oil, and a big pinch of salt to make a chunky rig (see page 30).

Serve with a hefty spoonful of the parsley rig.

sweet: # cream-stewed quince w/oatcakes

Cream works well for stewing because it has a lower protein content than milk, meaning that it won't curdle over a long cooking. The addition of water keeps the cream from reducing into an excessively thick and gloppy mess. The oatcakes, while not technically essential, are here for texture, and the honey flavor pairs well with the rosewater and lemon.

2 quince, peeled, cored, and cut into 1 in [2.5 cm] wide pieces

1 cup [240 ml] heavy cream

2 Tbsp honey

Pinch of salt

1 tsp rosewater or orange-flower water

Zest of 1 lemon

1 recipe Oatcakes (page 50) (optional)

Place the quince in a large saucepan where they fit snuggly in a single layer. Add 1 cup [240 ml] of water, the cream, honey, and salt. Bring to a simmer over medium-high heat, then lower the heat to low. Cover with a cartouche (see page 29), or slightly skewed potlid, and simmer until the quince starts to soften, about 20 minutes. Add the rosewater and lemon zest and simmer until the quince is pale pink and fully tender, an additional 10 to 15 minutes.

Serve warm with a hearty ladle of cream sauce and a plate of oatcakes, if desired.

POACHED

The smaller you cut quince, like anything, the faster it will cook. With the speed comes the increased risk that the fruit will fall apart during cooking. Cut quince is fairly sturdy, so while overcooked fruit shouldn't be much of an issue, it's still good to be aware.

savory:

sunday at the pub

This dish is more of a dinner party stunner than a quick, Monday night go-to. The combination of luscious poached quince, juicy medium-rare duck breast, crispy duck fat-fried potatoes, and the acidic hit of the hazelnut-orange relish is worth the effort. That said, you can poach the quince ahead of time and store it in the cooking liquid for at least a week, making a bit less to do on the given evening. The poaching liquid is delicious as a pre-dinner cocktail cut with some soda water (and a splash of gin, if you're so inclined).

2 cups [480 ml] dry white wine

2 Tbsp honey

¼ cup [60 ml] apple cider vinegar

1 to 2 quince, peeled, cored, and cut into 1 in [2.5 cm] wide pieces

½ cup [60 g] hazelnuts, toasted and skins half rubbed off

1 orange (about 3 oz [90 ml]), zest and juice

¼ cup [60 ml] red wine or sherry vinegar

¼ cup [60 ml] olive oil

Salt and freshly ground black pepper

4 duck breasts (about 20 oz [600 g] total), skin on

2 lb [910 g] potatoes, cut into cubes and boiled until tender

In a medium pot over high heat, combine the wine, honey, and apple cider vinegar and bring to a boil. Lower the heat to a simmer, then slip the quince into the liquid and poach the quince until they are pale pink and tender, about 20 minutes.

Meanwhile, roughly chop or smash the toasted hazelnuts.

In a medium bowl, add the hazelnuts, orange zest and juice, red wine vinegar, olive oil, and a big pinch of salt to make a chunky rig (see page 30).

Score the skin of the duck breast into thin lines or a diamond pattern (this allows the fat to render from under the skin, crisping the skin as it cooks) and then season all over with salt.

In a large frying pan, place the duck breasts, skin-side down, and turn the heat on to medium (starting the cooking in a cold pan allows the fat to melt evenly—a hot pan will cause the skin to burn before the fat has fully melted). Sear the duck breast until the fat is completely rendered and the skin is crispy and golden brown, about 8 minutes. Flip the duck breast to cook the flesh side to medium-rare, about 2 minutes. Remove the breasts from the pan and let rest for at least 7 minutes.

Add the potatoes to the hot duck fat with a big pinch of salt and several grinds of black pepper.

Fry the potatoes until they are crispy and golden brown, about 4 minutes, stirring after a few minutes to brown evenly.

To serve, divvy the potatoes among four dinner plates. Add a few pieces of quince, a duck breast, and a hefty spoonful of the hazelnut-orange relish to each plate. I also like a pile of bitter greens or spinach salad on the side, but up to you.

sweet: oeufs à la coing

Oeufs à la neige, the French dessert of poached meringue in custard, is a real thing. Poached quince is a thing. *Coing* is French for *quince*. So, logic goes that meringue poached along with quince would be a thing. It just didn't have a name yet, so I made one up. Note: You can make this with dry white wine too. Just increase the honey to ½ cup [170 g].

2 cups [480 ml] sweet wine such as late-harvest Riesling or Moscato d'Asti

2 Tbsp orange-flower water or rosewater

¼ cup [85 g] honey

1 lemon (about 1.5 oz [45 ml]), zest and juice

2 to 4 quince, peeled, cored, and cut into 1 in [2.5 cm] wide pieces

1 recipe Meringue (page 99)

½ cup salty pistachios (see page 78)

In a medium pot, combine the wine, orange-flower water, honey, and lemon zest and juice. Bring to a simmer over medium heat, then slip in the quince, lower the heat, and poach at a gentle simmer until tender and starting to turn pink, about 20 minutes. With a slotted spoon or spider, lift the quince from the poaching liquid.

Bring a fresh pot of water to a medium simmer and spoon big dollops of meringue into the simmering water. Cook until the meringues are firm, about 2 minutes.

To serve, divvy the quince among serving bowls, then top with a meringue, a big spoonful of the poaching syrup, and a generous sprinkling of salty pistachios.

PRESERVED

Quince last a good long time—longer than pears, not as long as apples—and so quince preserves end up in the "I make them because I want to eat them, not just to hold onto the fruit" category of preserves for me.

JELLY

Membrillo, Spanish for *quince jelly*, is probably the most well-known quince preserve. Unlike other jams, membrillo is cooked down to a thick paste and then set in a mold and sliced like Jell-O you can eat with your fingers. Classically, it is served alongside sheep milk cheese like Manchego and salty, dry-cured olives. I like it to top Chicken Liver Mousse (page 218) for an appetizer or lunch.

I use a 70:30 ratio of uncooked fruit to sugar, usually 4 lb [1.8 kg] of quince and 1¾ cups [350 g] of sugar. Peel, core, and chop the quince into chunks, then transfer to a pot and cover with cold water. Bring to a boil, lower the heat to a simmer, and cook until the quince is soft, about 25 minutes. Drain and then mash. Add the sugar and return to the heat. Cook over low heat, stirring regularly, until most of the moisture has evaporated and the mixture looks dry and deep red. Remove from the heat, taste, and add a splash of lemon or vinegar if it tastes too sweet. Cool in an oiled mold (a bread loaf or bowl) and then chill. When fully cool, turn out of the mold and slice to serve. Store covered in the fridge for up to a year.

PICKLED

Quince does well both in the Basic Fruit Pickle Brine (page 112) and in the more savory Traditional Pickle Liquid (page 113), though, if push came to shove, I'd prefer to use the Basic Fruit Pickle Brine made with sherry vinegar. I love the balance of sherry vinegar's wood-barrel flavor with a bit of sweetness but not as much caramel flavor as balsamic vinegar. I generally poach or roast the quince first and then top with the pickle brine, but it would make it a one-pot go if you poached the quince in the pickle brine itself. In short, there are options.

Uses: anywhere you might want a hit of tartness to counterbalance rich, wintery foods, or alongside seared pork chops or any sort of red meat or game bird. I also really love a small dice of pickled quince on top of roasted roots such as carrots, parsnips, and celeriac.

SYRUP

More often than not, quince syrup (or cordial) is the by-product of poaching quince in a sweet syrup. Instead of pouring the syrup down the drain, it can be bottled and stored in refrigeration for upwards of 6 months (or really as long as it still tastes good to you). Use the recipe for the sweet poached quince (page 364) or simply combine 4 cups [960 ml] of water, ¾ cup [180 ml] of honey (or 50:50 honey to maple syrup), and a pinch of salt and poach whatever volume of quince you have on hand. Use the poached quince elsewhere and save this gloriously pink syrup.

quince gin fizz

2 oz [60 ml] gin

¾ oz [22 ml] lemon juice

¾ oz [22 ml] quince syrup

1 egg white

2 oz [60 ml] soda water

Pour the gin, lemon juice, syrup, and egg white into a cocktail shaker and fill with ice.

Shaky, shaky for 30 seconds and then pour over ice and top with the soda water.

rhubarb

"Oh, I just love rhubarb!"

"You know, rhubarb is a vegetable. Just sayin'."

I find the phrase *just sayin'* to be one of the most feckless combinations of words to come into vogue. To employ this phrase is to make a point by way of declaration, but with complete and utter inaction; just sayin', yet doing nothing more.

Yes, rhubarb is technically a vegetable. It was declared classifiable as a fruit in 1947 by a New York court because it is most commonly used in the same way as fruit. It has been used medicinally in China and across Asia for thousands of years. It arrived in Europe in the fourteenth century, transported along the Silk Road, and was more valued than other imported luxuries like saffron, satins, jewels, and spices. Europeans began cultivating rhubarb as a way to increase supply. Increased abundance, in tandem with the decreasing cost of sugar produced on colonized land with enslaved labor, moved rhubarb from the medicine cabinet to the kitchen cupboard.

In the kitchen, I use it as an acidic foil, contrasting against buttery cakes or lusciously fatty roasts. It can be left raw in thinly sliced stalks as a bracing sour crunch. It can be stewed down into velvet strands layered into pillowy cream puffs. It can be baked underneath a whole chicken, giving punch to the comfiest of comforts. Rhubarb is a delight, a favorite no matter how you classify it, and that is all that needs to be said.

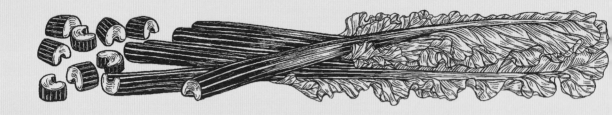

HOW TO SELECT

Look for stalks that are firm, not limp, with tight, even skin. Puckering or divots indicate loss of moisture either from age or improper storing.

SIGNS OF RIPENESS

Rhubarb doesn't really ripen, so there's not much to look for here. The color of the rhubarb has nothing to do with ripeness, nor does it change the flavor. Instead, it is specific to that variety. The color will carry through to the finished dish, so if you are craving bright red on the plate, seek it out at the market. If cutting rhubarb from a plant, wait until the stalks are at least 10 in [25 cm] long, ensuring that the plant has gotten enough sunlight through the leaves to not set it back when taking the stalks along with the leaves.

HOW TO STORE

Keep it in the fridge, wrapped in newspaper or plastic, to keep it from evaporating moisture through its stalks. If you have rhubarb with the leaves still attached, cut them away before storing.

NOTES

Rhubarbs are sun-loving perennials, so if you have outdoor space, grow the crown in plenty of light and in well-drained and fertile soil.

To harvest, simply cut or tug away the long stalks, never harvesting more than half the available stalks. Remember, rhubarb leaves are poisonous when eaten in quantity.

RAW

The first time I had raw rhubarb, it felt as against convention as eating raw beef and egg in steak tartare. Similar to lemon, raw rhubarb is mouth-puckeringly tart, so it's perfect to brighten up rich flavors. Either shave the long stalks to make thin ribbons for texture or blend into a paste if the long strands are distracting. Soaking the rhubarb ribbons in acidulated water (see page 29) will cause them to curl like real ribbon.

savory:

poached salmon w/rhubarb salad + pine nut relish

This dish is all about contrasts: buttery salmon, the crunch of rhubarb and fennel, peppery arugula, and the singular fatty texture of pine nuts. Fish can be poached in plain water or stock but fortifying the liquid with aromatics adds depth of flavor. Just don't let it deter you if you don't have any on hand. If doubling this recipe for a larger party, it may be easier to slow cook the salmon side rather than poach it. To do so, simply bake on a parchment-lined baking sheet, skin-side down, at 300°F [150°C] until cooked through, about 40 minutes. Then lift the fish from the parchment, leaving the skin (that probably stuck anyway) behind.

1 onion (about 8 oz [230 g]), cut into chunks

4 stalks celery (about 8 oz [230 g]), cut into chunks

3 bay leaves

5 sprigs thyme

1 Tbsp salt

4 fillets of salmon or one full side, skin on (about 2 lb [910 g] total)

4 Tbsp (2 oz [60 g]) butter

One 10 in [25 cm] long stalk rhubarb

1 head fennel (about 5 oz [140 g])

1 lemon (about 1.5 oz [45 ml]), zest and juice

½ cup [120 ml] olive oil, plus more as needed

¼ cup [30 g] pine nuts, toasted and roughly chopped

1 small shallot, minced

10 sprigs parsley

4 oz [115 g] arugula

continued

In a medium pot, place the onion, celery, bay leaves, thyme, and salt evenly across the bottom.

Lay the fish fillets, skin-side down, on top. Add enough water to the pot to just cover the fish fillets, then dot with the butter. Over medium heat, bring the poaching liquid to a simmer and then remove from the heat. Leave the fish in the liquid to carry over cooking until just cooked through, about 7 minutes, depending on the thickness of the fish. The fish will start to leach the white albumin from between the muscle layers. Lift the fish from the poaching liquid and gently peel the skin away.

Meanwhile, slice the rhubarb and fennel very thinly with a sharp knife or mandoline. Immediately dress with the lemon zest and juice, and a big glug of olive oil.

In a small bowl, combine the pine nuts, shallot, olive oil, and parsley with a big pinch of salt and stir to mix.

Drain the fennel and rhubarb, then toss with the arugula, a big glug of olive oil, and pinch of salt to coat.

To serve, top the fish with the salad and spoon the pine nut relish all over.

sweet:

parsnip panna cotta w/rhubarb, orange + olive oil relish

While I normally advocate for turning panna cotta out of its container to reveal its unapologetic jiggle, this is one time I prefer it served in a glass or jar. This dessert can be made with a traditional panna cotta recipe, but infusing the scalded cream with parsnip is next-level.

1 recipe Panna Cotta (page 84)

1 lb [455 g] parsnips, peeled and cut into chunks

One 10 in [25 cm] stalk rhubarb, cut into chunks

2 Tbsp sugar

2 oranges (6 oz [180 ml] total), zest and segments

¼ cup [60 ml] olive oil

Pinch of salt

¼ cup [30 g] candied almonds (see page 75)

When scalding (see page 31) the cream for the panna cotta, add the parsnip chunks and let infuse for 20 minutes, then strain before adding the sugar, milk, and gelatin.

In a food processor, blend the rhubarb, sugar, and orange zest into a paste, adding 1 Tbsp of water if needed.

In a medium bowl, dress the orange segments, and any juice, with the olive oil and salt.

To serve, spoon the rhubarb–orange zest paste on top of the panna cotta. Spoon the orange segments on top of the rhubarb paste and garnish with the candied almonds.

POACHED

Rhubarb can be poached in large batches and holds well in the fridge for ages, so there are very few reasons to not make it in quantity. The strings in rhubarb help it hold its shape during the poaching, so don't peel or string and avoid stirring to keep the pieces of rhubarb intact.

savory:
pork chops w/rye spaetzle, white wine–poached rhubarb + spinach

This recipe makes more spaetzle than you probably need for four people, but making spaetzle can be a bit of a project, and it freezes well. So, I make the full batch, serve what I want on the day, and pop the rest into the freezer for another time. When using from frozen, simply pull the container from the freezer and let thaw in the fridge overnight before using just as you would fresh spaetzle.

2 cups [480 ml] dry white wine	1 stalk lemon verbena (optional)	4 pork chops (about 2 lb [910 g])
½ cup [170 g] honey	3 cups [750 g] sour cream	Neutral oil
Salt	5 eggs	4 oz [115 g] spinach
1 lb [455 g] rhubarb, cut into 2 in [5 cm] pieces	4½ cups [500 g] rye flour, or all-purpose or buckwheat flour	Freshly ground black pepper

In a medium pot, bring the wine, honey, and ½ tsp of salt to a boil. Add the rhubarb and lemon verbena (if using), then lower the heat to a simmer and poach until the rhubarb is tender but not mushy, about 15 minutes.

In a large bowl, whisk together the sour cream and eggs until well combined. Add the flour and stir vigorously to combine into a thick batter.

continued

Bring a large pot of salted water to a boil. Lower the heat to a simmer and line a baking sheet with parchment paper or drizzle with oil. Place a colander over the simmering water and smear the spaetzle batter through the holes, letting it drip into the simmering water. When the spaetzle are cooked through, about 30 to 60 seconds (they'll float and look "cooked"), lift from the water with a slotted spoon and let cool on the baking sheet. Continue making the spaetzle in batches until you've worked through all of the batter.

Season the pork chops liberally with salt. In a large frying pan, heat a glug of neutral oil over high heat until smoking. Blot the pork chops dry and then sear on one side until well browned, 5 to 6 minutes. Flip and sear the other side, then remove to a plate to rest. Without degreasing the pan, add 1 cup [150 g] of spaetzle per person (more or less) and crisp in the pork fat until golden brown, about 2 minutes.

In a large bowl, dress the spinach with a glug of olive oil, pinch of salt, and grind of pepper.

To serve, divvy the crisped spaetzle among four plates and top with a pork chop, a couple of pieces of poached rhubarb, and a handful of the dressed spinach.

sweet: # rhubarb cream puffs

For dessert, I like to poach rhubarb in a heavy syrup, but if you've made a large batch of wine-poached rhubarb (see page 377), it will work just as well. This is my favorite flavor combination, but poached rhubarb is equally at home over a butter cake or as a garnish over yogurt and granola in the morning.

2 cups [480 ml] Citrus Syrup (page 110) or Marigold Syrup (page 111)	1 lb [455 g] rhubarb, cut into 2 in [5 cm] lengths 4 baked Cream Puffs (page 55)	2 cups [480 ml] Pastry Cream (page 85) or whipped cream Powdered sugar

In a medium pot, bring the marigold syrup to a boil over high heat. Add the rhubarb and lower the heat to a simmer. Poach until the rhubarb is tender but not mushy, about 15 minutes. Remove from the heat and allow to cool.

To serve, fill each cream puff with ½ cup [120 ml] of the pastry cream and top with three or four pieces of rhubarb and a drizzle of the syrup. Place the lid of the cream puff on top and dust with powdered sugar.

BAKED

As rhubarb bakes, it tends to collapse, yielding its structure into a pool of tart. Read: Controlling moisture content is definitely a consideration. If making something like a crisp or pie, a thickening agent will do the trick. I've highlighted two recipes here that absorb rhubarb's copious juices and will be better off for it.

savory: ## rhubarb one-pan chicken w/kale + poppy seed salad

I have a real deficiency when it comes to giving good recipes cheeky, hashtaggable names. (Insert shruggy shoulder emoji.) Chicken over bread doesn't really convey the beauty of this one-pan, complexly flavored, more-than-the-sum-of-its-parts dish, but it is all of those things. It is also one of my top dishes of all times. I hope you'll give it a whirl. Note: You can double your rhubarb and double your fun by taking ¼ cup [60 ml] of rhubarb (or any tart jam) and thinning it with a couple of tablespoons of water or vinegar to make a glaze and then brushing that over the chicken as it roasts. It isn't strictly necessary (very little is), but it is extra nice should you already have jam on hand.

1 whole chicken (about 4 lb [1.8 kg] total), cut into quarters

Salt

Neutral oil

1 cup [240 ml] hard cider or white wine

1 onion (about 8 oz [230 g]), thinly sliced

4 garlic cloves, roughly chopped

4 cups [120 g] cubed bread (any type, including sourdough, cornbread, milk bread, or a mix)

8 oz [230 g] rhubarb, cut into 1 in [2.5 cm] pieces

2 cups [480 ml] chicken stock or water

¼ cup [60 ml] apple cider vinegar

3 Tbsp sugar

2 Tbsp poppy seeds

1 Tbsp mayonnaise

1 tsp Dijon mustard

4 oz [115 g] baby kale or 10 leaves adult dino kale

4 radishes (about 2 oz [55 g]), thinly sliced

Freshly ground black pepper

Preheat the oven to 400°F [200°C].

Season the chicken all over with salt.

In a large, ovenproof frying pan, heat a glug of neutral oil over medium-high heat. Blot the skin of the chicken dry and then sear, skin-side down, until golden brown, 5 to 7 minutes, turning the chicken as needed to ensure good contact and even browning on the skin.

When the skin is thoroughly browned, remove the chicken from the pan and set aside.

Lower the heat to medium, deglaze the pan with the hard cider, and allow the hard cider to reduce by half. Add the onion, garlic, and a big pinch of salt and let sweat until softened, 3 to 4 minutes. Add the bread, rhubarb, and stock to the pan, then lay the chicken, skin-side up, on top. Place the frying pan in the oven and bake until the chicken is cooked through and the stock has evaporated by half, 25 to 30 minutes.

Meanwhile, in a medium container with a lid, combine the vinegar, sugar, and ¾ tsp of salt and whisk to dissolve. Add ½ cup [120 ml] of neutral oil and the poppy seeds, mayonnaise, and mustard and shake until the dressing is emulsified. Re-shake as needed to bring back together.

Just before serving, dress the kale and sliced radishes with ¼ cup [60 ml] of the poppy seed dressing, a pinch of salt, and a couple grinds of black pepper.

To serve, dish up a piece of chicken and a big scoop of the baked bread and rhubarb mixture. Pile a big handful of the kale salad on top.

sweet:

rhubarb upside-down cake w/ whipped cream + salty nuts

This buttery cake will absorb a good deal of the rhubarb's cooking juices but expect it to be a bit juicer than a traditional pineapple upside-down cake. The addition of a bit of cornstarch helps keep it from being a complete and total mess.

1 lb [455 g] rhubarb, cut into ½ in [12 mm] pieces

¼ cup [35 g] cornstarch

½ cup [100 g] granulated sugar

4 Tbsp (2 oz [60 g]) butter, melted

½ cup [100 g] brown sugar

1 recipe Upside-Down Cake Batter (page 68)

2 cups [480 ml] Whipped Cream (page 91)

½ cup [60 g] salty pecans (see page 78)

Preheat the oven to 350°F [180°C]. Butter a 9 in [23 cm] cake pan and line with a round of parchment paper.

In a large bowl, combine the rhubarb, cornstarch, and granulated sugar.

In a separate bowl, combine the melted butter and brown sugar, stirring until the brown sugar dissolves.

Pour the butter–brown sugar mixture into the prepared cake pan. Spoon the rhubarb mixture evenly into the pan. Top with the cake batter, ensuring that the rhubarb is entirely covered. Bake until the cake is golden brown and the knife test (see page 30) comes out clean when inserted into the center, about 30 minutes. Allow the cake to cool for 10 minutes and then loosen the edges and invert onto a serving platter. If any of the rhubarb mixture stays behind in the pan, simply spoon it back into place.

To serve, cut into wedges and top with a hefty dollop of whipped cream and a sprinkling of salty pecans.

PRESERVED

Rhubarb preserves like a champ, which is great because it has such a short season at the very beginning of spring.

JAM

Because rhubarb collapses so much when cooked, I usually assume a 2:1 ratio of rhubarb to sugar when making jam. Combine the cut rhubarb, sugar, and a pinch of salt in a heavy-bottomed, nonreactive pan and stew until the mixture reaches 220°F [105°C].

- Use anywhere you would use cooked rhubarb—to fill cream puffs, to make an upside-down cake, or to top a sweeter cake such as angel food, brown butter pound cake, or cornbread.
- Thin ½ cup [115 g] of rhubarb jam with ½ cup [120 ml] of water and use to glaze a roast chicken.
- Serve alongside richer cuts of meat such as roast lamb, pork chops, or chicken liver mousse.
- Pair with cheese on a cheese board or for a cheese course.
- Mix 50:50 with whole-grain mustard to use on sandwiches or alongside charcuterie.

rhubarb meringue pie

Make rhubarb curd with the Tart Fruit Curd recipe on page 95.

Blind-bake a pie shell using the recipe on page 60.

Fill the baked pie shell with the rhubarb curd. Tap the whole pie to encourage the curd to settle and to pop any air bubbles.

Top with soft Meringue (page 99).

To serve, burn the meringue with a blowtorch or under the broiler. I take it pretty dark, so don't be shy.

JUICE

Rhubarb juice is made quickly by whizzing up stalks of raw rhubarb in a blender or food processor and then straining the solids away. The resulting juice is great in place of lemon for lemonade or in sorbets and freezes perfectly.

rhubarb shrub

Use 2 cups [480 ml] of rhubarb juice and combine with 1 cup [240 ml] of white wine vinegar and 1 cup [200 g] of sugar. Stir until the sugar is dissolved. Use to spritz up sparkling water or as a base for a cocktail.

PICKLED

Because rhubarb can taste almost vegetal, I treat it like a savory pickle instead of a sweet fruit pickle and use poached rhubarb where I would pickled berries. To protect the rhubarb's structure, pour the hot pickle liquid over the cut stalks, but avoid bringing them to a boil. I also often cut rhubarb for pickling very thin, about an ⅛ in [4 mm]. Thicker often feels like a chore to chew.

- Add to grain or green salads for an extra hit of acidity.
- Serve alongside richer charcuterie or use to brine pork loin or chicken before cooking.

FREEZING

Because rhubarb is very dry as a raw ingredient, it does not need to be frozen as individual pieces. I usually just slice the stalks into ½ to 1 in [12 to 25 mm] pieces, place into a sealable bag, and freeze.

strawberries

Strawberry season looms large in the northern Midwest. Strawberries come on fast and head out just as quickly; you blink, you miss them. While they are here, their soft curves and sweet juices whisper assurances of hot nights and desserts cooled in a pool of icy cream.

Promise is so enticing because it isn't a guarantee. Unfulfilled potential lurks around the edges of expectation. Life's too short to cooperate. Vows are sometimes no more than wishes.

One year, the disappointment started with the strawberries. More accurately, it started with the unending spring rain, which bloated the red jewels, diluting their flavor and stretching their cells, making bruising and rot an almost near certainty. They simply tasted average, indistinguishable from the grocery store berries of winter. All the hopes we thrust upon the strawberries' gentle shoulders flitted away. It just wasn't a great year for berries, and since strawberries are fickle and best enjoyed unadorned, there was little to do. Nothing to hide behind: strawberries' charms are also their downfall.

That's the danger of the Delicious Movement—trumpeting local, seasonal produce as only better because of flavor alone. Sometimes, through no fault of the farmer, the strawberries suck. The other benefits of buying locally—money maintained in the regional economy, lowered carbon impact from not shipping such perishable items—hold true no matter the perfectness of the product. At the end of the day, these crops are still agricultural products whose quality reflects that year's growing season. They are not always the prize we crave.

But sometimes they are. The gambler's hope lives on.

HOW TO SELECT

Strawberries should be evenly colored and have tight, shiny skin. Avoid berries with puckered skin or with coloring that has faded to a bluish purple overtone. The size of the berry doesn't affect flavor as much as ripeness, though smaller berries tend to ripen more evenly.

SIGNS OF RIPENESS

Look for berries that appear to be red from the inside out. Underripe berries will show white underneath the red exterior. Overripe berries will have a more maroon coloring. Ripe strawberries will also be very fragrant.

HOW TO STORE

Strawberries don't store well, so buy in smaller quantities and eat them up. Store in the fridge if you won't eat them within a day or two. Just be sure to let them come back to room temperature before eating—cold dampens the aroma and flavor.

NOTES

Most strawberries are seasonal—ripened and harvested in a short window. There are everbearing varieties that continue to flower and set fruit throughout the season.

Excessive rain will dilute the flavor of strawberries and make them more prone to spoiling, so if you have had a lot of rain before buying berries, don't be surprised or disappointed.

Fraise des bois are the highly coveted, tiny, wild strawberries. If you see them, snap them up, notwithstanding the high price tag.

ROSALINDA GUILLEN

Rosalinda Guillen, daughter of immigrant farm laborers, is the founder of Community to Community. She represents farmworkers in the legislatures of California and Washington State and in ongoing policy- and movement-building dialogues on immigration issues, climate change, labor rights, trade agreements, ecofeminism, and strengthening the food sovereignty movement toward a solidarity economy.

Abra Berens: I'm fascinated by the idea of all of the "invisible workers" along our food chain, folks that the general public doesn't interact with. Most people know that crops are produced by migrant laborers, often Latino, but don't know much about that community. What does a year in the life look like?

Rosalinda Guillen: Yes, migrant workers are often not seen, and the hardships of that work often go unrecognized or unaddressed. My father was a migrant farmworker in this country from when he was ten years old. He used to move from Texas to Michigan and Wisconsin to pick fruit, cherries specifically, and then on to North Dakota to harvest potatoes, and then back to Texas. Those migration patterns are old but are changing now, especially due to climate change. Many families are settling in the northern states because the southern ones are just getting too hot to grow some of the crops they specialize in—berries mostly, especially blackberries and raspberries.

For migrating workers, it is a constant search for work. They have three to five farmers whom they know, either through word of mouth or local relationships, who will give them work at certain times of the season and that they can go back to year after year. Keep in mind, none of that work is guaranteed. Once the peak season for one grower is over, they jump into the peak season for the next crop.

There are sometimes gaps in that work and families have to decide whether to find more work in those gaps or use the time to rest. Most farmworkers don't see their families much in the summer because they are working all the time. After harvest time, it is often family time.

When the winter sets in, they're on to field maintenance: pruning, thinning, etc. All of this depends on their reserve, how much they've earned. That's their goal, to earn enough to survive the winter.

If the reserve isn't enough, they will find other work in the gaps to make it through—the seafood industry, flower industry, even the service industry. The father might have a job cutting fish at a fish processing plant, and the mother is working at a hotel laundry. Then they move out of that and back to field work. It used to be that in the gaps, families would travel home to Mexico to see their extended families, spend the month of Christmas together, and then return, but they can't do that anymore because of all of the troubles at the border and immigration issues. That's basically the year.

AB: Why is this population in need of organization and protection?

RG: Simply, these workers don't have a ton of leverage in the system. Community to Community is dedicated to addressing the reason the direct services are needed in the first place: lack of living wages, health care, child care, and decent housing.

We do a lot of work to support workers with injuries. There is a lot of injury in field work. I've always believed that small family farmers should be able to come together to purchase a medical plan to ensure basic access to health care across farms.

One of the hardest parts about farm work is child care. Schools are not in session and so, in reality, a lot of those kids are in the fields with their parents. It is a myth that children are not working in American fields. The families can earn more money if there are more hands harvesting, and most of the time there's no child care available or it isn't affordable. If there is child care it is often for the very young, infants up to maybe four years old. Between ages seven to twelve they go to the fields. Better wages would provide better options.

In Washington State, Familias Unidas para Justicia [the local farm union that came out of our work] just managed to get through a piece of legislation that removes the exemption for overtime for agriculture. By 2024, all farmworkers in the state of Washington will receive overtime for work over forty hours a week, which is pretty amazing and opens up options for things like child care.

AB: I bet the public doesn't know that agricultural workers are not entitled to overtime. Is the argument that it is such seasonal work, that there is a need for more work in the summer and not in the winter, and so the labor would even out over the course of the year?

RG: That's one of the rationales, but also the players argue that the market doesn't provide enough for the farmers to pay higher wages or afford to provide benefits. That's been the constant argument that the "special circumstances" of agriculture—seasonality, low prices—should be exempt from the benefits and protections that other workers in the United States get. That just doesn't make sense to us.

AB: Talk of raising wages always leads to conversation about raising prices and that we can't just make food more expensive because it precludes access. What do you think about that?

RG: That's been an ongoing discussion with the progressive parts of the food movement. When you look at what it takes to get this food to the store, it is a long line of workers, and unfortunately, farmers are often at the bottom. When you think of cherries, they are so expensive, but think about who picks a cherry. That is very skilled labor—to know the exact level of ripeness so that when it gets to your table, it is perfect—but that farmworker probably gets paid less than the other roles along the chain.

The United Farmworkers in California had a very successful boycott in order to raise wages. They got consistent feedback that folks would be happy to pay more if they knew that workers were getting a better wage. Much of this change is consumer driven. One of the programs we've worked on is a cooperative labeling system to identify food justice. If all of the growers in a county agree on a fair wage, then all of the food produced in that county is verifiably produced with workers in mind. Instead of providing supplies to farmworkers, we're working to ensure that they earn a decent wage, so they can buy what they need or want for themselves.

AB: What would you like to see in the future of food on a policy and infrastructure level?

RG: Food has to cost more if we're going to protect the land, if we're going to have a healthy food system, and if we consider farmworkers our neighbors. You can't grow a product without a loyal labor force. I always think about the farming tradition of this country. Family farmers founded the United States—let's get back to that tradition. Family farms were what created community in rural America: grange halls, farm bureaus, shared coolers, and so on. Why can't we go back to that tradition and build community in a new way together? I've always thought that the immigrant community of this country is the future of healthy, organic farming because the majority have peasant backgrounds and traditional food production knowledge that we're not leveraging. Instead of pushing that away, let's accept these traditions and blend them to make a new food system.

It's also on a human rights level. We are human beings in your community. There is a skilled labor force in every community where Latinos have settled. The majority of Latinos in the United States since the 1950s have a farmworker background. In terms of infrastructure, we are having conversations on how labor can strengthen the resiliency of family farms. When you look at most small farms, all of them probably are low income, living season to season, just like us. We need to work together, as landowners, farmworkers, and consumers, to ensure that farming families are doing better. And then you grow that. We refer to this as the solidarity economy.

It all boils down to the solidarity economy and participatory democracy. Many of the issues that farmworkers have to deal with are because of fundamental exploitation. We have to break down the silos of food production. We need to stop looking at food as an industry and look at it as a system that we need, as human beings, to nourish ourselves. Sovereignty for me goes from the individual to the collective.

It's a whole mind shift. I want to see a food system that is governed by the community that is living in that system and provides for all of us and the soil in all facets. Collectively we can do so much more, but there's a lot to do.

RAW

Strawberries, at their finest, need little more than to be rinsed, sliced, and gobbled up. Pairing them with similarly straight-forward ingredients allows them to shine beyond simply being eaten out of hand and is a suitable way to continue the celebration of a good strawberry season all the way from breakfast through the end of a meal.

savory:

beet carpaccio w/strawberries, flowers + candied fennel seed

There are little hacks that chefs use to create a sense of drama on the plate. Fiddly plating is one of them. Jewel-toned, monochromatic ingredients is another. Edible flowers and microgreens is yet another. This dish has all three, setting the stage to awe over great strawberries. Should individually plating not be in the cards for your party, cut the beets into larger pieces and toss the whole thing together like a big salad and carry on with equal exuberance.

1½ lb [680 g] beets, equally small or medium is ideal

Salt and freshly ground black pepper

1 lemon (about 1.5 oz [45 ml]), zest and juice

1 orange (about 3 oz [90 ml]), zest and juice

¼ cup [60 ml] olive oil

1 lb [455 g] strawberries, hulls removed

¼ cup [50 g] Candied Fennel Seeds (page 74)

Edible flowers

Preheat the oven to 375°F [190°C].

Wash the beets and place in a baking dish with ¼ cup [60 ml] of water. Cover tightly with aluminium foil and bake until tender, 20 to 45 minutes, depending on the size of the beet. When the beets are tender when pierced with a knife, remove from the oven and let sit, uncovered, until cool enough to handle. With a kitchen or paper towel, rub the skins off of the beets. Using a mandoline or

continued

sharp knife, cut the beets into ¼ in [6 mm] thick rounds. Lay the beets on individual plates overlapping a bit, like fish scales. Sprinkle the beets with salt and a couple grinds of black pepper.

In a medium bowl, combine the citrus juice and zest, olive oil, and a pinch of salt. Drizzle a couple of tablespoons over each plate of beets.

Slice the strawberries into halves or quarters depending on the size.

To serve, scatter the strawberries over the beets. Sprinkle the candied fennel seeds over the whole thing and garnish with edible flowers.

sweet:

strawberry sundaes: vanilla ice cream, pulsed strawberries + meringue

Through most of June, my favorite dessert is a bowl full of hulled strawberries, splashed with heavy cream, a spoonful of sugar, and a sprinkle of the coarsest salt. The salt acts as foil to the sugar and fat, lifting the whole bowl beyond the sum of its parts. When strawberries are hit-or-miss, blending them gives them safety in numbers. The crunch of the dry meringue lends texture to an otherwise ubiquitous treat. Note: This strawberry purée freezes wonderfully and is my preferred way to preserve strawberries for late-season sundaes.

2 lb [910 g] strawberries, hulled and halved

1 Tbsp sugar

1 qt [960 ml] Ice Cream Base (page 96), churned and frozen

½ to 1 cup (2 oz [55 g]) dry Meringue (page 99), broken into crumbles of various sizes

Coarse salt, such as Maldon or fleur de sel

In a food processor or large bowl, combine the strawberries and sugar and then either pulse or mash with a fork until coarsely chopped.

Divide the ice cream among four bowls.

To serve, top with a hefty ladle of the strawberries and several crumbles of meringue. Sprinkle each bowl with a pinch of salt.

ROASTED

In its essence, roasting achieves two things: 1) It removes excess water from the ingredient, thus concentrating the flavor, and 2) it caramelizes the inherent sugar within the ingredient, creating depth of flavor. Both help less-than-stellar strawberries along. The key to roasting strawberries is a screaming-hot pan, which helps sear the outside of the fruit before all the juice releases.

savory:

lamb chops w/buckwheat + black pepper strawberries

By using the same pan to roast the lamb chops and sear the strawberries, you're using the juice in the berries to deglaze the flavorful fond into the sauce as well as creating one less pan to wash.

1 cup [180 g] buckwheat, bulgur, or other grain of your choosing

10 stems chard, cut into ribbons

1 rack of lamb (8 lamb chops, 1 to 2 lb [455 to 910 g] total)

Salt and freshly ground black pepper

Neutral oil

1 lb [455 g] strawberries, hulled and halved

½ cup [120 ml] dry red wine

Olive oil

Bring a medium pot of salted water to a boil over high heat. Whisk in the buckwheat, return to a boil, lower the heat, and simmer until tender, about 12 minutes.

Place the chard ribbons into a medium bowl. Drain the buckwheat and then pour it over the chard, letting the heat from the buckwheat wilt the chard.

continued

Season the lamb chops liberally with salt and black pepper. In a large frying pan, heat a glug of neutral oil until smoking hot. Sear the lamb, flat side of the rack down, until deeply browned, about 5 minutes. Flip and sear the other side for another 2 to 3 minutes or until the chops are medium-rare. Remove the lamb from the pan and let rest.

Tip any excess fat from the frying pan into a heatproof dish to discard once cooled. Return the frying pan to high heat and add a glug of neutral oil. When smoking, add the strawberries and a couple grinds of black pepper (be warned, the moisture in the strawberries will cause the oil to pop and spit). Allow the strawberries to sear until the juices just start to leach, about 2 minutes. Remove the strawberries from the pan, then add the red wine to deglaze, scraping up any of the browned fond on the bottom of the pan. Let the wine reduce by half, then pour over the roasted strawberries.

Toss the buckwheat-chard mixture with a couple good glugs of olive oil.

To serve, slice the rack of lamb into eight individual chops. Dish the buckwheat-chard salad among four plates, place two chops per plate atop the buckwheat, and spoon the roasted strawberries over the whole thing.

sweet: # dutch baby w/sherry vinegar strawberries

The easiest way to be sure that your pan is hot enough to both roast strawberries and bake a Dutch baby successfully is to heat it in a very hot oven. Heating two pans at once makes for a very fast breakfast indeed. Note, too, that the batter for the Dutch baby can be blended a day in advance and held in the fridge, making for a lightning-quick breakfast or a no-fuss, dinner-party dessert.

3 Tbsp butter

1 recipe Dutch Baby Batter (page 45)

1 lb [455 g] strawberries, hulled and halved

Neutral oil

¼ cup [60 ml] sherry, balsamic, or red wine vinegar

Powdered sugar, for dusting

Salt

Preheat the oven to 425°F [220°C].

Place two large, ovenproof frying pans in the oven to heat through, 7 to 10 minutes. Once preheated, add the butter to one frying pan and let melt, watching to make sure it doesn't burn. Pour in the Dutch baby batter and let bake until cooked through and golden brown, about 20 minutes.

Toss the strawberries with a glug of neutral oil. Pour the strawberries into the second preheated frying pan and return to the oven to roast until their juices release and reduce, 5 to 7 minutes. Remove the strawberries from the oven. Add the vinegar and stir to combine.

To serve, either spoon the vinegar-roasted strawberries into the center of the whole Dutch baby or cut it into wedges and top with the strawberries. Dust with powdered sugar and a pinch of salt.

PRESERVED

Someone once scoffed at my reticence to preserve strawberries, saying, "They are strawberries! It's not like they're lettuce!" But despite the ubiquity of strawberry jelly, I find strawberries the least satisfying fruit to preserve, second only to melon, because they are watery and lack the acidity to not be cloyingly sweet.

JAM

Strawberry jam is often unsatisfying to make because the fruit is low acid, making it one-note sweet, high in moisture, and low in pectin, requiring either a long cook to reduce the amount of juice or a setting agent to make the jam firm.

PICKLING

Pickling ripe berries tends to yield very mushy results, though pouring a Basic Fruit Pickle Brine (page 112) over frozen fruit helps some. Recently, there has been a lot of to-do about pickling green strawberries. The unripe fruit is tarter, having not yet developed its sugars, and the flesh is firm enough to withstand the acidic brine. These pickled berries taste more vegetal to me, so I use them in places where I'm craving more of a traditional pickle than the sweet-sour combination of other pickled fruits.

FREEZING

Freezing is my preferred way of preserving strawberries, either as whole berries or pulsed strawberry sauce. Freezing as whole berries gives you more options—blend into a smoothie, thaw and roast, or pulse into sauce later—but it takes up space. To freeze: Wash, dry, and hull the strawberries, then place on a baking sheet lined with parchment or a silicone mat and freeze. Once the berries are fully frozen, transfer to a sealable bag and store frozen. This ensures that the berries will freeze as individuals and not as a big lump, making it easier to use a portion when the time comes.

Frozen strawberry sauce takes up less space and tastes just as sparklingly bright as in season. To make the sauce, blend a couple of handfuls of washed and hulled strawberries with a spoonful of sugar and pinch of salt to taste. Transfer to small containers (I like 8 oz [240 ml] deli containers) and freeze.

tart round fruits: cranberries, currants, gooseberries, lingonberries + autumn olive

When I was a line cook, one of the greatest pleasures was stepping outside after the last order had been served but we hadn't yet started to break down and clean the line. We could, for a moment, leave the unending heat generated by the burners and ovens that had been on before noon. My favorite nights were in the winter, when steam would rise from our skin in the bitingly cold air. We'd stand in a loose circle, no coats in the subzero air, and talk about service—what went right, what went wrong. There was more than a little complaining, and in that icy air, we'd finally stop sweating.

One of these hundreds of nights, when a particularly cold gust of wind whipped through our stand, Spencer-the-Intern said, "That's as refreshing as red currant jelly." Teasing ensued because it was a weird thing to say, but it always stuck with me. It's a good way to sum up the role acid plays in a particularly rich meal—to cut through and balance the richness. I think about that offhand, and endearingly earnest, comment often.

I don't know what Spencer-the-Intern is doing now. I don't work in typical restaurants anymore and probably never will again. I don't want to sweat buckets digging out of the stack of tickets that pile up every night at 7:15 p.m. because everyone wants to eat at the same time and reservations aren't spaced out. I don't want to earn $85 a shift no matter how long I'm there. I don't even want to stand outside in the refreshingly cold wind with a bunch of line cooks smoking cigarettes and ribbing each other at 1 a.m. anymore. I still miss it from time to time. I miss the incredibly smart people from all walks of life who make this food and conquer the everyday hurdles to make a restaurant go. I still think of that crew when I spoon a bit of cranberry relish onto my Thanksgiving plate, when I layer lingonberry jam onto my butter-laden crepes, or when I add a wobble of red currant jelly to my Sunday roast.

There are several fruits that cut through a world more and more fixated on sweetness—fruits where the acidity is the point. I often use cranberries, currants, gooseberries, lingonberries, and autumn olive interchangeably because each has its own preciously short season and varying degrees of availability.

CRANBERRIES

HOW TO SELECT

Look for berries that are bright in color. They start to fade to a maroon as the cells break down. Avoid berries that have excessive browning or mushy parts. Don't be put off by cranberries that show white under the red pigment—that's how they are. They will turn all red when those internal cells break down, either by cooking or curing with sugar. Fresh cranberries are generally available in late fall; frozen are very easy to use and often available year-round.

SIGNS OF RIPENESS

You aren't really selecting for ripeness because the berries will have been deemed ripe by the farmer before harvesting. Cranberries begin to ripen in September but aren't usually harvested until late October–early November to maximize sweetness. Most cranberries are wet-harvested by flooding the bog in which the berries grow and then mechanically shaken from the bushes and collected as they float to the surface.

HOW TO STORE

Store covered in refrigeration, avoiding excess moisture, which can contribute to premature rot. Cranberries will store in the fridge for months, but also freeze perfectly, so don't be shy about popping them into the deep freeze.

CURRANTS

HOW TO SELECT

Currants have an incredibly short season toward the end of July in my area and are only around for a couple of weeks. I find currants generally still on their clusters and look to make sure that the majority of fruit has taut skin and a vibrant, almost sparkly color. Because of how densely packed currants normally come, check for signs of mold or mildew on the underside of the package if it is clear, or in the center of the package if you can access it. Black currants are the same, but will have a duller, almost blueberry-like dustiness to them.

SIGNS OF RIPENESS

All currants are very tart, but their ripe tartness will have an underlying fruitiness, for lack of a better term. Their unripe tartness is more vegetal and astringent. The best way to get a sense of ripeness is from the color. It should seem to be coming from within the fruit itself. The fruit doesn't give off much fragrance.

HOW TO STORE

Currants store surprisingly well for their short season. The skins seem to hold their shape and moisture easily. Keep in loose layers, covered and in the fridge, if storing for a length of time. Currants also freeze well. I usually freeze as whole clusters and then shake them loose from their stems after frozen.

NOTES

Currants are very high in pectin and so make incredible jelly and syrups for homespun sodas.

GOOSEBERRIES

HOW TO SELECT

Gooseberries hit their sour splendor in mid- to late June, give or take a few weeks depending on the region. Look for either green, yellow, or red varieties that have a firm, even shape and don't show any signs of wrinkling. I use the same criteria in evaluating grapes when checking out a box of gooseberries.

SIGNS OF RIPENESS

Like grapes, gooseberries show cooler-hued colors—greens and purples. Look for the color to be as warm as possible, knowing it will never quite glow like a peach or melon.

HOW TO STORE

Gooseberries last in the fridge for a week or two without starting to collapse. Store them there to pro-long their shelf life or freeze quickly. Frozen gooseberries are, to my mind, indistinguishable from fresh, especially when cooked, so don't be shy about buying in quantity during their short season and freezing with abandon.

NOTES

Gooseberries are very high in pectin and so do well as jams and jellies. The most classic combination is with elder-flower infused into the syrup, as elder is often flowering as gooseberries are ripening. Gooseberries are another fruit, like lingonberries and currants, that originated in northern climates, so often their best seasons are on the cooler, wetter side, which can be a silver lining for when that same season produces disappointing strawberries.

LINGONBERRIES

HOW TO SELECT

It's very rare to find lingonberries at a fresh fruit market; I've only ever been able to order from online sources. Frozen berries are showing up in more and more places because of their high level of antioxidants, which gives them "superfood" potential. Like most berries, look for even, tightly stretched skin and no obvious signs of browning or decay. Lingonberries originated on the boreal tundra and prefer colder areas. They often don't come ripe until late summer or early autumn. If you do happen upon fresh ones, look for even skin and a deep claret color, remarkably like North American cranberries but juicier in texture.

SIGNS OF RIPENESS

Lingonberries only turn that ruby red color with time (and ripeness), so look for that. I've never particularly noticed a rich fragrance, so this is one of the few cases where you're truly evaluating a book by its cover.

HOW TO STORE

Traditionally, lingonberries were stored in a jar of water at room temperature for months—their naturally occurring benzoic acid and pectin keeping them fresh throughout the winter. These days, I simply pop them into the freezer or, more realistically, buy them frozen and keep them that way.

NOTES

Lingonberries are packed with vitamin C as well as other micronutrients, all the rage with homeopaths. Traditionally, lingonberry water (literally the water that the lingonberries were floated in as preservation) was used as a cure for scurvy. Today lingonberry extract is used to treat urinary tract infections and ward off seasonal colds and flus, especially when paired with elderberry or cranberry.

AUTUMN OLIVE

HOW TO SELECT

Autumn olive is an invasive species to North America and the devil du jour for native plant folks around here. The berries turn deep red with the most amazingly beautiful golden splotches in mid- to late October. I've never seen them in a retail setting, so you'll have to go foraging. Look for that dark red color and taste a few to see if they have sweetened to the point of being edible.

SIGNS OF RIPENESS

Ripeness only comes with time, so wait for the color to deepen to a dark reddish pink. Taste a few berries and see if they are palatable, then pick ad nauseam, because once you identify an autumn olive bush, you'll see them everywhere.

HOW TO STORE

Autumn olive will store for a few weeks covered in the fridge, but to be honest, I've never really harvested them to keep them, mostly just to eat on a walk or for a specific canning project.

NOTES

Autumn olive is considered an invasive species in many areas, and the plant is quite a headache to remove. Enjoying the berries due to their proliferation, is, for many, really grasping at a silver lining.

RAW

Holiday recipes make their rounds, and I got this cranberry relish from my friend Liz Hollinger's family. The first time I read the recipe, I texted her, "This recipe is insane. No cooking?! Whole oranges?!" It works and is delicious. It graces our Thanksgiving table every year, but I like it best throughout the weeks after turkey day. The acidity braces even the most cloying comfort foods. The orange marries well with the other yuletide flavors, including the dreaded warming spices. It also works well with other tart fruits, such as fresh currants, gooseberries, even rhubarb.

savory:

roasted carrots w/lentils, spinach + cranberry relish

I'm a big fan of dots. Not the little, haute cuisine dots made with a variety of squeezy bottles, but big globby dots. So let this be your encouragement to dot with abandon. Release your Jackson Pollock, but please don't drive so recklessly. Note: This makes more relish than you will need for the dish, but it keeps in the fridge for weeks, so I didn't reduce the amounts.

1 lb [455 g] fresh cranberries, washed and nasty ones removed

1 orange, cut into chunks (skin and all, but seeds removed)

2 apples, cored and cut into chunks

1½ cups [300 g] sugar

Salt

¼ cup [60 ml] neutral oil

½ cup [100 g] cooked lentils

2 to 3 lb [910 g to 1.4 kg] carrots, any variety, left whole or cut into large pieces

Olive oil

Ground black pepper

2 oz [55 g] fresh spinach

In a food processor, combine the cranberries, orange, apples, and sugar with a big pinch of salt and blend into a rough paste. Taste and add more sugar if it's too tart. Remove from the food processor and let macerate at room temperature for 1 hour, then refrigerate to store.

Preheat the oven to 400°F [200°C].

In a large oven-safe frying pan, heat the neutral oil over medium-high heat until shimmering. Add the lentils (the drier they are, the less they will spit) along with a pinch of salt and pan fry until brown and crisped, 7 or 8 minutes, stirring occasionally to brown the other side. Remove from the pan and let drain on a paper towel–lined plate. Wipe the frying pan clean to prepare to roast the carrots.

In a medium bowl, toss the carrots with a glug of olive oil, a big pinch of salt, and a couple grinds of black pepper and place into the large frying pan. Roast in the oven until tender and deeply caramelized, 45 to 60 minutes.

In a medium bowl, dress the spinach with a glug of olive oil, a pinch of salt, and black pepper.

To serve, lay three-fourths of the cooked carrots on a serving platter, scatter the spinach and three-fourths of the crisped lentils on top, then dot cranberry relish all over. Add the remaining salad ingredients and finish with a few more dots of cranberry relish to serve.

sweet:

eton mess

Eton mess is one of my favorite desserts. At its heart, it has three ingredients: dry meringue, something creamy, and some sort of tart, red fruit. You can build it as tidy, individual pavlovas, or bake the meringue in a giant thin sheet just to smash it and make a big unruly pile in a serving bowl or jar. Traditionally, the English make it with strawberries (you know they have a thing with strawberries and cream), but I want a more jolting fruit. My favorite way to make this is with the raw cranberry relish from the previous recipe, but I have also made it with fresh currants or gooseberries, gently smashed with a spoonful of sugar to loosen their juices.

1 recipe Meringue (page 99)

1 cup [240 ml] Maple Whipped Cream (page 93) or Custard (page 81), whipped to hold soft peaks

¾ cup [180 ml] Cranberry Relish (page 412) or other gently macerated tart fruit

Bake the meringue as two large circles, roughly 8 in [20 cm] across, until fully dry, about 45 minutes.

Place one circle of meringue on a cake plate or serving platter. Spoon three-fourths of the cream into the center and gently push out to within 1 in [2.5 cm] of the edge. Spoon three-fourths of the cranberry relish on top. Place the second meringue disc on top and layer with the rest of the cream and cranberry relish. Serve immediately and encourage messy eating.

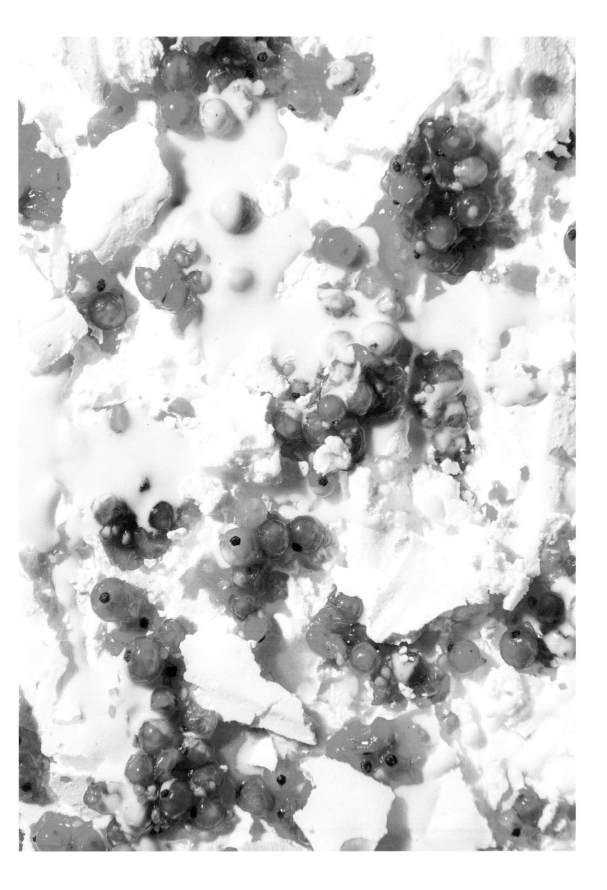

STEWED

Stewing is likely the most popular treatment of tart round fruits because the heat softens the fruit while not collapsing their texture entirely, and combining the fruit with sugar takes the tannic edge off the astringent fruit. This can be done in large batches when the fruit is in season and freezes perfectly as a compote.

savory:

squash claws w/stewed currants

I pull currants from the freezer right as I'm ready to switch gears from summer to fall, which just so happens to be exactly the best time to eat acorn or delicata squash. This dish can be made with any variety of squash and also made with cranberries, or frozen currants or gooseberries, if their season has come and gone. Note: I would also add a few spoonfuls of cooked wild rice, buckwheat, or lentils to make it more hearty, but this dish is perfectly good on its own, so don't feel compelled to add heft.

2 acorn squash (about 4 lb [1.8 kg] total)

Olive oil

1 tsp smoked paprika

Salt and freshly ground black pepper

1 lb [455 g] red or black currants, stems removed

½ cup [100 g] sugar

¼ cup [60 ml] white wine

2 Tbsp butter

1 cup [180 g] cooked wild rice (optional)

4 oz [115 g] goat cheese

¼ cup [60 g] salty pecans (see page 78)

Preheat the oven to 400°F [200°C]. Line a baking sheet with aluminum foil.

Cut the squash in half, remove the seeds, and cut into large, claw-like wedges. In a large bowl, toss the squash with a big glug of olive oil, the paprika, a big pinch of salt, and a couple grinds of black pepper. Transfer to the prepared baking sheet and roast until tender and beginning to caramelize, about 40 minutes.

In a medium, nonreactive saucepan, combine the currants, sugar, wine, and a pinch of salt over medium heat. Cook until the currants start to release their juice and the liquid reduces by 25 percent, about 8 minutes. Remove from the heat, add the butter to the currant mixture, and stir to blend.

To serve, spoon the wild rice (if using) into the center of a large serving platter, arrange the squash wedges on top, spoon the currant sauce all over, dot the goat cheese irregularly around, and finish by sprinkling the salty pecans across the whole lot.

sweet:

gooseberry fool w/tortas de aceite

I remember learning about fool when I was in cooking school and, like the impetuous student I was, raised my hand and said, "So, it's just whipped cream and stewed fruit?" One of the other students chimed in, "Well, it's nicer than that sounds." It's true. Fools are dead simple but more than the sum of their parts. Gooseberry fool is my favorite, maybe because it reminds me of my time in England, but more likely because gooseberries are so tart that they foil perfectly against billowy whipped cream. I do like to pair fools with some sort of crunchy business. Tortas de aceite are little more than squares of puff pastry brushed with olive oil and sprinkled with salty sugar before baking. Any other cookie thing would sub in perfectly.

8 oz [230 g] gooseberries, the tarter the better	2 cups [480 ml] heavy cream	4 Puff Pastry Tortas de Aceite (page 73)
¼ cup [50 g] sugar	1 tsp vanilla extract	

In a small, nonreactive saucepan, combine the gooseberries and sugar over medium heat. Cook until the gooseberries start to bubble and burst, about 5 minutes. Remove from the heat and mash with the back of a fork until pulpy. Let cool.

In a medium bowl, combine the cream and vanilla. Whip until soft peaks form, about 2 minutes.

To serve, layer the whipped cream and stewed gooseberries in pretty glasses with the tortas de aceite alongside.

BAKED

The warming of winter foods can often languish in the comfort doldrums of heavy starches, luscious fats, and endless root vegetables brought on by dark, cold nights. Thankfully, like on the Thanksgiving table, the tart fruits are there to add a shock that balances all that soft-edged cosseting.

savory:

winter casserole

Too often bread casseroles, most often called stuffing or dressing during the winter holidays, are relegated to just then—the winter holidays. This one is for anytime. Serve alongside a dinner party roast or as a midweek meal next to a big green salad.

4 lb [1.8 kg] parsnips or another root vegetable like carrot or sweet potato, peeled and cut into chunks

½ loaf Pumpernickel (page 39), cut into large cubes

1 small red onion (about 2 oz [55 g]), thinly sliced

1 cup [100 g] tart round fruit (frozen is fine)

2 to 4 oz [55 to 115 g] Manchego or Cheddar cheese, cut into cubes

Olive oil

Pinch of salt

Freshly ground black pepper

3 cups [750 ml] chicken stock or water

Preheat the oven to 350°F [180°C].

In a large bowl, toss together all of the ingredients except the chicken stock with a big glug of olive oil, salt, and several grinds of black pepper. Transfer to a baking dish and pour the stock all over. Press the casserole down to encourage the bread to absorb the stock; it should be quite juicy. Cover with aluminium foil and bake until the parsnips are tender, about 35 minutes. Remove the foil and bake for an additional 10 to 15 minutes to crisp the top.

Note: My favorite way to reheat the leftovers is to slice off a slab of the casserole, which should hold together pretty well, heat a large glug of neutral oil in a frying pan, and pan fry to get a deeply browned crust, flip, repeat, and eat.

sweet: # january cake

This is one of my favorite winter desserts, not only because that is when we have oranges in the house consistently, but also because this cake satisfies my desire for slightly more austere sweets throughout the January-return-to-normalcy after the holidays. It is sweet enough to work for dessert. It isn't too sweet to preclude being eaten for breakfast (especially crumbled into a bowl of yogurt). Plus, it keeps for more than a week on the counter in case you find yourself with fewer houseguests after ringing in the new year. My favorite way to eat this cake is lying in the afternoon winter sun as it streams through my bedroom window while I pretend to be in the tropics.

1 recipe Almond Orange
   Cake (page 62)

1 cup [100 g] tart round
   fruit, fresh or frozen

Follow the instructions for the cake, but add the fruit to the filled cake pan before baking.

PRESERVED

Tart round fruits are great candidates for preserving for several reasons. Their seasons tend to be short, so preserving keeps them in more regular rotation. They are self-contained (unlike, say, a melon), so they freeze well. They often contain a good deal of pectin and so do well as jams and jellies. They also dehydrate well because they aren't the juiciest of fruit and they are small enough to dry down quickly.

JAM

Because of the tart fruit's inherent tartness, I like to use a 50:50 ratio of fruit to sugar when making jam. The process is simple: Weigh the fruit, weigh the sugar, combine in a nonreactive pan over medium heat, and cook until the berries burst and the mixture cooks to about 220°F [105°C]. Because the fruits are generally high in pectin, I usually don't measure the temperature of the jam; when it starts to wrinkle as you stir it, that is good. The wrinkle test (see page 31) is also a useful method.

The difference between jam and jelly is that jams contain the fruit pulp, jellies do not. I generally prefer the thicker texture of a jam, but also often strain currants and make jelly, as it is the most efficient way to remove all the little seeds and stems.

To make Magenta Mustard: mix 50:50 red fruit jam and Dijon mustard to make a hot pink mustard that is beautiful and delicious. This is my favorite accompaniment to any sort of cheese-charcuterie platter. It also dresses up a plate of cooked sausages or an average deli turkey sandwich. Feel free to vary the ratio to suit your tastes.

DRIED

The tart fruits dry well and result in a pleasantly sweet and tart snack. Lay out in a single layer in a dehydrator or in a low oven until the fruit is leathery. Use anywhere you would raisins or dried cherries.

FREEZING

Again, the tart, round fruits freeze very well and are my most common way of preserving them. Lay them out on a parchment- or silicone-lined baking sheet and, when entirely stiff, transfer to a sealable bag. For currants, I often freeze the whole clusters and then knock them off their stems as I transfer to the storage bag. The reason I process the fruit this way is that it is quick and most of these recipes work just as well with frozen fruit, including making jam, so there's really no downside and it's not worth the risk of forgetting about the fruit in the fridge until it's too late.

acknowledgments

Thank you to all of the people who worked the line with me along the way and who helped, unwittingly, craft this book: There are too many of you to name but hopefully you see yourselves in these pages.

To the growers, producers, and advocates who bring fruit to our tables, but especially those who took the time to talk to me and share their perspectives: Agatha Achindu, Gene Garthe, Rosalinda Guillen, Mike + Pete Laing, Nikki Rothwell, and Abby Schilling.

These folks made the book possible: Kari Stuart, Sarah Billingsley, EE Berger, Mollie Hayward, Lucy Engleman, Sara Schneider, Vanessa Santos, Tia Rotolo, Ilana Alperstein, Cynthia Shannon, Keely Thomas-Menter, Jessica Ling, Tera Killip, and Steve Kim.

Thank you to Debbie Carlos Ceramics, Danielle Chutinthranond of Monsoon Pottery, Jen Bernstein of Meilen Ceramics, and Abigail Murray Studio for lending your ceramics to us to create such beautiful photos.

For the people who fed me and kept me company while writing this book: Laura Piskor, Heidi Joynt, Molly Kobelt, Erin Stanley, Johannah Freiler, Molly Brewe, Wes Rieth, Andrew Harris, Pat + Ellie Mullins, Emma Brewster, Joe Lindsay, Jesse Rosenbluth, Sara Burns, Bryan Morrison, Samantha Lee, Betty Barnes, Sarah + Mickey Humpula, Hannah Isreal, Rose Hollander, and Eric Gerstner.

To everyone who has eaten my food over the years. Without you, it would have just been me at the saddest farm dinners of all time.

Tim Mazurek, thank you for being a friend. You've traveled down the road and back again. Your heart is true. You're a pal and a confidant.

A special thank you to Jo Karyl Witte Berens and Lee Berens for being the trees this apple didn't fall quite so far from, and to Lark for being the apple of my eye.

Erik, you're a peach, and I want to squeeze you.

index